STAFF
DEVELOPMENT

STAFF DEVELOPMENT

ENHANCING HUMAN POTENTIAL

Donald C. Orlich

WASHINGTON STATE UNIVERSITY

ALLYN AND BACON
Boston, London, Sydney, Toronto

Copyright © 1989 by Allyn and Bacon
A Division of Simon & Schuster
160 Gould Street
Needham Heights, Massachusetts 02194

Library of Congress Cataloging-in-Publication Data

Orlich, Donald C.
    Staff development : enhancing human potential / Donald C. Orlich.
        p.   cm.
    Bibliography: p.
    Includes index.
    ISBN 0-205-11827-5
    1. Teachers—In service training—United States.   2. Continuing
education—United States.   3. Career development—United States.
I. Title.
LB1731.O75   1989
371.1'46—dc19   88-22268
                                                                    CIP

Printed in the United States of America

10   9   8   7   6   5   4   3   2   1   92   91   90   89   88

CONTENTS

TABLES

MODELS AND FIGURES

PREFACE

Staff Development: Enhancing Human Potential presents the total spectrum of concepts, issues, and practices relating to staff development and in-service education. The book focuses on the most humane and productive means for continued school renewal at the local level. Staff developers and school administrators will gain new insights into processes associated with in-service education and will find the book most useful as they conduct local in-service projects.

The book is most appropriate for the university community, especially for those involved in adult education, continuing education, staff development, and personnel management. Topics are explored in depth, with the more significant research and published studies smoothly integrated into each treatment. The book discusses emerging trends and ideas in a comprehensive statement that will be of interest to all policymakers.

Staff Development: Enhancing Human Potential is based on the assumption that if schools are to succeed in their many goals, then school personnel must continuously expand their knowledge and skills, be made aware of new challenges, and be encouraged to solve problems—especially those related to student achievement. The essence of this work is to encourage school district policymakers and administrators to view the people in their organizations as having the capacity to solve *all* problems in the schools. Teachers are encouraged to become active participants in planning and conducting projects in this emerging and dynamic arena.

This book will undoubtedly cause many staff developers to reevaluate their current practices. The enhancement of human potential is growth oriented, and the concept implies that every administrator, teacher, or nonteaching support person is crucial for bringing success to a troubled institution.

The text begins by showing the importance of in-service education and providing a rationale for conducting systematic, if not empirically based, programs.

Chapter 2 details needs assessments and explains why it is critical to address individual and organizational needs for success.

Chapter 3 discusses the many delivery systems available to staff developers, including the reborn teacher center, and describes peer coaching as a powerful and innovative training mechanism. Chapter 4 stresses the many ways of evaluating in-service projects. The presentation of the Temporary Systems Approach here is a first for any staff-development book. Incentives for staff development are the subject of Chapter 5, where detailed illustrations are given so that those who excel in staff development can be recognized. Funding is the topic of Chapter 6. The concepts of direct and indirect costs are highlighted, again for the first time in such a book.

The most creative aspect of this book is presented in Chapter 7, A Paradigm for Staff Development. The chapter offers a novel, dichotomous key to the profession by which to select the most appropriate model for success. Using this paradigm will ensure that program planners reflect a systematic and holistic vision. Readers are urged to join in creating and testing an emergent theory.

Chapter 8 illustrates the many options available to administrators for continued staff-development efforts. Chapter 9 is a biting critique of reforms that tend to sap the energy of personnel in educational and noneducational circles. The final chapter is an overview of issues that impinge on staff development and need resolution.

This book offers a clear, but nonlinear vision for continuously preparing professional and classified staff for the never-ending dream of school improvement and for truly educating all youth to their highest potential. This is a noble vision to be sure, but it is an attainable one.

Several people have helped bring this text to fruition. Daniel L. Duke inspired me to use the metaphor of "vision." Hiram G. Howard, Gerald Bauman, and Louis J. Rubin provided encouragement to complete the manuscript. Continued support and help came from my wife, Patricia. Students in my graduate class, Inservice Programs, critically examined the first complete draft of the book; their suggestions as practitioners are reflected here. Judith Leet, Sandra Tyacke, Paula Perron, and Wendy Thayer all helped in production phases.

The staff-development movement has established a self-identity, as witnessed by the growth of the National Staff Development Council, the National Council of States on Inservice Education, and many emerging state and local councils. Finally, I compliment the Washington State Staff Development Council for its efforts to include in-service education as an integral part of the education process.

DONALD C. ORLICH

CHAPTER 1

REALIZING
THE VISION

Welcome to Singapore: Where Our Only National Resource is Our People
Sign in the Singapore International Airport

Staff development is a basic and necessary component of the continuing preparation of teachers, administrators, and other staff as they extend their professional or technical knowledge. Educational leaders, school trustees, and concerned citizens have been aware of the benefits of staff improvement for many years. As a result, thousands of papers have been written on the topic, and the publications relating to staff development and in-service education are voluminous. Such a plethora of published material should not be surprising, since schools in all countries are labor-intensive industries often representing the single largest national, state, or local industry.

CARINGNESS,
ORGANIZATIONS, AND THE VISION

The educational enterprise is a "helping" profession. People who enter teaching in elementary or secondary schools tend to do so for altruistic reasons. Regardless of the adequacy of one's preservice or university preparation, no one in the teaching field—from kindergarten teachers to graduate faculty in universities—will ever be adequately prepared at an entry level to remain current for an entire career. In fact, preservice training, regardless of its length or intensity, may not even be adequate to prepare teachers for a successful first year without some in-service education. Thus all educational planners need a vision—a rationale—to increase the effectiveness of the services offered in order to enhance the human potential of their organization.

One persisting problem in the schools is that of helping persons achieve their maximum potential. Staff developers must encourage line or staff administrators and trainers to show that the organization cares about all individuals. That *caringness* adds the human element to impersonal organizational structures.

1

The above problem seems to be commonplace rather than an isolated incident. By not caring, morale problems emerge; or worse, an attitude of "I couldn't care less" persists. This condition is debilitating to educational institutions and ultimately affects the services to children. The problem seems to emerge when leaders—usually line administrators such as principals, superintendents, department heads, and deans—ignore the importance of continuously nurturing all personnel. Institutions with caringness exhibit a strength of organization far greater than one would expect.

Institutions are first and foremost people—far more than the fiction of an "organization." Schools consist of systems and subsystems of individuals who collectively conduct the business of schooling. The human interactions between leaders and teachers, and subsequently between teachers and learners, forge bonds of trust and mutual support. The purpose of in-service training projects and staff-development programs is to enhance human potential so that every person can achieve a higher standard of attainment, success, or excellence than would otherwise be possible. That vision will be expanded throughout this book.

Chapter 1 provides a context for this vision of staff development. Next is a very brief historical overview of in-service education, followed by a discussion of the need for a precise definition of in-service education. The concept of staff development is then established, and deficiency and growth perspectives are developed, with the latter linked to the tenets of adult learning theory. The chapter closes with a set of criteria by which to build programs and a short analysis of the concepts being treated. Now on to that historical footnote.

HOW WAS IN-SERVICE EDUCATION INSTITUTIONALIZED?

The concept of in-service education developed over a century ago. Since the advent of public education in the United States, school administrators have seen the need for additional training for their staff. Many teachers in the mid-1800s were not prepared to be teachers, but were simply recruited for classroom service as greater numbers of children entered the schools. This condition resulted from a commitment to universal elementary education.

Much of the in-service training at the time consisted of short two- or three-day institutes, evening work sessions, and various courses to remedy teacher deficiencies. Ralph W. Tyler (1971) observed that institutes were largely remedial and attempted to help teachers learn more practical ideas for classroom application.

Between the early 1900s and World War II, in-service programs for many teachers consisted of summer sessions at normal schools. This again was primarily to overcome grave deficiencies in teachers' entry preparation. As the commitment to universal education was implemented, states assumed regulation of teacher certification, and many teachers then had to complete a bachelor's degree. This led to college or university correspondence and extension courses designed to meet college degree requirements as well as, or in addition to, state certification. Early in-service education was not designed for individual teacher growth but was apparently based on external institutional or agency requirements developed by state departments of public instruction and colleges or universities.

Certification requirements are continually being upgraded, with education beyond the four-year degree now required. Current trends in in-service programs show many teachers working toward fulfillment of certification requirements and many others working beyond a fifth year. Permanent certification in several states requires a master's degree or its equivalent.

Until the 1930s, in-service education was basically "remedial" in nature. However, the classic Eight-Year Study, which began in 1933, was a time of major change. Tyler (1971) recalled that this period was one of unusual excitement, as teachers in a select group of thirty schools made the transition from "remedial" to "creative in-service education." This era also gave rise to the popular "workshop" format used so extensively for in-service projects.

Unfortunately, the results of the Eight-Year Study were published in 1942, when the world was engulfed in World War II. The Second World War brought in its wake a very severe teacher shortage, and in-service education and staff development became remedial once again, as thousands of "teachers" were certified under emergency certificates to staff the nation's classrooms. The period after World War II (1945–1960) witnessed subtle changes in in-service education: the programs became oriented toward personal and curriculum development rather than simple remediation.

New purposes for in-service education have since emerged that expose teachers and other staff to specific training in implementing new programs successfully. In many cases, teachers have needed to learn different roles in order to work effectively with new programs and technologies.

For example, in elementary science curricula, teachers learned through in-service projects to evolve from a content to a process orientation. A *content* orientation for elementary science emphasizes the acquisition of facts and concepts. A *process* orientation emphasizes intellectual skills, such as classifying, inferring, predicting, controlling variables, formulating hypotheses, and defining operations. Further, teachers adapted to new roles, such as using the investigative methods of scientists rather than just traditional lectures and class discussions. Thus "processes" became the carriers of science "content." The idea of learning processes has become very widespread, and it underlies the emphasis on "teaching thinking skills."

Implementation of new programs often involves developing different skills, techniques, and roles. A great variety of new skills and techniques may be needed as a result of some major new programs, such as the national emphasis on computer literacy.

New programs affect the continuing education of teachers significantly, but the impact of rapid change in society impinges on in-service education even more vividly. That we live in a period of rapid change almost goes without saying.

In addition, there are at least ten movements and trends that require renewed and massive local initiatives for staff development:

1. Focus on the "effective schools movement"
2. School-based staff development
3. Locally negotiated agreements relating to in-service education
4. Increased state requirements for renewal of teaching credentials
5. Restructuring of the concept of the middle school
6. Renewed emphasis on instructional processes
7. Growth of professional organizations such as the National Staff Development Council, which focus on in-service issues
8. Emergence of the microcomputer as an instructional tool
9. National debates about teacher preparatory programs
10. Tendency to use staff development as a means of enhancing teacher compensation

Collectively, these issues are creating staff development as an emergent cause that will definitely reach new heights in the last decade of the twentieth century.

There are two critical needs relating to staff development. The first is to inculcate a vision of what the *best* professional and classified staff might be and might develop into as they teach or support student endeavors. The second is to encourage a sense of history and trends. One needs to know what was done in the past and why. The history of educational practices and instructional technologies shows a continuous evolution of ideas, while trends forecast pending changes. The vision and historical understanding are implicit in the way in-service education is defined and delivered. Let us examine that point.

IN-SERVICE EDUCATION— A CONCEPT IN NEED OF DEFINITION

There are various terms to describe the concept of in-service education. Those commonly used are *professional development, in-service training, professional growth, staff development,* and *in-service education.* Each of these seems to be used with the same frequency in the literature, with the term chosen more as a matter of author preference than for any significant difference in meaning. Yet the need for a standard definition and description of in-service education is critical for policymakers.

A rather detailed analysis of about 2,000 documents relating to in-service education was carried out by Alexander M. Nicholson and associates (1976). His group had a difficult time determining both a definition for in-service and a common descriptor for it. Showing a sense of humor, the team prepared a grid by which one could invent one's own descriptor. Simply mix or match any three terms from columns A, B, or C:

DESCRIPTORS FOR IN-SERVICE—GENERATE YOUR OWN TERM*

A	B	C
Continuing	Staff	Development
Continued	Professional	Growth
	Teacher	Education
	Personnel	Renewal
		Improvement

During the period between 1957 and 1987, virtually every major publication in the field of staff development provided some definition of the term. The ideal definition of in-service education contains at least the following four elements: (1) orientation of training, (2) clientele to be served, (3) agency affected, and (4) financing of the program. To meet those criteria, an eclectic definition is offered.

In-service education denotes programs or activities that are based on identified needs; that are collaboratively planned and designed for a specific group of individuals in the school district; that have a very specific set of learning objectives and activities; and that are designed to extend, add, or improve immediate job-oriented skills, competencies, or knowledge with the employer paying the cost.

If all policymakers and all educational groups and agencies were to accept this definition (or one similar to it), then any discussions or policies on in-service education would immediately be defined with a consistent interpretation of the program's means and ends. In-service education must have a condition of immediacy about it: this essential criterion differentiates in-service activities from all other categories of professional education.

To repeat, in-service education must be job oriented, must be of immediate use to an individual, must improve or extend job-related skills, must focus on a specific group of individuals, and must be paid for by the employing organization. That definition will be used consistently throughout this book.

A TOTAL STAFF-DEVELOPMENT PROGRAM

Up to this point, the vision has been limited to the concept of in-service education. But if you examine the options available for more comprehensive training programs, then the vision encompasses a broader ideal: staff development. Whereas in-service education is oriented toward immediate training objectives, staff development implies persistent and personally significant activities. In essence, staff development subsumes in-service education projects and also addresses the larger issue of developing organizational problem-solving capacities

*Used with permission of Floyd T. Waterman. Reprinted from *The Literature on In-Service Teacher Education: An Analytic Review*, p. 79.

and leadership skills. The totality of building human and institutional resources in the organization becomes the goal of staff development.

One Staff-Development Plan

E. Lawrence Dale (1985) developed a major planning document that deals with the essential requirements of staff development. Table 1-1 illustrates the six major functions of Dale's developmental model: (1) in-service education, (2) organization development (OD), (3) consultation, or internal development of local

TABLE 1-1.

SIX FUNCTIONS OF A STAFF-DEVELOPMENT PROGRAM

1. In-service education
   Improving skills
   Implementing curricula or instructional procedures
   Expanding knowledge of subject matter
   Instructional planning and organizing
   Increasing personal effectiveness
2. Organization development
   Improving the building and program climate
   Solving problems
   Increasing communication among staff
3. Consultation
   Conducting (or arranging for the presentation of) workshops, clinics, special projects
   Assisting with building staff-development planning, implementation, and evaluation
   Assisting with administrative planning
4. Communication and coordination of resources
   Assisting with interbuilding communications
   Organizing and providing information regarding resources
   Assisting with communications between administration and staff
   Providing central coordinating service and coordination of efforts
5. Leadership training
   Providing suggestions for new curricula, instructional approaches, and communications about innovative approaches
   Identifying problems and making suggestions for resolutions
   Researching to evaluate new practices or procedures
   Providing assistance with processes of innovation
6. Evaluation
   Conducting (or arranging for the conduct of) needs assessments
   Evaluating resources—e.g., quality of programs, personnel, and media providing in-service education or organization development
   Evaluating or arranging for the evaluation of staff-development efforts
   Organizing for systematic feedback

Source: E. Lawrence Dale, "Proposed Staff Development Model," (Pullman: Unpublished paper, Washington State University, 1985). Used with permission.

human resources, (4) communication and coordination of resources, (5) leadership training, and (6) evaluation.

The typical school district usually deals with in-service education, some minor leadership functions, and evaluation as mandated by state law or state board regulation. The concept of staff development is *not* widely implemented. Perhaps one might speculate that a district embarking on a staff-development program is *proactive;* that is, the leadership (typically the superintendent and administrative cabinet) seek to develop human and organizational resources in anticipation of emerging trends, needs, or changes in the social milieu.

In contrast, district personnel who ignore or choose not to build staff-development models are *reactive.* These administrators wait until crises occur or until outside forces demand changes. Generally, the administration quickly establishes some contingency plan or technique to alleviate these crises or placate external forces. Reactive responses tend to be inadequate, poorly planned, and in the long run, inconsequential. This is not the vision for success.

Adding the Staff-Development Vision

The two major concepts—staff development and in-service education—must be institutionalized to enhance human potential. The all-encompassing one is staff development. It is a broad concept, it is a general or global plan, and it is a process; protected under its umbrella are all in-service education activities or projects. The goal of staff development should be to provide thoughtful and guided enhancement of human talent in the schools by means of a long-range working model.

To use this model, school district planners prepare staff-development plans describing sets of options and processes similar to Dale's model. This model incorporates well-conceived strategies for enhancing the long-term human development of the organization. Staff development requires close collaboration with the personnel department, principals, and curriculum specialists. Ellen R. Saxl, Ann Lieberman, and Matthew B. Miles (1987) have suggested a similar, expanded model for staff development.

Concomitantly, in-service education projects are planned and implemented to rectify specific needs emerging from the staff-development process. It is imperative to keep these two concepts separate as operational definitions. In this manner, institutional resources—financial, human, material—can be planned and committed on a more systematic basis. As a process, staff development connotes a condition of "nonimmediacy." It implies training for the future, whereas in-service education is training for the "right now."

By understanding these two concepts, all educators will be able to communicate their intentions more accurately, purposefully, and effectively—with better results.

A Perspective to Guide the Vision

Philip W. Jackson (1971) synthesized two perspectives from which in-service education may be viewed: the defect view and the growth approach. These perspectives are not mere semantic exercises; they establish the underlying vision for staff developers. Jackson argued eloquently that, from the receiver's frame of reference, the *defect view* is a negative and damaging one. If staff developers and administrators (or planners) imply that the in-service project is to fix some intellectual or technical "defect," then those participating in the training project are viewed as unprepared or incompetent. Jackson also observed that the typical defect-oriented project is arbitrarily assigned; it emphasizes the simple or behavioral aspects of teaching, stresses fast-acting tricks, uses prescriptive techniques, and usually stresses the latest educational fads. Administrators and staff developers with this perspective assume that "the teacher" is out of date, but can be "fixed"—just like last year's microcomputer.

The long-range, or even short-range, consequences of the defect view are to inhibit human potential. The planner draws the specifications, and that is that. Teachers may be reluctant to admit that they do not understand the value of some concept or technique; the main thing is to use it, whether or not it is appropriate.

The *growth approach,* conversely, implies that teaching and learning are complex activities in which no one ever masters the totality of the profession. Everyone enters the profession with skills and knowledge that will continuously expand with experience gained both inside and outside the classroom. The motive for participation in in-service activities is to gain an artistry of teaching, as Louis J. Rubin (1984) advocated. Jackson's growth approach is the keystone by which human potential is enhanced: it recognizes teachers in a humanistic, not mechanistic, perspective. This approach, as did Rubin, recognizes that every educator is a continuous learner who wants to solve organizational and instructional problems, wants to be involved in educational decision-making processes, and recognizes that staff or personal development is an imaginative, inventive on-going process, not a singular event.

Closely allied with Jackson's growth approach is Malcolm S. Knowles's (1984 and 1986) concept of *andragogy.* Knowles emphasized that adult learners are, in fact, different in degree and kind from young learners. He assumed that adults have a great degree of self-directedness, have experiences that form a knowledge base, and learn by solving problems. The important implications of this concept for staff development are:

1. Adults enjoy planning and conducting their own learning experiences
2. Experiences are the key to self-actualization
3. The best learning takes place when the need to know coincides with the training
4. Adults need opportunities to apply what they have learned
5. Adults need some independently structured options

The andragological model is a process to enhance adult learning. Experience, concluded Knowles, is the critical element for adult education programs. Likewise, Stephen D. Brookfield (1986) advocated that adult learning activities be (1) self-directed, (2) practical, (3) andragological, (4) formal and informal, and (5) facilitative. Refer to Brookfield's book *Understanding and Facilitating Adult Learning* for a comprehensive treatment of how adults best learn. The concepts are easily translated and incorporated by those responsible for staff development.

When planning and conducting in-service programs, persons aware of adult learning theory should (1) include program planning periods with the participants, (2) establish clearly defined goals and objectives, (3) include the participants in the actual instruction, and (4) allow individuals to identify alternatives even though specific program elements have been planned and scheduled (Verduin, Miller, and Greer 1986).

Summing up these points, Alan B. Knox (1986) stated that working with adults is a "unique and fulfilling experience." He further noted that effective adult learning is an active search for meaning where content and personal experience are blended. The implications for staff development are monumental.

P. C. Wu (1987) strongly urged staff developers or responsible administrators to approach the teaching of teachers with tenets from adult learning theory and with a growth perspective, so that in-service education can have a real impact on teachers or their students. Further, the highly prescriptive manner in which the typical in-service project is conducted may have failure built into the design. Such projects are usually too global and tend to neglect felt needs. Meeting the "needs" of a specific group of teachers is paramount for in-service project success, as shown in repeated surveys on the success or failure of in-service projects. That topic will be expanded in Chapter 2.

CRITERIA FOR STAFF-DEVELOPMENT PROGRAMS

The administrator can forge a vision of what school personnel can be if he or she subscribes to a set of criteria by which to build a program. Criteria are guidelines that are applied when staff-development programs are planned and evaluated. There are several sets of criteria to use in planning or judging a program. For example, Gary D. Fenstermacher and David C. Berliner (1983) prepared a conceptual framework by which to judge staff-development programs. Their framework has three dimensions: worth, merit, and success. Under these dimensions are listed twelve necessary conditions. The framework is an interrogation piece by which a staff developer can prepare an in-service education plan and then ask a series of questions about it. The dimension of *worth* emphasizes relevance; *merit* relates to design and delivery; and *success* focuses on planning, resources, and structure. The criteria are of use in asking the question, "Is this program what we really need?"

A more comprehensive list of criteria was prepared by Meredith D. Gall and Ronald S. Renchler (1985). Their research monograph of in-service education criteria contained twenty-seven dimensions or elements. The model consisted of

TABLE 1-2.

CRITERIA FOR EFFECTIVE IN-SERVICE EDUCATION PRACTICES

DIMENSION	EFFECTIVE PRACTICE	BASIS
Teacher Objectives		
Target competencies	Teacher should use instructional methods validated by research	Basic skills experiments
Operationalization	In-service program should have operationally stated objectives for teacher behavior	Implementation research
Complexity	If the skills to be learned are complex, introduce them gradually	Implementation research, in-service research
Expected level of performance	Teachers should be told specifically how much to use particular instructional behaviors	Basic skills experiments, implementation research
Student Objectives		
Target objectives	In-service program should have improved student performance as its ultimate goal	Basic skills experiments
Expected level of achievement	Teachers should be helped to believe that students' academic performance can be improved	Basic skills experiments, teacher expectations, research
Delivery Systems		
Readiness activities	Hold meetings that deal with teacher concerns about the in-service program and build consensus to participate in it.	Implementation research
Instructional process	Teachers should be given manuals describing the methods covered in the in-service program, should discuss the methods in group meetings with a trainer, and should receive observation and feedback on their skills performance	Basic skills experiments; in-service research
Maintenance and monitoring	In-service program should have follow-up component to maintain and monitor gains made on initial training	Implementation research
Training site	In-service program should use the teacher's own classroom as a training site at least part of the time	Basic skills experiments; in-service research
Trainers	The trainer should have credibility with teachers	In-service research
Scheduling	Schedule in-service sessions at times that do not interfere with teachers' other obligations	In-service research
Organizational Context		
Purpose of participation	In-service program should focus on school improvement rather than on personal professional development	In-service research

TABLE 1-2 (continued)

DIMENSION	EFFECTIVE PRACTICE	BASIS
In-service cohorts	In-service program should provide activities that allow teachers to work with and learn from each other	Survey research
Concurrent organizational changes	Principal should participate in and support teacher in-service activities	Implementation research; research on principals' behavior
Other in-service activities	None identified	

Governance

Governance structure	None identified	
Teacher participation in governance	Teachers should have the opportunity to help plan the in-service program	Survey
Recruitment of participants	Participation should be mandatory in order to bring about schoolwide improvement	In-service research
Incentives	Provide incentives such as released time, expenses, college or district credits, approval by school principal	Survey research; implementation research
Sanctions	None identified	
Costs	None identified	

Selection and Evaluation

Policy	In-service program should be selected because of its demonstrated effectiveness in improving students' academic performance	Basic skills experiments
Needs assessments	In-service program should be targeted to areas of student performance demonstrated to be in need of improvement	
Relevance to participants	Content of the in-service program should be relevant to the classroom situation	Survey
Measurement of teacher competence	Teachers' classroom performance should be assessed to determine their implementation of in-service content	
Measurement of student objectives	In-service program effectiveness should be assessed by student performance on relevant measures and in such a way that teachers do not feel threatened	Research on achievement testing

Source: Meredith D. Gall and Ronald S. Renchler, *Effective Staff Development for Teachers: A Research-Based Model,* (Eugene: Clearinghouse on Educational Management, University of Oregon, 1985) Table 1, 3–5. Used with permission of Meredith D. Gall.

a grid containing three components: dimension, effective practice, and basis. Gall and Renchler organized their criteria into six major dimensions, or subsets: (1) teacher objectives, (2) student objectives, (3) delivery systems, (4) organizational context, (5) governance, and (6) selection and evaluation. Their list was well documented. By examining the research summaries, you can quickly determine if the context is applicable. Table 1-2 provides their criteria in short form.

Using Criteria
Staff developers usually have an intuitive grasp of desired outcomes or goals for a sponsored project. However, by applying the criteria in Table 1-2, a planning grid can easily be constructed. For example, relevance is a key criterion for in-service education (Orlich and Ezell 1975). You could determine if an in-service project is relevant by referring to the dimensions of teacher and student objectives, organizational context, governance, and selection and evaluation. Are the applicable criteria being met? Positive responses to that question soon provide a staff developer with the probability of program success.

Over the years, staff developers have discovered that projects attempting to solve a pressing problem or meet felt needs are the most successful.

The need for collaboration (governance) is widely acclaimed. Jay C. Thompson, Jr., and Van E. Cooley (1986) noted the need for collaboration among planners, administrators, and recipients of staff-development efforts. Bob Pickles (1988) urged that parity be an agreed-upon principle when groups collaborate to plan in-service projects. A collaborative model ensures that needs and interests are converted into action projects.

These concepts have long been documented in the literature on effective staff-development programs (see Edelfelt 1977; Harris 1980; Lawrence 1982; Joyce and Showers 1988). By establishing well-identified and documented needs, and using collaborative planning, the staff developer can apply the criteria for successful in-service projects with a sense of empiricism.

In *Continuing to Learn: A Guidebook for Teacher Development*, Susan Loucks-Horsley, Catherine K. Harding et al. (1987) have compiled sets of characteristics and critical attributes that can be used when planning staff-development programs. The writers also discussed a selected set of models, concepts, and delivery systems. Highlighted in each discussion are the assumptions, conditions necessary for success, benefits, and exemplars related to the topic. Collectively, the various summaries could be used as a comprehensive set of criteria by which to guide staff developers.

Other Considerations for the Vision
The probability of success for staff-development programs can be enhanced by following the findings and conclusions of major research studies. Six published syntheses of research on in-service education yielded a list of empirically

TABLE 1-3.

FIFTEEN EMPIRICALLY BASED TRAITS FOR SUCCESSFUL STAFF-DEVELOPMENT PROGRAMS

1. Needs derived
2. Clearly stated objectives
3. Diverse groups with different needs
4. Collaborative planning
5. Flexibility in scheduling
6. Relevant protocols
7. Options for individuals and groups
8. Intensity of training
9. Problem-solving orientation
10. Involvement of principal
11. Concrete activities
12. Participant skills practice
13. Assistance for classroom transfer
14. Long-range development
15. Rewards and incentives structure

based traits, as shown in Table 1-3 (see Korinek, Schmid, and McAdams 1985; Nickolai-Mays and Davis 1986; Thompson and Cooley 1986; Good and Grouws 1987; Wu 1987; Joyce and Showers 1988).

APPLYING THEORY TO PRACTICE

The general topic of how theory relates to the vision of staff development will be introduced at this point and expanded on in Chapter 7. For the most part, staff-development planning and implementation are usually conducted in an atheoretical environment, although one could argue that these practices reflect an implied application of pragmatism. Even so, a series of training projects may often be conducted without someone placing the activities in a global framework or theoretical perspective. Using selected sets of criteria by which to guide program development is really an entree into operating under a theoretical mode. Completing this step alone, however, may not lead to a theoretical analysis unless the developer is required to justify the models being used or the training modes chosen. Again, such a call is infrequent.

One mission of this book is to provide a testable and theoretical statement relating to staff development that fills an apparent void. The paradigm, described in Chapter 7, reconciles the criticism of Donald R. Cruickshank, Christopher Lorish, and Linda Thompson (1979), who asserted that there is a lack of theoretically oriented in-service education projects. This general statement attempts to establish relationships among various kinds of in-service education models, illustrates their conceptual bases, and describes how they are related.

The paradigm is described in Chapter 7 so that detailed descriptions of the components of effective staff-development programs can be presented first. These components include needs assessments, activities and delivery systems, evaluation models, incentives, and funding. By introducing the elements of staff development first, the paradigm can be examined and applied more critically. Further, by then, the staff developer is ready to establish the components and subsystems of his or her comprehensive staff-development program, formulate a set of implicit or explicit characteristics of successful programs, and be in a position to verify or refute some testable inferences.

Thinking about a paradigm for staff development helps the planner state the assumptions being accepted as valid and test those assumptions within an established theoretical framework. All of these elements fit into the vision of a comprehensive staff-development program—a program that is well thought out, is logically consistent, and enhances the growth and potential of every member of the school community.

My vision for staff development is a positive one. Yes, there are mounting problems in the schools. Each problem must be identified and the best possible solution applied to address the problem. By subscribing to more rational and empirical concepts on which to base staff development, the planner continuously tests and refines grounded theory. There is a science associated with staff development, but the art of humanizing the science is incorporated in the vision: a "toast" to the visionaries!

CHAPTER CHECKLISTS

Each chapter concludes with a checklist, designed to help review key concepts. The checklists should be considered as "working lists" that can be expanded for specific contexts.

IN-SERVICE VISION CHECKLIST

_____ 1. The planning of in-service is relevant to anticipated outcomes.

_____ 2. Programs are planned collaboratively.

_____ 3. A definition of staff development is understood.

_____ 4. Staff growth and experience form the training perspective.

_____ 5. Sufficient resources are committed to staff-development efforts.

_____ 6. The intended audience is carefully selected and is appropriate for the in-service training.

_____ 7. Goals and objectives of staff-development programs are consistent with identified needs.

_____ 8. Local staff specialists are used to conduct appropriate programs.

_____ 9. A set of criteria is developed for all in-service programs.

___ **10.** Adult learning principles are incorporated in all in-service projects.

___ **11.** Relevant, empirically tested traits are integrated in program planning and implementation.

___ **12.** Staff-development visions are articulated to the educational community.

CHAPTER 2

DETERMINING NEEDS FOR SUCCESSFUL STAFF-DEVELOPMENT PROGRAMS

Plan Your Work. Work Your Plan.
          Sign on the door of Superintendent of Schools George E. Haney

Staff-development programs are enthusiastically supported when they are adequately developed, well planned, competently managed, and systematically evaluated. Conversely, the literature is replete with unsuccessful case studies, reflecting poorly planned and managed programs. One criterion that stands out among all those discussed in the previous chapter is that in-service projects be "needs driven." Needs-driven projects are based on the clearly defined needs of the school and are relevant to educators and meet their personal and professional desires. These are the programs highlighted in the literature as successful models.

Preparing successful needs assessments combines the art of sensing what needs improvement and the science of collecting accurate data on which to base predictions. Thus, needs assessments depend on planning, on determining what data to collect, and on providing decision makers with coherent statements spelling out how certain schools have well-identified areas requiring new or continued fiscal or material support. In addition, it is most important to identify the human resources already in the organization. Untapped human resources should be marshalled to remedy identified problems or needs. And since state and federal grant proposals require a needs assessment to justify the funding, you should learn to prepare them effectively and persuasively. The "tips" described in this chapter are tested techniques that can be adapted to specific staff-development programs or grant proposals.

AN ASSUMPTION AND SOME SUPPORTING STUDIES

When this book was being reviewed by outside readers, as is the industry practice, one school practitioner wrote that this chapter ought to be left out. His reasoning was that "everybody knows that needs assessments are conducted regularly, but promptly ignored." This comment illustrates the skepticism and lack of understanding that abounds in backward-looking school-district central offices. The assumption that undergirds this chapter is that in-service education programs are effective only because they meet the real or perceived needs of the intended recipients. It is obvious that this reviewer's school district plays unprofessional games with its teachers and subscribes to the deficiency view.

The vision of successful staff-development programs reflects thoughtful and comprehensive planning. Elayne M. Harris (1984) observed that data gathered from needs assessments illustrates the gaps or discrepancies in knowledge and skills in the respondents. Jon C. Marshall and Sara D. Caldwell (1984) reported that systematic formal or informal assessments yield valid data on which to make program decisions. Joan Kingrey (1987) described how the objective use of needs assessments led to a five-year program addressing equity needs across a wide variety of school-related issues.

Providing student test data as a measure of success, Georgea Sparks and her associates (1985) described a comprehensive school-improvement initiative involving nineteen elementary and secondary schools in Michigan. The writers stated that needs assessing was the second step in their strategic planning. Peter J. Murphy (1985) implied that needs assessments were important for collaborative school-based improvement projects. Fred H. Wood, Sarah D. Caldwell, and Steven R. Thompson (1986) presented an "audit" concept that was field-tested in the St. Paul and Fort Worth public schools. Their audits, while being most thorough in collecting data, were sophisticated needs assessments. They wrote that the audit team identified material and human resources in the district, and that their focus was to discover practices and perceptions which district personnel evidenced about school-based staff development. From the audits emanated longitudinal and detailed improvement plans.

James Franco and Donald Zundel (1986) reported on "Project Impact," a Sitka, Alaska, comprehensive staff-development program. Used as part of their needs assessment was the "audit" concept of Wood, Caldwell, and Thompson. The needs assessment culminated in a three-year program that included five phases: awareness, training, implementation, maintenance, and evaluation.

The state of Connecticut has mandated that five-year professional-development plans be prepared by all school districts. Addressing that requirement, the Madison, Connecticut, schools plan (1985) specified continuous needs assessments.

In the same vein, Ann Lieberman (1986) described how the Maine State Board of Education cooperates directly with local school districts to assess needs. Lieberman viewed the cooperation as one means of encouraging collaboration and as a key to successful educational reform.

Two major reviews on in-service education focused on needs assessments as a critical element for successful in-service projects. Hershot C. Waxman (1985) indicated that new programs tend to fail if teachers are omitted from the planning process or when needs are not objectively collected. Jay C. Thompson, Jr., and

Van E. Cooley (1986) studied effective staff-development programs in the fifty states and concluded that the first prerequisite for success (being effective) was a comprehensive assessment of needs.

In conclusion, it is valid to assume that a proper needs assessment is one of the critical elements that ultimately leads to successful in-service projects. And the converse is also valid: no needs assessment leads to a low probability of success. Therefore, we begin with the testable hypothesis that needs assessments are essential for successful in-service programs.

CONDUCTING NEEDS ASSESSMENTS

There are many methods by which to assess needs. A few selected techniques in the process are:

- Surveys—interviews or questionnaires
- Testimonials from knowledgeable individuals
- Committee reports
- Planning documents
- Reviews of literature
- Statements from professional or scientific societies
- Scores on objective or standardized tests

While the above seven techniques are far from all-inclusive, this chapter will focus on the following techniques:

- Evaluation data from tests
- Surveys
- Delphi Technique
- Discrepancy models

These general methods are highlighted because they tend to be those most easily and widely used by school districts or universities as well as those most economical to conduct and interpret.

A *need* may be defined as some condition that requires attention, or some desire or value that is not present or not being met. In many cases, needs are simply what someone or some group "wants." Educational needs tend to arise from changing conditions or circumstances, and they are "discovered" as "needs" relatively late.

The identification of needs is an essential element in planning for and in involving the community in educational goal setting. A *needs assessment* is a method of discovering gaps between what "is" and what "ought" to take place in the schools. The difference between reality and desire is frequently referred to as a "discrepancy."

Needs assessments are conducted and needs are identified for the following reasons:

1. To discover strengths of programs or personnel
2. To identify perceived weaknesses in programs or personnel
3. To determine discrepancies in programs or curricula
4. To identify "unmet" concerns
5. To assist curriculum development through evaluation
6. To set priorities for future or immediate actions
7. To illustrate a novel local want
8. To justify renewal of special areas
9. To provide for community consensus
10. To share the general decision making among various constituencies

Needs assessments often have multiple foci. Assessments are commonly used to determine administrator, teacher, or classified staff in-service educational needs; to identify the many needs of students; and to inaugurate recommended curriculum changes. In short, a needs assessment is one method by which school administrators can plan more efficiently to meet changing conditions in a world where change is the norm.

ORGANIZATIONAL CONCERNS

Carrying out a needs assessment requires that school decision makers continuously plan ahead—at least one or more years. Generally, a school district might conduct several different needs assessments during a year, each one focused on a single issue. However, a district could combine several emerging issues and conduct fewer assessments.

Identifying the Focus

When conducting needs assessments for in-service programs, it is imperative to focus on one or more of the following groups:

- Classified staff members
- Elementary school teachers
- Junior and senior high school teachers
- Principals
- Central office administrators
- School board members
- Citizen committees and students

Seldom, if ever, will all of these groups participate in the same in-service program—except perhaps for a bond issue or mill levy.

The first step is to identify the group or groups that require future growth. The second step, to identify the focus, can be accomplished by making one individual in the central office responsible for collecting possible topics or issues that could be converted into needs assessments.

Once a topic or issue has been selected, all the specifics of a needs assessment must be determined. These specifics include (1) the model or technique to be followed, (2) the focal group (or groups) to be included, (3) the type of data or information required, (4) the specific forms or instruments for conducting surveys and the questionnaires to be used, (5) the people who will collect the data, (6) the method for analyzing and synthesizing the data; (7) the people who will receive copies of the report with recommendations or options, and (8) the plans for implementing the options.

Contextual Considerations

A needs assessment is profoundly affected by "contextual conditions." The time, place, and circumstances of the assessment have an important effect on the results. Emotional or value-laden issues will prove more difficult to assess, even under the most scientific conditions. These issues include sex education in the schools, AIDS educational programs, family planning, or controversial areas that relate to evolution, interscholastic sports, or teacher evaluations.

Further, specific needs change as the context changes. For example, there may be a strong perceived need for a specific in-service program. Once that need is met, a different set of needs may emerge that relate to the original program, but in a different context. For example, if teachers identify a need to learn about inquiry teaching models, predictably a future need will be how to apply inquiry-related teaching materials across the curriculum.

ASSESSING LOCAL RESOURCES

Another preliminary step in a needs assessment is determining just what kinds of resources are present in the organization. The resources are of many varieties: human, material, fiscal, and cultural. Identifying these resources is important if you are to maximize the available human talent and nonhuman resources.

This book reflects the growth approach to staff development. But before teachers (or anyone else) can grow, they need to be guided in that growth, perhaps even coached. Therefore, staff developers should conduct an assessment of internal, and particularly human, resources. Basically, the staff developer needs to locate everyone with some educational specialty, whether or not it is being used in current assignments. School decision-makers should incorporate these talented people in planning future in-service projects.

In addition to collecting this information, planners should put to use specific or esoteric specialties. For example, most school districts have personnel with in-depth experience or training in selected topics such as science, writing-across-

MODEL 2-1.

HUMAN RESOURCE FILE ASSESSMENT

We are establishing a human resources file and we need your help. (1) Please nominate someone in the school district who you know has some expertise that could enhance our staff-development program. (2) Please list your own special expertise that you would be willing to share with others or that you might use to help others extend their skills in our staff-development program. (3) If you know any of our students with a specialized skill, please share that information.

Name of Colleague:
Area of Expertise:
School Location:
Your Name:
Date:
Please return this form to the Director of Staff Personnel, using our internal mail system.

Note: The same form could be modified to seek cultural resources that are located in the district—museums, art galleries, public collections, and the like.

the-curriculum, critical-thinking programs, questioning strategies, organizational development, human-relations training, PERT charting, computer simulations, lunchroom management, care and maintenance of floors, boiler repair, asbestos removal, and so forth. Use questionnaires or nomination forms for initial identification of human resources. Include bus drivers, secretaries, custodians, security personnel, administrators, teachers, and even students. Yes, students are usually ignored as a human resource in the schools. Just remember that many young students are the whiz kids of computers and many other forms of electronic gadgetry. (Hey! We are all in the business to learn and to teach.)

Once the information is collected, it needs to be referenced, catalogued, and cross-referenced for ease of use. Of course, individuals should be contacted so that they can decline nomination if they so desire. The resources catalog might be published every year or every two years, with a copy provided to every school and administrator in the school district.

The data-collection form can be elaborated with checklists, or it can be as simple as Model 2-1.

That is how simple it can be. Several school districts in the United States conduct such an inventory on a regular basis. Nearly every state has such an inventory sponsored by the National Diffusion Network (NDN). Needless to say, the NDN has a talent bank that expands intellectual resources far beyond expectation.

The first step in enhancing human potential in any school organization, then, is to survey the existing resources. How satisfying it is to be recognized by one's professional peers. The esteem of one's colleagues is a very powerful motivating force. And that motivation comes virtually cost-free.

ACHIEVEMENT TESTS

Achievement tests are constructed to assess a student's terminal behavior or the expected behavior or attainment of the student after completion of an assignment, unit, module, or course. Achievement tests are developed to assess the degree to which the desired behavior or performance takes place. Such tests scores tend to illustrate levels of skills development.

Use the data from any state or nationally normed test with great caution. The first question to ask is, "Did we teach that content before the test was taken?" If not, any poor showings on the subscales of the test can be ignored. However, if major concepts have been taught and the students still did poorly, examine the quality of instruction (the teachers) and the quality of the curriculum being used. To improve achievement-test scores requires detailed analyses of scores on a school-by-school basis. Further, the fastest possible gain on normed tests is usually two years. Assuming valid tests, the data should be interpreted by the school's in-service education task force. The task force can isolate topics or concepts requiring curriculum revision or development, as well as the in-service education needed to implement the improvement plan. Thus, the curriculum can be aligned with in-service projects. This process stresses the importance of maximizing student achievements through specific, data-based interventions.

SURVEYS FOR NEEDS ASSESSMENTS

The typical school-conducted needs assessment is usually a short questionnaire distributed to all teachers in a school district. It may contain open-ended and forced-response items. Both techniques will be discussed here, after a short statement about advantages and disadvantages of surveys.

General Advantages of Questionnaires

If surveys are used, then multiple sets of needs questionnaires must be administered to subgroups. Such a method approaches a marketing concept for determining concerns and for providing successful programs. It is important that decision makers carefully examine the relative advantages and disadvantages of forced-response questionnaires in determining apparent needs.

The following list summarizes the overall general advantages of using a questionnaire to collect needs data:

1. Many individuals can be contacted at the same time, usually through the school district's mail service.
2. A questionnaire is less expensive to administer than a personal interview.
3. Each selected subgroup respondent receives identical questions.

4. A written questionnaire provides a vehicle for expression without fear of embarrassment to the respondent.
5. Responses are easily tabulated, depending on the design of the instrument.
6. Uniform data are gathered that allow for long-range research implications and for program development.

The above advantages must be carefully analyzed for each needs survey. Further, the timing of a survey is critical. The months of September, December, January, May, and June are very poor times in which to distribute questionnaires. The summer months of July and August are inappropriate for mailing questionnaires to school personnel, since they are on vacation. In addition, many school districts, for example, have policies which specify that no one in the district is obliged to complete a questionnaire not officially approved by the district.

Disadvantages of a Needs Questionnaire
For every advantage of a forced-response questionnaire survey, there is an accompanying disadvantage. A summary of disadvantages includes the following:

1. The investigator is prevented from learning the respondent's motivation for answering questions.
2. Respondents may be somewhat limited in providing free expression of opinions, owing to instrument design.
3. Not all questionnaires are usually returned.
4. Complex designs cause poor responses, or no response at all.
5. A question may have different meanings to different people.
6. Selections of the sample, per se, may cause biased results; that is, the sample may not be representative of the whole.
7. Respondents may not complete the entire questionnaire.

Open-Ended Questions
An open-ended question typically does not include predetermined, or forced-response, categories and the respondent therefore is free to answer in any manner desired. There are at least five reasons for using an open-ended question: (1) to probe an idea further, (2) to accommodate categories that are incomplete or inadequate in a forced-response list, (3) to provide projective situations, (4) to generate items for forced-response surveys, and (5) to elicit items for a Delphi Technique. Open-ended questions are inappropriate when forced-response categories are needed to clarify some point.

Tabulating and quantifying results, and determining meaningful generalizations, tends to be more difficult when using open-ended questions. These questions require a more complex and more subjective coding system than do forced-response questions. Tabulating open-ended results involves examining each respondent's answers on an individual basis. Categories for some characteristic

MODEL 2-2.

EXAMPLES OF OPEN-ENDED QUESTIONS

When Addressing Teacher In-Service
1. What problems does this school (or district) have in conducting in-service programs?
2. How do these problems affect you?
3. What can be done and who can solve the identified problem?

When Addressing Curriculum Needs
1. What is our most pressing curriculum need in
   (a) elementary schools, (b) high schools?
2. What do you think contributed to these problems?
3. What can be done and who can solve the identified problems?

When Addressing Organizational Needs
1. What policies or procedures are most in need of change to improve the schools?
2. How do these policies or procedures affect the way in which you do your job?
3. Who could solve these problems?

---

of the responses must also be developed, and each of the open-ended responses is then classified into one of the appropriate categories. In contrast, the categories for classifying forced-response questions are already developed by virtue of the response patterns provided by the respondents. In some cases, the investigator can combine both types of questions.

Open-ended questions can identify topics that a staff-development committee might not have generated. Thus respondents identify needs, problems, or concerns that can later be translated into forced-response questions. Open-ended questions can be asked in either personal or telephone interviews, or in mailed surveys. Model 2-2 shows several different examples of open-ended questions that address "needs."

Forced-Response Questions

As the term implies, in this question type a respondent can logically select only one category, because the responses are already established and are mutually exclusive. Further, the question presents an equal number of positive and negative responses. The item is simple, written as a positive statement. If negative statements are used, respondents quickly become confused.

Likert scales. One of the more commonly used response continua was developed by Rensis Likert. Note how the following examples use his response patterns; any of these could be used in needs assessments:

1. More writing experiences are needed in the high-school curriculum.
   ( ) Strongly Agree
   ( ) Agree

( ) Undecided
( ) Disagree
( ) Strongly Disagree

2. I would encourage the school board to promote programs aimed at providing job skills for the physically and mentally handicapped.
( ) Encourage Very Much
( ) Encourage
( ) No Opinion
( ) Discourage
( ) Discourage Very Much

3. How well do you like attending workshops as compared to other instructional procedures?
( ) I like workshops much better
( ) I like workshops a little better
( ) I like all instructional procedures about equally well
( ) I like other instructional procedures a little better than workshops
( ) I like other instructional procedures much better than workshops

The respondent is requested to select only one category of a Likert-scale item. The categories must be exhaustive and mutually exclusive. These models, as well as other models used here, are provided for your use; feel free to adapt them as you prepare items for needs assessment you conduct.

Model 2-3 illustrates how a Likert scale could be applied to a checklist, so that the respondent can make a finer discrimination for each item. (Note that when using weighted scores, the positive responses have higher numerical values.)

MODEL 2-3.

COMBINING CHECKLIST AND LIKERT DESIGNS

Kindly respond to each item by circling the number that represents your attitude regarding each part of the question. The coded numbers mean:

5 = Strongly Agree   3 = No Opinion   2 = Disagree
4 = Agree   1 = Strongly Disagree

1-6. To what extent do you agree that students at each specified grade level should be taught about careers and the world of work as a part of the school program? Please respond to each grade level.

	STRONGLY AGREE	AGREE	NO OPINION	DISAGREE	STRONGLY DISAGREE
1. Grades 1–3	5	4	3	2	1
2. Grades 4–6	5	4	3	2	1
3. Grades 7–8	5	4	3	2	1
4. Grades 9–10	5	4	3	2	1
5. Grades 11–12	5	4	3	2	1
6. Post-secondary schools	5	4	3	2	1

MODEL 2-4.

ELEMENTARY SCIENCE NEEDS SURVEY

Please indicate the grade level(s) in which you teach science classes _____.
On the scale at the right, please circle the number that best describes the intensity of
your reaction to each of the questions.

	STRONGLY AGREE				STRONGLY DISAGREE

1. Children in my school enjoy science. — 6 5 4 3 2 1
2. My school has excellent materials for scientific activities. — 6 5 4 3 2 1
3. Children in my school would like more hands-on activities in science. — 6 5 4 3 2 1
4. Our school district should adopt an activity-centered science program. — 6 5 4 3 2 1
5. My school has excellent texts for studying science. — 6 5 4 3 2 1
6. Our school district should adopt a textbook-oriented science program at my grade level. — 6 5 4 3 2 1
7. My preparation in science courses is strong. — 6 5 4 3 2 1
8. My preparation in science methods courses is strong. — 6 5 4 3 2 1
9. An in-service training program for teachers should be provided when the district is adopting a new science program. — 6 5 4 3 2 1
10. If an intensive in-service program could be provided during the summer, I would be interested in attending. — 6 5 4 3 2 1
11. Our school district should establish a system for maintaining and distributing living and consumable materials, which are used in elementary-science instruction. — 6 5 4 3 2 1

Please place any other comments on the reverse side.

Model 2-4 shows a needs survey originally developed by David R. Stronck, which I later adapted. As a demonstration of a need for a revised elementary science program in a large school district, the instrument shown here was administered to over 400 elementary school teachers. Data were tabulated and graphic illustrations were prepared for each item. The results were then appended to a grant application to the National Science Foundation, and subsequently, the project was awarded $50,000. The needs for that grant were so well documented that the proposal reviewers rated the project higher than one might have expected.

Observe that Model 2-4 requests three types of information: (1) policy statements, (2) factual statements, and (3) personal judgments. These elements typically are used in any needs assessment to justify a grant.

While Model 2-4 was designed for a grant proposal, it has subsequently been used to determine teachers' perceptions of teaching science as well as other specific subjects. It can easily be adapted to other subjects by dropping the word *science* and substituting some other subject; note how the model questions can easily be generalized.

Rank-ordered items. Another common needs-assessment technique is that of providing a set of items and requesting the respondents to rank them. Model 2-5 illustrates this technique as applied to teacher concerns about in-service education. By comparing the responses of various subgroups of teachers, planners could devise a set of appropriate in-service activities. However, notice that the needs as expressed in Model 2-5 are too general to be implemented. A collaborative group of administrators and teachers would have to establish the details: objectives, procedures, techniques, and times. Model 2-5 simply yields a ranking of general statements as evaluated by the respondents. Again, note that each item could also be judged independently by providing a scale similar to Model 2-4.

Model 2-5 is illustrative of a common form. The ultimate interpretation of the results might require speculation, and it may be prudent to use some type of small-group prioritizing technique as a follow-up activity.

MODEL 2-5.

RANK-ORDERED ITEMS TECHNIQUE

Below is a list of in-service items. Please rank these items from 1 to 9. No. 1 has the highest priority, No. 2 is the second highest, and so on, with No. 9 the lowest priority. These items are submitted to you so that the school district in-service committee can plan for next year.

RANK	ITEM
————	A. Districtwide workshops conducted during school time for the improvement of instruction.
————	B. In-service programs set up for selected teachers on the teaching of inquiry.
————	C. In-service programs needed to implement the district's new mathematics program.
————	D. Released time allowed for work on curriculum development.
————	E. Gifted-student program models arranged for the middle school.
————	F. Pilot microcomputers introduced in mathematics classes.
————	G. Questioning strategies workshop arranged for teachers at all levels.
————	H. Small-group tutorial techniques demonstrated.
————	I. Cooperative learning techniques.

Through systematic collection of opinions from students, teachers, administrators, and citizens, school decision-makers are better able to determine the relative support and opposition to proposed projects, activities, or goals. There is practically no limit to the kinds of needs surveys that can be conducted. Among the topics that can be surveyed are (1) attitudes toward selected programs, (2) attitudes toward changing a specific curriculum, (3) opinions about programs and program goals, (4) suggestions for possible curriculum expansions or deletions, (5) feelings about anticipated evaluation methods, (6) ideas for determining long-range program priorities, and many, many more.

THE DELPHI TECHNIQUE

The preceding sections emphasized the basics of needs-assessment construction: communication, precision, objectivity, simplicity, clarity. The designs of the instruments just discussed are rather traditional. There are, however, other information-gathering techniques that may be of value as alternative models for, or as components of, a needs assessment. The Delphi Technique has emerged as an excellent method of determining valued or desirable requirements which are lacking in the schools.

General Model

The Delphi Technique was developed and popularized by the RAND Corporation (Helmer 1967). RAND originated the system as a method of identifying group opinions, initially about defense needs, and named it Delphi after the great oracle of Apollo. Basically, the respondents participate in three or more rounds of needs surveying, in which they receive their own data and the data for the entire group prior to each round. Delphi provides a continuous feedback system to all participants, but through a privileged design. That is, each respondent knows how he or she has responded, but does not know how any other individual responded. As such, the Delphi Technique (1) allows professional judgments to be made, (2) avoids personality conflicts and interpersonal politics, and (3) reduces the possibility of high-position people forcing judgments in group discussions in the direction they deem desirable. The Delphi Technique is one means of identifying organizational consensus, determining problem areas, and establishing priorities by providing detailed feedback and systematic follow-up.

One of the problems in making decisions is predicting what the future will hold. It may therefore be prudent to establish priorities for goals that have already been identified through other needs assessments, opinionnaires, or small-group task techniques. To this end, the Delphi Technique provides a methodology for organizing and prioritizing the collective judgments of the polled group, or of those who are concerned with planning and implementing the change. This technique is an excellent way to seek consensus on what may be the most useful means of effecting change.

Implementation Procedures

In the Delphi Technique, the initial procedure is to prepare and distribute a series of questions or problem statements for evaluation. For example, a planner might distribute a questionnaire that contains a series of problems, statements, opinions, activities, or predictions of future probabilities. In the first round, respondents provide a rank ordering, a priority, or an evaluation of each item. One modification of this first step is to prepare a general statement that elicits specific responses which can ultimately be converted to items for judging.

All selected participants then receive a second list of items and are asked to either rate the list by selected criteria or reevaluate their original list in reaction to the responses of others provided in the initial ranking. Depending on the method used in the initial round, the lists are returned to each respondent with detailed group rankings plus adverse comments, new ideas for consideration, and minority reports. Typically, the group mean or mode per item is computed and fed back to all participants.

The tabulator of the instruments (a list of rankings, in this case) reanalyzes the data and prepares yet a third instrument for distribution to the selected sample. This procedure continues through at least four rankings. By working with multiple submissions of the same set of data, each respondent reaffirms original opinions, modifies some, or adds additional needs to the list. The technique aids in forming a clearly defined convergence pattern of major needs, plus a well-outlined minority opinion.

The Delphi Technique is easily adaptable to needs-assessment surveys designed to analyze the desirability of innovative programs or projects. A series of needs, for example, might be rated as to their significance. In addition, all respondents are encouraged to provide statements about the impact that the programs might have if instituted. For example, the Delphi Technique is most effective in initially determining whether a group can identify issues, concerns, problems, or suggested courses of action.

Another organizational problem—the formulation of educational policies and plans that allow for alternative future options—can be solved by Delphi analyses. In such cases, preference statements can be written by a task force. The list can then be distributed to the selected subgroup for their initial responses. The complete Delphi Technique then follows. Consensus can easily be identified for those items that have higher or lower means, or modes.

In summary, the Delphi Technique is a feedback mechanism by which selected members of an organization have an effect in shaping organizational goals and policies. It is a very systematic method, nevertheless. (See Appendix A for an example.) Directors of staff development need a detailed understanding of survey methods, since needs assessments are a special case in the methodology. Let us now examine an array of other techniques by which to carry out the process.

MODEL 2-6.

DISCREPANCY MODEL NEEDS ASSESSMENT: IN-SERVICE QUESTIONNAIRE

Please respond twice for each statement listed in the center. In the left column, labeled "What Is," circle the number that indicates your perception of the current circumstances in your school or district. Then circle one number in the right column, "What Ought To Be."

1 = I strongly disagree
2 = I disagree
3 = I concur
4 = I strongly concur

WHAT IS	STATEMENT	WHAT OUGHT TO BE
1 2 3 4	**1.** Teachers are offered a wide variety of in-service offerings.	1 2 3 4
1 2 3 4	**2.** The district's in-service offerings meet my professional needs.	1 2 3 4
1 2 3 4	**3.** Objectives of our district's in-service offerings are well known to all teachers.	1 2 3 4
1 2 3 4	**4.** My in-service needs are met through college-sponsored extension courses.	1 2 3 4
1 2 3 4	**5.** In-service in this district is conducted during the regular school day.	1 2 3 4
1 2 3 4	**6.** In-service activities are generally incorporated into my teaching.	1 2 3 4

SELECTED DISCREPANCY TECHNIQUES

Needs-assessment designers often use a *discrepancy analysis* as an alternative technique. A discrepancy exists when respondents perceive that "what ought to take place" is different from "what seems to take place." For example, teachers have long participated in in-service activities after school hours, and usually in some type of university extension course. If district administrators want to shift some in-service activities to be "job-embedded" (activities that take place during the school day or in a teacher's actual class), then they can determine potential teacher support through a needs-assessment instrument similar to Model 2-6.

Note that in Model 2-6 the statements are drawn from experience and tend to reflect some dimension of current practices. By requesting two specific sets of responses, planners can make comparisons among respondent groups. Where discrepancies are observed, additional decision making and interpreting are required.

Models 2-7 and 2-8 illustrate modified forms of discrepancy instruments. These two models show an attempt to determine (1) how much educators apparently know about a set of topics, (2) their interest in becoming more proficient in the topic, and (3) their highest priorities for growth. In many needs-assessment instruments, however, respondents are *not* asked to prioritize items, the designers implying that all items are of equal value. Quite obviously, such an assumption is usually invalid.

REVIEWS OF THE LITERATURE OR RESEARCH

Nonbiased research or other published literature can provide general information on state-of-the-art needs. By reviewing such published papers, school decision makers can determine trends that may ultimately reflect their specific needs. A review of the literature begins with a set of referenced generalizations. Next, the

MODEL 2-7.

MODIFIED ADMINISTRATOR'S NEEDS ASSESSMENT DISCREPANCY INSTRUMENT

The Council desires to provide more direct administrator-staff development activities. To aid in planning that process, we have developed an instrument to elicit specific responses to specific topics. The items in the left-hand column list specific topics related to administration. The column entitled "Your Self-Rated Proficiency" asks for your own evaluation of your proficiency for each specified topic. "Your Desire" asks if you want to learn more about the selected administrative topic. "Your Highest Priority" asks you to indicate your FIRST, or top, priority within each group.

Please circle a number that is coded for each of the three areas, as is described:

Your Proficiency:
1 Indicates that you already know the topic and are using it.
2 Indicates that you know of the topic, but *do not* use it.
3 Indicates that you are *not* knowledgeable on that topic.

Your Desire:
1 Indicates that you desire to become proficient in using that topic in your administration.
2 Indicates that you do *not* desire to become proficient in using the specific topic in your administration.

Your Priority:
1 Indicates YOUR HIGHEST priority, you desire most to attend a staff-development program for that set of topics.

RANK ORDER ONLY THE TOP PRIORITY ITEM FOR EACH OF THE MAJOR SECTIONS OF THE IDENTIFIED TOPICS.

Please circle your proficiency AND your desire for each specific topic. Do not omit any items. Also circle a "1" in the right-hand column to indicate your highest priority for staff-development programs within each major section. This technique allows you to identify your administrative strengths and areas for future professional growth. The prioritizing allows you to establish your true "wants."

MODEL 2-7 (continued)

TOPIC Section I PERSONAL MANAGEMENT STYLES	YOUR SELF-RATED PROFICIENCY FOR EACH TOPIC			YOUR DESIRE TO KNOW MORE ABOUT EACH TOPIC		SPECIFY YOUR HIGHEST PRIORITY TOPIC BY CIRCLING ONLY ONE OF THE NUMBERS BELOW
	1 Know & Use	2 Know, But Do Not Use	3 Do Not Know	1 Desire	2 Do Not Desire	
Organization Development (OD)	1	2	3	1	2	1
Stress Management	1	2	3	1	2	1
Time Management	1	2	3	1	2	1
Problem-Solving Techniques	1	2	3	1	2	1
Other (Specify)	1	2	3	1	2	1

TOPIC Section II MANAGEMENT PLANNING SKILLS	YOUR SELF-RATED PROFICIENCY FOR EACH TOPIC			YOUR DESIRE TO KNOW MORE ABOUT EACH TOPIC		SPECIFY YOUR HIGHEST PRIORITY TOPIC BY CIRCLING ONLY ONE OF THE NUMBERS BELOW
	1 Know & Use	2 Know, But Do Not Use	3 Do Not Know	1 Desire	2 Do Not Desire	
Delphi Technique	1	2	3	1	2	1
Management By Objective (MBO)	1	2	3	1	2	1
Program Evaluation Review Technique (PERT)	1	2	3	1	2	1
Other (Specify)	1	2	3	1	2	1

MODEL 2-8.

TEACHER NEEDS ASSESSMENT INSTRUMENT*

TOPIC Section I TEACHING TECHNOLOGIES	YOUR SELF-RATED PROFICIENCY FOR EACH TOPIC			YOUR DESIRE TO KNOW MORE ABOUT EACH TOPIC		SPECIFY YOUR HIGHEST PRIORITY TOPIC BY CIRCLING *ONLY ONE OF THE NUMBERS BELOW*
	1 Know & Use	2 Know, But Do Not Use	3 Do Not Know	1 Desire	2 Do Not Desire	
Learning centers	1	2	3	1	2	1
Criterion-referenced evaluation	1	2	3	1	2	1
Computer-assisted drill work	1	2	3	1	2	1
Tutorial techniques	1	2	3	1	2	1
Other (Specify)	1	2	3	1	2	1

TOPIC Section II CLASSROOM MANAGEMENT TECHNIQUES	YOUR SELF-RATED PROFICIENCY FOR EACH TOPIC			YOUR DESIRE TO KNOW MORE ABOUT EACH TOPIC		SPECIFY YOUR HIGHEST PRIORITY TOPIC BY CIRCLING *ONLY ONE OF THE NUMBERS BELOW*
	1 Know & Use	2 Know, But Do Not Use	3 Do Not Know	1 Desire	2 Do Not Desire	
Behavior Modification	1	2	3	1	2	1
Desist Strategies	1	2	3	1	2	1
Reality Therapy	1	2	3	1	2	1
Transactional Analysis	1	2	3	1	2	1

*Directions, omitted from Model 2-8, are almost identical to those shown for Model 2-7. If you have any doubts that the respondents are *not* familiar with any technique that is being rated, then *do* prepare a short abstract on all the techniques. (For example, in the listing of classroom management techniques, most teachers are probably not familiar with the last three.) Then accompany the needs instrument with an added page concisely explaining each technique.

33

methodology of each study is examined to reject those papers having questionable or contrived designs. Finally, a set of conclusions about the topic are written. These reflect an interpretation of how applicable the findings are to the *local educational context*. Elliot W. Eisner (1984) calculated that the experimental treatments in school settings for an entire year averaged only seventy-two minutes of actual student use! "Educational commando raids" was Eisner's reaction to this situation, where he reviewed all fifteen experimental studies published in the nation's leading educational research journal.

Reviews of research are helpful when you propose implementing a new technique, instructional model, or educational technology. By reviewing the research, you'll avoid the pitfalls, and the programs may be more successful. Of equal importance, you'll reject the fads, brief enthusiasms, and other questionable programs as a result of this review process..

CONCLUSION

One hallmark of organized activity is the process called *planning*. If effective changes are to be made in any educational enterprise, a substantial amount of time and energy must be concentrated on planning sessions. With planning, changes can take place in a more systematic fashion, not just by random activity. Researchers in all disciplines have long known that if a well-devised research plan has been prepared, then results can be predicted with a high degree of probability. Only occasionally are outcomes unanticipated. The results of staff-development programs should also be anticipated in such a manner, that is, predicted. Successful in-service education is not always the development of inspired or creative projects; often it is the result of thoughtful prior needs assessments and careful analysis.

If the needs assessment is not a reasonably accurate predictor, then those associated with the planning function will be discredited and considered unreliable. Assessing needs requires continued reevaluation of data, circumstances, and conditions. Needs identification is a relativistic process, not an absolute one. Needs assessments worth their mettle should be continuously modified—but this is unfortunately the exception. As a general rule, needs plans are seldom distributed and infrequently rechecked to determine success ratios.

Assessing the many apparent needs of the schools is not a simple activity. Actually, assessing needs is an extension of evaluation in its broadest context. Judgments are made after data are collected. These judgments lead to decisions and plans. The more valid the needs assessments, the more valid will be the decisions and the plans. Needs assessments are tools that improve the problem-solving capacities of educational institutions. When observed from a problem-solving frame of reference, the total process of systematic planning can be one of the most important administrative activities, enabling educators to solve problems as they emerge. Through such planning, institutions evolve from reactive to proactive organizations, with staff development emerging as a highly valued activity.

In the last analysis, John I. Goodlad's *A Place Called School* (1984) was the ultimate model for a needs assessment. He illustrated that multiple sets of needs exist in the school, all of which can be met. The quality of schooling is really the one aspect that we as professionals control.

CHECKLIST FOR NEEDS ASSESSMENTS

_____ 1. Information on needs is collected systematically.

_____ 2. Needs assessments are keyed to specific groups within the organization.

_____ 3. Local resources are assessed.

_____ 4. Student outcomes are examined critically to determine specific priorities for in-service projects.

_____ 5. The staff-development team is well trained in survey methodologies.

_____ 6. Delphi or similar techniques are used to arrive at a consensus when prioritizing in-service projects.

_____ 7. Discrepancy analyses are used to judge needs.

_____ 8. Appropriate literature is reviewed which relates to anticipated in-service projects.

_____ 9. Needs assessments lead to staff-development programs for targeted groups.

_____ 10. Needs relate to curriculum, instruction, or work-related activities.

CHAPTER 3

DELIVERING STAFF-DEVELOPMENT ACTIVITIES

When teachers attend a workshop they expect a professionally conducted performance—not excuses.

Presenter at the National Staff Development Conference, Seattle, 1987

The actual conduct of any in-service activity and the subsequent implementation of the learned behaviors (or content) in the classroom constitute the bottom line in staff development. Chapter 1 presented the concepts of planning effective in-service projects and establishing a vision for an overall staff-development program. If you make use of the various well-tested criteria, practices, and models, as described in Chapter 2, then your in-service vision is virtually assured of success. Presenters must always remember that the participants are professional adults. The participants are themselves educators who know how to teach and who know what constitutes appropriate instructional technique.

Yet in-service education has had a relatively poor reputation among recipients. In 1986, that point was again reiterated by Samuel B. Bacharach, Scott C. Bauer, and Joseph B. Shedd, who reported that data from a national study showed that in-service training was ranked at the bottom of effective ways to increase job-related knowledge or skills. From this finding and earlier negative findings (Neil 1985), we may reasonably conclude that the content and delivery of in-service activities have been inadequate. How to improve the quality of these programs through better organization is the subject of this chapter.

SPECIFIC ACTIVITY FORMATS AND CONTEXTS

Staff-development activities focusing on group needs take place in many different formats: workshops, clinics, short courses, seminars, institutes, and conferences. The format selected should have an organizational characteristic that makes it the best possible choice. Table 3-1 shows how these group formats can be used with various-size groups and also shows the optimal use of each format. Recall that you can use a self-directed or individualized format, too. However, the emphasis here is on group needs.

Format should follow function; that is, after the needs are assessed, the planning accomplished, and the participants identified, a format should be selected that best accomplishes the goals and objectives of the activity.

The general use of workshops, clinics, short courses, seminars, and institutes should be derived from identified needs. The conference is an exception. Professional associations conduct conferences as a major source of revenue as well as an arena in which to share ideas and expand knowledge.

Conference planners do not conduct needs assessments to determine what knowledge or skills need expansion. Most planners do, however, attempt to forecast trends for conference themes. Yet the conference also holds a potential for incidental or unstructured learning in a staff-development program. That is, participants will always pick up something new, while not actually seeking it.

Professionals and classified staff attend conferences for a variety of reasons, one of which is to establish a network of personal contacts. It is through networking that participants create an awareness of the expertise and human potential that exist in some specific disciplines, such as administration, science education, social studies education, or counseling. Personal contacts become a powerful source of "knowledge about field happenings" as well as a way of disseminating and diffusing information on innovations.

The people constituting a specific network maintain an oral tradition. Professionals tend to call on colleagues who hold similar positions to determine possible solutions to problems rather than refer to the literature. Thus the conference serves a dynamic social function, allowing those in attendance to become acquainted with practitioners, professors, researchers, writers, and consultants. Personal evaluations of various projects, staff-development programs, and even the presenters themselves typically are discussed at professional meetings. A school district or regional conference serves the same social purpose as does a well-established national convention.

As early as 1976, Bruce R. Joyce and his colleagues provided a set of five contextual modes relating to staff development. The *job-embedded mode* usually consists of committee work, team work, or work with consultants. The critical point of this mode is that it takes place right on the job, during the regular work-

TABLE 3-1.

FORMATS FOR STAFF-DEVELOPMENT ACTIVITIES

FORMAT	OPTIMAL SIZE	OPTIMAL USE
Conference	None	Awareness—information giving
Institutes	24–36	Longitudinal and detailed study
Seminar	8–12	Group study on one topic
Short courses	12–36	Detailed study of some area—typically university sponsored
Clinic	12–24	Intensive study of one or two techniques, some application
Workshop	8–24	"Make it and take it"—hands-on, activity oriented

ing day. Teachers, administrators, or classified staff are released from duties to participate in sponsored activities.

The *job-related mode* focuses on workshops, centers, exchanges, or other delivery systems. The essence here is that topics are related directly to the participant's job. Relevance is the key concept for a job-related workshop; that is, administrators, teachers, or classified staff apply the concepts they learn as quickly as possible.

The *credential-oriented* and *professional-organization* modes are self-explanatory. Bruce Joyce's *self-directed mode* was amplified by Maureen A. Sullivan (1987), who presented a successful case study of an adaption of the self-directed mode by teachers in the East Lansing Public Schools (Michigan). She described a successful seminar approach that provided teachers with a mechanism for detailed discussions that had not taken place previously on in-service topics. Marc S. Reigel (1987) reported a similar project in which teachers demonstrated motivation and commitment to a project through the self-directed mode of in-service education.

A sixth type needs to be added: the *school-based mode*. There is now a trend toward shifting staff-development responsibilities from the school district to the school itself. These six modes will be referred to as we discuss delivery systems.

In summary, these modes—job-embedded, job-related, credential-oriented, professional-organization, self-directed, and school-based—will predictably be the subject of professional negotiations as staff development is considered even more important for continued teacher education. The implications will be more fully observed as teachers, administrators, and classified staff use staff development as an extension of compensation practices.

Now let us focus on some of the mundane, but important, elements that conference and in-service planners must determine so that the presenters know what is expected of them.

GENERAL ORGANIZERS FOR PLANNERS

Assume that a needs assessment is completed, analyzed, and interpreted before the format or context of a conference or in-service activity is selected. A study of local human resources should also be completed to determine if a local activity leader is available. If no one can be found, arrangements must be made to retain an outside presenter or consultant. Regardless of the locale, collaborative planning and goal setting must be done with the presenter before the activity ever begins. Following is a brief list of organizational considerations that should be discussed in detail.

Goals
- Goals of activity
- Specific training objectives

- Activities to be accomplished
- Commitments

Logistics
- Location
- Number of hours or days
- Dates and times
- Format
- Context

Participants
- Type of participants
- Number of participants
- Incentives for participants
- Participant fees
- Prerequisites for participants

Outcome
- Expected outcomes
- Evaluation
- Anticipated follow-ups

These considerations require preplanning by the staff-development coordinator. When the preplanning is completed, some publicity must be distributed. Information on the items listed must be sent to those invited to attend. In many cases, attendance will be voluntary. Since voluntary attendance is difficult to predict, it may be prudent to ask each principal to make a quick check of how many people plan to attend the session.

Guidelines for Presenters
Presenters should be given as much information as possible about the staff-development activity. Following is a brief list of such information.

- Those who will attend
- The reasons they will attend
- The format or mode that the presenter can expect
- The laboratory experiences, simulated teaching, or print materials the participants are anticipating

Presenters should also be given a list of available resources, materials, and personnel, as well as an idea of the experiences that are expected to take place during the activity.

Incentives, briefly noted, will be addressed in detail in Chapter 5. However, if continuing-education units, college or university credits, or district in-service credits are to be awarded, then school district representatives must make arrangements with all involved agencies so that appropriate time commitments may be made. Any required checklists, forms, or applications should be prepared well in advance. Further, if registration fees are to be charged, these fees should be administered by the school district rather than by the presenter.

For their part, presenters should provide the staff-development coordinator with a list of materials required to conduct the activity. These include:

- Materials (lab equipment)
- Space requirements
- Resource books
- Nonprint resources (films, video tapes)
- Media (microphones, projectors, computers, screens)
- Duplicated handouts
- Suggested time schedules
- Teaching strategies to be used
- Activities to be accomplished

Schedules

All schedules should be prepared and distributed in advance of the activity. The schedule should provide realistic time requirements and a list of activities as the planners intend them. During long-range institutes or college or university courses, adjustments can be made to the schedule to accommodate participant needs.

The schedule should also contain the organizational considerations previously presented, particularly the logistics of time, place, length of session. Collectively, all the components of detailed planning are needed for successful staff-development activities.

Appendix B presents a detailed conference-planning guide—an In-Service Activity Organizer. This guide illustrates how in-service planners can focus systematically on all aspects of the scheduled activities or programs. The sponsor should complete the form in collaboration with the in-service activity provider. By addressing the elements in Appendix C, planners almost guarantee a successful in-service activity.

Determining specific formats is an integral part of the planning process. When you reach the next section, which deals with delivery systems, you will note that there are many ways in which to present an activity or project. Planning makes the difference between projects that are successful and those that simply are acceptable (and therefore, probably unsuccessful), as well as those that are flat-out failures.

USING DELIVERY SYSTEMS EFFECTIVELY

Staff-development programs and in-service projects just don't happen; they require planning and, ultimately, delivering the services. We frequently refer to

TABLE 3-2.

PARTIAL LISTING OF IN-SERVICE DELIVERY SYSTEMS

1. Amplified telephone	21. Microteaching
2. Cadre system	22. Oral tradition
3. Classes	23. Paired teaching
4. Class observations	24. Professional association meetings
5. Clinics	25. Professional association training
6. Coaching (peer)	26. Professional journals
7. Committees (task group)	27. Programmed instruction
8. Computer-aided instruction	28. Resource persons
9. Conferences	29. Role modeling
10. Consultants	30. Role-playing
11. Continuing education	31. School/university cooperatives
12. Discussion groups	32. Simulations
13. Educational centers	33. Staff meetings
14. Films	34. Study groups
15. Extension courses	35. Teacher visitations
16. Institutes	36. Teacher association briefings
17. Instructional TV	37. Team teaching
18. Internships	38. Two-way telecommunications
19. Laboratories	39. University courses
20. Lectures	40. Workshops

this provision of the services as the *delivery system.* Table 3-2 lists forty different delivery systems currently used by providers of in-service education in the schools. To select the best possible delivery system, planners must determine the goals and objectives of each in-service project. But they must also decide whether the context is job-embedded, job-related, self-directed, credential-oriented, professional-organization related, or school-based. The context should be compatible with the delivery system.

As an in-service or staff-development director, you must consider how to apply adult learning theory. Recall that adults prefer learning in programs that provide (1) active participation, (2) application of skills or knowledge, (3) job relatedness, (4) relevance, (5) sparing use of time, (6) flexibility, and (7) an experiential outlet.

It is no easy task to conduct an in-service project that meets these seven criteria. Obviously, staff-development planners should work to provide multiple in-service opportunities for adults, as suggested earlier. Add to this list the demands that staff development also provide experiences in organizational development, development of specific consulting skills, and leadership development, and you begin to fathom just how broad the scope of staff development can become.

Among the dozens of delivery systems from which to choose, two emerging general systems—teacher centers and peer coaching—will be discussed further. These systems were selected because there is a tendency nationwide to rank experience in the classroom and collegial interactions as among the best mechanisms by which teachers learn on the job (Joyce and Showers 1988).

Courses within the field of specialization are ranked very high as a delivery system, if not highest, by secondary school teachers. However, university courses are under the total control of university faculty, and little collaboration is possible. Teacher centers and peer coaching may be emerging visions for staff-development planners.

TEACHER CENTERS

There is a general trend toward collaborative arrangements for in-service governance, which attempt to decentralize teacher education. One major innovation in in-service education is the *teacher center*. A teacher center is often administered by teachers themselves to meet their perceived needs. Usually they are voluntary; that is, teachers elect to go to the centers for special classes, workshops, and individualized or group help—all in a noninstitutional environment.

The teacher-center movement, which was brought to the United States by American teachers visiting British schools, has grown tremendously. Because of their autonomy, teacher centers have differing objectives and organizational patterns. According to Harry Bell, Jr., and John W. Peightel (1976), and writers in the Spring 1980 issue of *Action in Teacher Education,* three general classifications describe a majority of teacher centers.

Types of Teacher Centers
Consortium. These include three or more agencies or institutions who join in a cooperative effort to meet common goals. Examples are the Catskill Regional Teacher Center in Oneonta, New York, linked with its surrounding school districts and regional colleges to sponsor in-service projects. The center also awards mini-grants to faculty and teacher teams for classroom-oriented projects. The New York City Teacher Center Consortium delivers a wide array of staff-development services to its constituent districts (Report by the Commissioner, 1987).

West Virginia developed a network of eight regional centers, one of which has become the prototype for a number of intensive in-service programs designed to meet the needs of West Virginia's supervising and student teachers. Rhode Island also has a statewide consortium, while North Dakota's Center for Teaching and Learning attempts to integrate preservice training with in-service programs to bridge the gap between higher education and the public schools. The Oregon Consortium for Instructional Coaching reflects the continuing development of consortia (Gomery and Crouse 1987).

Partnership teacher center. This is a cooperative unit of two institutions, generally an institution of higher education and a public school system, designed to improve both pre- and in-service training and to share mutual resources. Another type is a parent-teacher center; one in Philadelphia, for example, offers all-day workshops and after-school and Saturday-morning activities. Teachers are free to avail themselves of a wide range of resources at the center, including a mathematics laboratory, a collection of early-childhood materials, and courses applicable toward certification.

Cooperative relationships with local businesses have been formed by the Cayuga Onondaga Teacher Center and a local computer corporation, and the Mid-Hudson Teacher Center (New York) and a local utility. Such cooperatives extend the resources of the public and private sectors.

Autonomous teacher center. Patterned after the British model, this type is administered by teachers for the benefit of teachers. The center functions primarily to review current and proposed curricula and teaching practices, and to encourage teachers to effect needed change. The rationale for this type of center rests on three premises: (1) classroom reform comes about only through the teachers who must implement such changes, (2) teachers are unlikely to change how they teach simply because they are told to do so, and (3) teachers change only when they define their own problems, determine their needs, and voluntarily seek help.

Wayne State University's science-mathematics center focuses on specialized topics. The Syracuse Teacher Center has provided a Frontiers of Science project for selected teachers and has helped others become mathematics and science teachers.

A number of autonomous centers operate in the United States and Canada. Participants generally have evaluated their programs favorably. Robert M. Pruzek (1987) prepared an evaluation of the New York State centers and stated that almost universally they are perceived positively by participants. Positive evaluations were common for both urban and rural centers. New curriculum materials, extended use of computers, and access to other technologies were attributed to the centers. In short, there have been extended services to the youth of the state.

Teacher Center Considerations

Financing. There are several ways in which teacher centers are financed. In some areas, the centers are supported by state appropriations, as in Florida and New York, or by local district funding, as in Boise, Idaho. Other sources of financing include combined public school and university funding (Wayne State University); grants from private and public foundations (Pittsburgh); cooperative funding by boards of education, school districts, and national teacher organizations (Vancouver, British Columbia); private and public donations; the federal government; or combination of these various sources.

Governance. Governance varies from informal agreements to legal contracts. All centers funded under the Higher Education Act, Title V-B, were governed by an advisory or policymaking council, of which teachers constituted a majority. A similar structure exists for the New York state centers (Report by the Commissioner, 1987). Actual control ranges from extremely loose-knit and informal to rather elaborate structures. Centers tend to be governed by their constituencies—teachers or principals.

Problems. The major problem facing those seeking to extend the teacher-center concept to be a solution to in-service needs is often the lack of trust by constituents of the various sectors comprising the educational community. Teachers, administrators, and school boards have tended to act as adversaries in governance. Teacher-center advocates view the establishment of trust and communication among all segments concerned with education as the first step in improving not only teacher in-service but also education in general. Of course, funding a center is a chronic problem.

Florida's Teacher Centers

A leader in the teacher-center movement is Florida, whose Teacher Education Center Act of 1973 established a comprehensive, statewide effort to organize and coordinate teacher in-service education. The 1973 act was established on the principle that teacher education is a career-long process, carried out most effectively by a collaborative arrangement among colleges, universities, schools, and communities. The act provided for the establishment of centers planned, financed, and staffed jointly by one or more school districts and by one or more colleges or universities.

Each Florida teacher center is charged with seven primary duties:

1. Assisting with in-service training as determined by teachers, district personnel, and others.
2. Developing programs based upon those needs.
3. Providing the human and material resources for such training by the most suitable agents.
4. Assessing needs and providing resources for clinical preservice teacher training.
5. Facilitating entry or reentry of personnel into the teaching profession.
6. Utilizing training programs that are based upon needs assessments, developing experiences to meet those needs, and evaluating the extent to which the expressed needs are met.
7. Facilitating internal and external evaluations, which include data gathering, process evaluation, product evaluation, and validation of teacher competency.

The Florida teacher centers are directed by a state council, of which half the members are classroom teachers. On the local level, each center is administered by a council appointed by the local school board, a majority of whom must be classroom teachers. (This distribution of membership was reflected in the federally funded centers.)

Funding for staff development in the Florida program has been rather liberal. During the academic year of 1975–76, the state appropriations amounted to $9.4 million. The state amount for the 1987–88 academic year increased to over $21 million (Morelli 1987). Funding for the centers supports four basic missions: (1) staff support for teacher-education centers, (2) school district staff-development activities, (3) beginning teacher-enhancement projects, and (4) summer institutes for teachers.

All sixty-seven school districts in Florida have established teacher centers. Observers of the Florida model report the importance of client ideas, plans, and projects when designing and implementing in-service programs. The programs obviously reflect the needs of the teachers, since approximately 95 percent of the state's teaching force utilize the centers, including those very hard-to-reach secondary school teachers.

It is not just Florida's school districts that have undergone a major change in perspective toward teacher in-service programs. The state's universities and colleges also have been forced to make preservice *and* in-service education dual major priorities. These institutions have formed a close association with local schools and districts to collaborate on solving organizational and instructional problems. As a result of this collaboration, the planning focus of the districts is moving slowly from short-term, large-group in-service activities to long-term commitments based on needs for school improvement. The State Council for Teacher Education Centers has taken the responsibility for improving program evaluations.

Teacher-Center Prospects

In 1984, the state legislature of New York passed a law supporting the Teacher Resource and Computer Training Centers. Adele Wenz (1987) described the New York centers and reported that seventy-four exist. The centers have budgets ranging from $20,000 to $750,000, but with legislative authorization to increase to $2 million. New York law requires that the governing boards have a majority of teachers on them, be constituency based, and control the management and organization. Four general patterns have emerged: (1) a New York City consortium, (2) local district centers, (3) small school or rural consortia, and (4) principal centers.

The statutory purposes of the New York centers are to:

1. Assist teachers in diagnosing learning needs, assessing student outcomes, and planning appropriate teacher strategies.
2. Provide demonstration and training sites.
3. Develop curriculum materials.
4. Improve the instructional skills of teachers.

5. Provide a site for sharing of ideas.
6. Retrain teachers for mathematics, science, and computer technology (Chapter 53, Laws of 1984).

The impact is being felt: in 1987, a total of 569 (74 percent) of the state's 768 school districts were participating in the movement. State funding during 1986–87 was $10 million. Further, the number of teachers who participated rose from 141,297 in 1984–85 to 177,590 in 1986–87. There are approximately 170,000 public and nonpublic educators in the state (Report by the Commissioner 1987).

Jean Fontana (1986) viewed the New York centers with "guarded optimism," noting that the centers can make changes where needed. She observed that a positive impact is being made on district policymakers.

In 1984, the U.S. Department of Education funded the Leadership in Educational Administration Development (LEAD) technical centers. The fifty state LEAD centers have structures, functions, and programs very similar to teacher centers. However, the focus is on developing and expanding the leadership skills of school administrators.

Intermediate educational service units are also establishing renewal institutes patterned after teacher centers. Rachael Heath and colleagues (1987) described one eastern Pennsylvania teacher renewal institute that combines the resources of the public schools, the intermediate unit, and the private sector.

One of the truly distinguished teacher centers of North America is located in Vancouver, British Columbia. This center illustrates the success of a locally funded center when there is genuine fiscal and management collaboration between the local school board and the teachers' bargaining association. However, for any center to flourish, teachers must be committed to the concept. This commitment is noticeably missing from secondary school teachers: it appears that the vast majority of teacher-center participants are elementary school teachers and administrators.

The secondary school teacher constitutes a very real dilemma for both teacher centers and staff-development programs. The orientation to "disciplines" rather than toward a common educational goal causes the secondary school teacher to act more like a university professor than another teacher in the public schools. That the professor model is inappropriate for high school teachers needs no discussion. (The professor model might even be inappropriate to the university's instructional mission.) However, staff developers must realize that high school teachers need special consideration and encouragement (see Lynne Miller 1980, and William E. Bickel et al. 1987).

For one thing, it is almost impossible to conduct an in-service program after school hours with high school faculty because so many are involved in extracurricular activities. In some small schools, *every* high school teacher is involved in an after-school activity! In large high schools, between 40 and 50 percent of the teachers are engaged in some after-school activity. Thus the context for delivery of high school in-service programs is a major problem requiring a creative resolution.

The second problem affecting high school teachers is that the high school is "loosely coupled." Karl E. Weick's (1982) concept can be applied to high schools, meaning that teachers act somewhat independently and are not directly affected by others in the organization. It takes a very strong high school principal to "couple" the high school faculty more tightly. Daniel L. Duke (1987) suggested that high school in-service programs be departmentally focused.

A third problem compounds the dilemma. High school teachers are oriented toward teaching a discipline, and they tend to shun any in-service projects that have an aura of general "improvement of instruction" or "staff development." Physics teachers want more physics; mathematics teachers want more math—*ad infinitum*.

These three problems are not without solutions. For example, Schenley High School in Pittsburgh, Pennsylvania, engaged in an instructional improvement project that brought together and involved all teachers. Of course, it took much effort, time, and even foundation money to accomplish it (see Bickel et al. 1987). The Bay Area Writing Project illustrates the effectiveness of a powerful model in revolutionizing the way writing-across-the-curriculum has been implemented in a very successful staff-development model. School-improvement or school-change projects have been successful with high school teachers (Caruso 1985; Moye and Rodgers 1987).

The model and concepts associated with teacher centers are powerful and will become more powerful as professionals assert their demands for more autonomy.

PEER COACHING

Staff-development programs and in-service projects are only as effective as the fidelity of their implementation to the original teaching model. Michael Fullan and Allen Pomfret (1977) concluded that most innovations fail to be implemented in the classroom with any degree of fidelity; that is, they are not used in the manner in which they were described by the developers or in the actual training programs, nor in the manner in which they were originally modeled. Much in-service education focuses on gaining new skills or procedures, so it is important to treat the implementation of these skills as "personal innovations." The Concerns-Based Adoption model describes reactions to learning new skills as "stages of concern." Individuals are concerned about how a new technique or skill will affect them personally (Tillman 1985).

If any learned behavior or skill is to have the intended impact, then it must be used as designed. *Fidelity of use* means that teachers or administrators follow precisely the model, strategy, or theory. A critical problem for any in-service project director is that teachers often do not learn the skill or behavior adequately to implement it with a high degree of competence or fidelity.

How can you improve the actual learning that takes place in an in-service project? One technique with the potential of becoming one of the truly exciting developments in staff development is coaching! But before the details of coaching are presented, we must understand one fundamental of learning and teaching: transfer.

Concept of Transfer

Bruce Joyce and Beverly Showers (1988) recognized the critical importance of *transfer*—that is, how a skill is learned by a teacher and then is incorporated into classroom instruction. They concluded that to learn a concept or skill, a teacher must transfer the newly learned information, knowledge, or behavior to a context that differs from the environment in which that knowledge was initially learned. To stimulate retention and transfer, an extensive variety of new tasks must be provided. In turn, learners apply the new behaviors. The greater the repetition, the greater the potential for mastery of the behavior or for fidelity of implementation.

How can in-service program planners or trainers ensure that effective transfer takes place? Coaching may be one process that ensures transfer.

Elements of Coaching

Benjamin S. Bloom (1982), Bruce Joyce and Beverly Showers (1982 and 1988), and Beverly Showers (1983 and 1985) critically examined the acts of great teaching and great learning. Bloom studied the traits of world-class performers and their coaches; Showers and Joyce examined teachers and learned how they could implement the transfer of learning to students by the concept of coaching. Coaching helps in the retention and transfer of learning. Thomas R. Guskey (1986) described a model that may account for desirable changes in teacher behavior. Guskey proposed that staff development be a process that leads to changes in teacher classroom practices and to changes in student learning outcomes, which in turn cause a change in teacher beliefs and attitudes. Guskey asserted that success in some teaching technique takes place prior to changes in teacher attitude.

In many cases, it is difficult to observe a direct link between in-service education and student learning outcomes. Richard L. Williams (1978) conducted one such study on the impact of metric-system learning and in-service education of teachers. He found a direct correlation between improved student outcomes and the knowledge that teachers gained about the metric system through in-service education. Thomas Good and Douglas A. Grouws (1987) described similar success with mathematics instruction. Forrest W. Parkay (1986) reported a very successful secondary school and university project that ultimately raised students' standardized writing scores by almost 18 percent.

The direct link between in-service education and other techniques is not always so well correlated. Cognitive gains by students often do not have a direct cause-and-effect relationship. A teacher might teach selected concepts of physics brilliantly to young children, but the children probably will not learn the concepts. Young children function at the "concrete-operations level" of thinking, not the formal level that is required to understand physics. Cognitive outcomes are affected by many factors, of which teacher in-service education is but one.

Bloom (1982) reported that the coaches of world-class Olympic swimmers and concert pianists tended to teach very few fundamentals. Williams (1978) implied that the fundamentals of metrics were stressed by the teachers in his study. Showers and Joyce (1982 and 1988) collectively illustrated that specific fundamentals must be learned and repeated by teachers in order for them to retain or transfer a new skill. These fundamentals are related to (1) understanding the theoretical basis of the new skill, (2) observing experts using the skill, (3) practicing the skill, and (4) being coached in it. Thomas R. Guskey (1984) concluded that successful in-service programs help teachers master new skills. But more important, their respective students then exhibit specific achievement outcomes as a consequence of teacher participation in the in-service program.

Referring to coaching, Bloom discussed the personal relationships that developed between coaches and students. As he noted, few close relationships developed. The coaches set very high expectations for their students, and the students performed up to them. Coaches were remembered with gratitude, but rarely with love or affection. The masters were "distant," but held in awe by the students.

The relationship described by Bloom is very different from that described by Joyce and Showers. They concluded that five distinctive traits must be assimilated by "teacher-coaches" before the Peer-Coaching model can be successfully implemented. The five behaviors are (1) providing companionship, (2) giving technical feedback, (3) analyzing applications, (4) adapting to students, and (5) facilitating practice. A description of each follows.

Companionship. Showers and Joyce concurred with Judith Warren Little's (1982) conclusion that a collegial atmosphere is one of the elements that leads to successful staff development. They called the element "companionship." It implies that teachers who are learning a technique for the first time need to establish friendly and supportive groups. These groups discuss ideas, successes, problems, frustrations, and strategies. Little described activities of companionship in those schools that she identified as having successful in-service programs and as being collegial. Similar elements were described by Joseph C. Dimperio (1987).

Technical feedback. Providing technical feedback is a key element of coaching. The term implies that judgmental comments are not given. Technical feedback involves a positive, constructive, and objective set of comments. If a new technique needs additional skills, then these comments are presented. The coach or coaching partner of the team observes the application of new skills and provides explicit feedback relating to the technique, as it is observed.

Showers (1983) commented that teachers need to achieve near-perfect trials to become comfortable with a new behavior. Joyce and Showers (1982) cited that it could take as many as ten to fifteen trials before a high level of skill development becomes apparent!

Obviously, coaching as an in-service delivery system is time consuming and requires a great deal of individual trust and courage. Feedback is critical if a teacher is to improve those new skills. The concepts of trust and feedback are closely correlated. Barney M. Berlin and associates (1987) observed these traits in the Palatine, Illinois, peer-coaching project called T-2-T.

Application. During the in-service training period, participants need to know why a model or technique is important and when (and when not) to use the technique. As individuals practice the technique, the coach and "player" need to consider when and how to use the skill (Westhoff et al. 1987). Additionally, the coaching team should examine curriculum materials and textbooks so that appropriate learning materials are available for student use.

Student adaptation. As the model is implemented, the teacher and coach must realize that it takes time to achieve student success with a new technique. There usually is a need to adapt and modify some strategies so that students can behave as predicted in the model.

Showers (1983) observed that teachers, in the usual process of learning a new technique, initially feel frustrated and uncomfortable. They actually feel that they do a poor job when first implementing new techniques. But as the teachers gain experience and receive feedback and support from their coaches, they begin to feel more successful and more comfortable. Noting this evolutionary process is important. If the early experiences are stressful to teachers and students alike, then there is a tendency for the teacher to revert to the old ways. The coach and "player" need to understand this phenomenon.

Facilitating. The coaching process requires facilitation by the staff-development director. The process needs to be planned, and those individuals involved in the process must receive training in the entire spectrum of skills needed to coach properly. Principals, supervisors, colleagues, and department chairs must be involved in the total facilitative and supervisory processes (Wood and Lease 1987).

Introducing the peer-coaching process requires a change in the school's organization. New norms must be established that foster collegial action. Proactive behaviors by teachers must be recognized and rewarded! Time must be scheduled for those involved in the in-service project to meet and reflect on what is taking place (Gomery and Crouse 1987). Little (1982) commented that teachers who work together on a project and discuss it often, and who spend time evaluating their efforts, illustrate a higher degree of success with in-service training than do teachers who are isolated in their in-service efforts. These observations are similar to those reported by Maureen A. Sullivan (1987).

Institutional resources must be provided to the individuals participating in peer-coaching programs. These resources include the all-important element of time. Peer coaching is a job-embedded in-service mode. Financial or personnel resources must be committed to *team building*. Team building requires learning cooperative-process skills: openness, honesty, trust. These skills are facilitated through various interpersonal techniques (see Saxl et al. 1987). In some cases, school counselors or school psychologists can expedite team building. In others, outside consultants have to be brought in to initiate a team-building effort. In-service planning must allow for multiple practice trials before new skills are applied in the classroom. Further, effective praise and intrinsic rewards must be provided by the principal or staff-development director. These aspects seem to be incorporated in the Oregon Consortium for Instructional Coaching (see Gomery and Crouse 1987).

A coaching process requires top-level organizational decisions and support. Enough resources must be allocated so that the program can succeed, which can be relatively low cost if options are fully explored (Joyce and Showers 1987).

Critique of the Process

Peer coaching requires a long-range approach to staff development. It requires a high level of intensity and direct teacher participation. Theory and practice are integrated in the process. In-service educators are very quick to condemn anything that "smacks of educational theory." But for the coaching process to be successful, teachers must be very much aware of the theoretical aspects of any skill or process that is being learned or transferred, including coaching itself.

Peer coaching implies that curriculum change brings about appropriate change in teacher behavior. Similarly, it is critical that curriculum materials be compatible with the teaching techniques being learned or extended. If inquiry models are being implemented, it is essential that appropriate classroom materials be made available to students. The current enthusiasm for "critical-thinking skills" is doomed in most schools because there simply is nothing provided to the students or teachers about which to think critically. Carl D. Glickman (1986) noted a concomitant problem and suggested that only through intensive study, evaluation, and staff development with various models can teachers implement critical thinking in their professional decision making.

Observation of the teaching act is a mandatory element of the peer-coaching process. Again, observing teachers requires accommodation by the school organization. The building principal never has the time to coach all the involved teachers. He or she therefore must establish the norm of collegiality. Observational skills and checklists need to be developed collaboratively, so that objective data can be provided by faculty during feedback sessions. All of this requires time. Job-embedded in-service education is implied in the coaching process. The real payoff is found in appropriate student outcomes. And that alone is worth the cost and effort of enhancing human potential.

RESOURCE PERSONNEL

Throughout this chapter there is an explicit endorsement of local resource personnel in planning, conducting, coaching, and evaluating in-service projects. By developing a cadre of in-service providers, a school district can begin the longitudinal process of becoming self-sufficient for most activities. In some cases, however, outside resource personnel must be brought in to conduct intensive training programs. When consultants are brought into the district, local instructors must be identified and trained to work with the consultants so that they can develop into specialists for specific projects—as "trainers of teachers." This adaptive strategy is a must for any peer-coaching program.

Administrators, staff developers, and principals must avoid identifying the same personnel for assignment to every project. The secret to enhancing human potential is conducting personnel assessments continuously so as to identify new specializations among the staff. Yearly evaluations of all personnel files should be conducted. In metropolitan school systems, evaluation requires decentralization of the process. Resource rosters are easily placed on computer networks and revised on a continuous basis. Small school districts will undoubtedly find that a few individuals can be called upon to conduct the bulk of in-service functions.

School districts should also utilize the expertise of local colleges and universities. One familiar institution usually neglected is the local community college. Community college faculties are usually well prepared in specific subject areas. It makes sense to ask the earth science instructor at the local community college to conduct intensive short courses for district teachers who lack formal earth science preparation. The director of staff development can "contract" with the local community college or university to provide a specified type of program. If so, a special short workshop could be required of community college and university faculty who participate in staff-development activities, so that they understand the theory behind teaching adult learners and realize that the school district has a vision and a rationale for staff development. Any professor associated with an institution of higher education should subscribe to the tenets established by the staff-development unit, or he or she simply should not be allowed to participate in the program.

Finally, we should recognize that many options are available for staff-development and in-service projects. The more options and the wider the variety of delivery systems used, the greater the probability that every specific learning style will be addressed. Then teachers will look forward to their in-service experiences as truly enhancing their potential. And that is a vision well worth our collective efforts.

DELIVERING STAFF-DEVELOPMENT ACTIVITIES CHECKLIST

___ **1.** The selected activity format is optimal for the topic and size of group.

—— **2.** Collaboration takes place between the in-service provider and the project leader.

—— **3.** Delivery systems are systematically evaluated before selection and use.

—— **4.** The contextual mode for the in-service project is identified.

—— **5.** Detailed organizational planning is evident in the total delivery process.

—— **6.** The selected delivery system supports the goals and objectives of the intended project.

—— **7.** Criteria are developed before initiating any educator or teacher center.

—— **8.** A training program for peer coaching is established prior to using the model.

—— **9.** Internal resource personnel are groomed to become specialists for selected models or programs.

—— **10.** A specific model is followed for each in-service activity.

CHAPTER 4

SELECTING AN APPROPRIATE EVALUATION MODEL

Whatever exists at all exists in some amount. To know it thoroughly involves knowing its quantity as well as its quality.

Robert L. Thorndike, 1918

The evaluation of staff-development programs and activities is time consuming and requires a commitment in materials, human resources, and real costs. However, evaluations of all activities of any in-service project should be carried out to ensure the following:

- Staff reactions and perceptions are obtained
- Adjustments can be made as needed
- Successful activities can be identified for future use
- Outstanding presenters are identified and used again
- Poor presenters are not reused
- Success or failure of the project can be determined
- Long- or short-range "profiles" are compiled
- Participants learn that their evaluations have an impact on staff development
- Impact on student achievement is verified

A vision for all in-service education, given adequate resources, is to offer the highest quality programs possible. If staff developers are to achieve and maintain high-quality programs, they must collect trustworthy information so that their immediate and future decisions are based on empirical data. There are a variety of general evaluation models from which staff developers can select a means of assessing their programs and their visions.

Ernest R. House (1978) identified eight major evaluation models, their assumptions, and their uses. These eight models are applicable to staff development, and they subsume the program evaluation strategies described by Bruce W. Tuckman (1985) and Ben M. Harris (1986). The models described in House's taxonomy are as follows:

1. Systems Analysis
2. Behavioral Objectives
3. Decision-Making
4. Goal Free
5. Art Criticism
6. Accreditation
7. Adversary
8. Transaction

According to House, models 1 through 4 attempt to provide "objectivity," or explicit measures. Models 5 through 8 tend to provide a more subjective or implicit knowledge about that which is being judged.

For the purpose of this book, three major models are discussed in detail, since these tend to be the most practical and efficient means for evaluating staff-development programs: Behavioral Objectives, Decision-Making, and Transaction. The remaining models are briefly described at the end of this chapter.

One assumption here is that any evaluation must ultimately lead to better decision making. If any evaluation model is to be helpful, it must be viewed as a process by which programs are improved through rational decision making based on objectively collected data. Now, those models.

BEHAVIORAL OBJECTIVES MODELS

The Behavioral Objectives, or Tylerian, model was originally devised as a curriculum-evaluation model during the 1930s for the classic Eight Year Study. The basic methodology was introduced by Ralph W. Tyler and his associates (Smith and Tyler 1942; Tyler 1951) and has been broadly applied to staff development. A second technique subsumed under this model is the single-subject design. Each model is discussed.

Tyler Model

Tyler's model focuses on learner behaviors: the ends of instruction, and not the means or processes, are important. There are six steps in the Tylerian Evaluation model:

1. *Formulate objectives.* Determine the broad goals of the program.
2. *Classify objectives.* Organize the objectives in order to achieve an economy of thought and action.
3. *Define objectives in behavioral or observable terms.* This feature has become the cornerstone of the Tyler model. "Modern" methodologies of evaluation, which rest heavily upon the specific behavioral statement of objectives, have not moved beyond Tyler's thought on evaluation in the Eight Year Study (so much for modernism).
4. *Suggest situations in which achievement of objectives can be shown.*

5. *Develop or select appraisal techniques* (standardized tests, ad hoc tests, questionnaires).
6. *Gather and interpret performance data.* The final steps in the evaluation process involve measuring student performance and comparing performance data with behaviorally stated objectives.

The Tyler model has pervaded educational thought since at least 1955. It has shifted the focus of instructional planning from *process* to *product*, and it has made explicit the need for clearly defined goals in terms of learner behaviors, even though direct learner influence is difficult to assess. Tyler's model has been used in packaged learning approaches, in determining accountability by objective plans, and in many state program-evaluation efforts. Its key appeal, as it relates to in-service program evaluation, is its direct definition and assessment of learner behaviors.

Single-Subject Design Model

Although the emphasis in staff development is usually on using groups as participants, there has emerged a rather novel evaluation technique commonly called Single-Subject Design. This technique is most closely associated with contingency management and time-series research so frequently used in the behaviorally oriented paradigm. The evaluation technique is a special adaptation of Tyler's model, but is in reality an extension of B. F. Skinner's behavioral model. Its popularity stems from the rationale that an individual provides both baseline and follow-up behaviors that reflect (1) the original status and (2) the results of the in-service intervention. The evaluation process contains at least five major steps.

The initial step is to determine some "inappropriate" behavior that the teacher or administrator demonstrates, or perhaps some behavior that is deemed useful or appropriate but which the subject lacks. The second step is to count the actual times that the inappropriate behavior or action is displayed by the subject. This step is called establishing a *rate count,* or a *baseline* (number of responses divided by time). See Figure 4-1 for an example.

The third step is to intervene with some specific *contingency* (a specific behavior to be used or a designated instructional technique), which may cause the participant to accelerate or decelerate the initial behavior or action. Rate counts are maintained during all phases. If the new behavior changes in the direction desired away from the baseline, then you may have found the correct "reinforcer."

The unique aspect of this model is not to stop at step 3 but to add step 4: reversal back to the conditions as they existed initially. Such a reversal should then cause the participant to revert to the original behavior or action and to show a rate count approximating the baseline. If you observe that the desired direction continues even after the intervening variable has been withdrawn, then you can assume that learning has taken place by means of a very powerful reinforcer (or extinguisher).

FIGURE 4-1.

SIMULATED CHART ILLUSTRATING THE NUMBER OF
TIMES PER PERIOD THAT A TEACHER USES "WAIT-TIME"
IN QUESTIONING, USING SINGLE-SUBJECT DESIGN

Periods of observation

	Baseline	Treatment	Reversal	Reintervention

Number of times
per period teacher
uses "wait-time"
in questioning

1 2 3 4 5 6 7 8 9 10 11 12 13 14 15 16 17
Number of periods observed

Note: "Wait-time" refers to a technique whereby the teacher asks a question, pauses three to five seconds (thus allowing students to think about a response), and then calls on a student or students to answer.

Finally, reintroduction of the intervening variable used in step 3 is often the last experimenter action. If the appropriate reinforcer has been determined, then the subject will once again exhibit behavior and a rate count similar to that seen in step 3.

By using a Single-Subject Design model, you can select small numbers of individuals to act as an intact "group" for control and follow-up phases, respectively, for evaluation. This model allows for easy replication or duplication. It requires observation or supervision, or adaptation of peer-coaching techniques. The model is excellent for evaluating in-service projects that stress skill development (Litzenberger 1979).

Critique of the Models

Although the Tylerian point of view was initially creative, it has gradually evolved into a mass (or mess) of hastily written behavioral objectives. Even after years of experience with this model, educators still encounter three unsolved problems:

1. For a significantly large portion of in-service education, the actual behaviors that are desired cannot be observed directly. Training and instruction must be evaluated through classroom tests, by observation in role-playing situations or simulated exercises, and through the learner's written or spoken reactions. These behaviors do not fully represent real performance.
2. Behavioral models, instrument development, and validation are still at primitive stages, requiring massive amounts of time to implement.
3. The Tyler model has been used now for nearly half a century. Although it still has ardent defenders, it is inadequate as a *single* model. It is ill suited

for evaluating outcomes of instruction and training. It is ill suited for evaluating problems related to organizational development, thinking skills, or computer-aided instruction. It has made, and continues to make, a significant contribution to educational thought, in that it emphasizes the central importance of learner performance.

Bruce R. Tuckman (1985) wrote that the trend for instruction to follow a process-product-outcome model is well established. However, the evaluation processes that accompany such a model are complex. He noted that evaluators must recognize that the model has an implicit assumption: there is some simple cause and effect. Prescribe an objective, and presto, the student demonstrates the defined behavior.

Not exactly so, observed Showers (1985). A teacher must first incorporate the behavior that was learned in the in-service project into a new context. Transfer between contexts is not a simple task. Then, consider the students: (1) they must be able to transfer the teacher's newly taught knowledge to their cognitive structure, and (2) they must apply that knowledge to some multiple-choice standardized test item a year later.

I am not being facetious. The translations that take place between behaviors learned in an in-service project and student test performance are not simple causal relationships, nor are they simple linear ones.

Ernest R. House (1983) cautioned that the metaphors used in an evaluation model shape our concept of what we are describing or valuing. For example, the industrial-production metaphor is most commonly used with the Tylerian model. Input, output, product, monitoring, assessment of outcome, and discrete elements are all metaphors from the industrial sector. The application of mechanistic or assembly-line concepts to social programs—staff development—is probably inappropriate. As of this writing, I've yet to see House's philosophical caution discussed in any published paper about staff-development evaluation!

Susan Ellis (1982) suggested that all evaluators focus evaluations on the objectives of an in-service project. Just as numerous projects prescribe behavioral, learner, or performance objectives, so the Tylerian model is most appropriate as an evaluation model, humanistic ideals or philosophy notwithstanding. Schools that implement "mastery learning" models would appropriately apply the Tyler model, since mastery learning is convergent with the basic tenets of that evaluation model.

Both Behavioral Objectives models have inherent weaknesses. For example, the models are difficult to apply when learning is a process or where knowledge and skills approach the higher domain of any cognitive taxonomy. They are *inappropriate* models for human-development projects or those that approach Abraham Maslow's notion of "self-actualization." The basic model requires a reductionist mentality: every act is reduced to some simple, if not inane, behavior.

Yet the Behavioral Objectives model has become the darling of accountability enthusiasts, and therefore it should be used when a project meets its basic assumptions. The model certainly provides quantifiable data.

DECISION-MAKING MODELS

This type of model has several proponents: Daniel L. Stufflebeam (CIPP model), Marvin C. Alkin (CSE model), Michael Scriven (Formative and Summative). Each of these models is explained, with its application to staff development.

CIPP Model

The CIPP evaluation model was originally developed by Daniel L. Stufflebeam (1970 and 1971) as a mechanism for improving both the planning decisions being made about programs as well as the actual decisions about programs. Stufflebeam perceived evaluation as having at least two major ends: (1) determining planning decisions, and (2) judging and reacting to what has actually taken place—so-called recycled decisions. Further, the CIPP model views the procedures as a "means" by which decisions are implemented.

Stufflebeam suggested that evaluations reflect a continuous and systematic process. To conduct the systematic evaluative processes, there are four major components: (1) context, (2) input, (3) process, and (4) product—the acronym CIPP. Each component leads to specific decision-making actions. Stufflebeam viewed the decision-making process as one that modifies, adjusts, sustains, or discontinues any program or any of its parts.

Context evaluation, according to Stufflebeam, is conducted where the activity takes place, so that the evaluator can gather information concerning needs, problems, and objectives. The context evaluation is a "reality" check. For example, in-service projects are often conducted after school on a short-term basis. You could evaluate that context alone by providing projects that are job-embedded. Analysis of teacher perceptions could help determine which project is best regarded by the staff and which has the greatest impact on the intended audience. There is probably a context that maximizes the use of both models. By using the CIPP model, you'll find out.

The evaluator uses *input evaluation* to gather data on the strengths and weaknesses of alternative strategies, each of which could probably accomplish the program's objectives. Thus context evaluation identifies the best possible objective to accomplish a desired end. Input evaluation requires judgments about relative strengths and weaknesses of the procedures for implementing those objectives. For example, if a series of workshops were to be conducted about preventing accidents in sports, then you could consider what resources would be needed to achieve the project's stated mission.

Process evaluation methods are used to determine the various techniques, strategies, events, and designs by which procedures are utilized in a program.

Product evaluation refers to a final, overall decision-making process in which the evaluator decides whether to (1) continue to use a project as is, (2) modify the project and continue to use it, or (3) terminate the project.

To use the CIPP model, a school district must have personnel who can identify the specific elements of each of these CIPP components. These personnel have to specify exactly what they consider the context, input, process, and product components. Second, personnel have to be identified to collect the data for each of the four areas. Finally, a series of standards must be developed by which the evaluation itself is judged either meaningful or useless.

Elaine Hackman (1982) described the evaluation model used at The Detroit Center for Professional Growth and Development. Evaluators collect data on a series of traits included in the CIPP model. Indices were then computed to have some standard for comparison of one variable or trait. She noted that the center views evaluation as a longitudinal process.

Stufflebeam and Hackman viewed evaluation as proactive. *Proactive* in this context means that the evaluation is conducted so that it provides information for decision making throughout the course of the project. The CIPP model cannot be used just as a final evaluation technique.

There is a major problem involved in using the CIPP model: it uses a very complex methodology. CIPP also tends to overvalue the efficiency of educational processes and undervalue teacher goals and aims. However, the CIPP model allows for either inside staff evaluators or outside educational auditors. In essence, the model's strength lies in its continuous focus on evaluation to guide decision making.

CSE Model

Marvin C. Alkin (1970) suggested the eclectic CSE evaluation model. (The monogram CSE is UCLA's Center for the Study of Evaluation.) The basic principle behind the CSE model is that evaluation is an on-going process which helps decision makers select in a more informed way among alternatives (this element is found in all models in some form). Yet it should be noted that "to select among alternatives" means that viable alternatives are in fact available. Evaluation must be viewed, argued Alkin, as a means by which directions can be changed, programs can be modified or eliminated, and personnel can be reshuffled as need be. In most cases, staff developers do not use evaluation to specify alternative directions. They tend to seek some final judgment about an event and lose sight of the process.

Alkin identified five decision areas and their concomitant evaluation requirements. The five dyads, if you will, are:

Decision	Evaluations
1. Selection of objectives or problems	Needs assessments
2. Programs to meet objectives	Plans
3. Program operations	Implementations

4. Program improvement   Progress
5. Program certification   Outcomes

Alkin stresed that each of the five dyad areas requires collection of information, evaluation of that information, and a decision based on the quantifiable information. In all steps, the evaluator must realize that the judgments are based on a probability of success.

When you judge a staff-development program, the first two dyads are most critical; that is, objectives/needs assessments and program/plans. However, judging instructional components of the program relies chiefly on the last three dyads: operations/implementations, improvement/progress, and certification/outcomes.

Judith Warren Little (1982) suggested that staff developers use a wide array of evaluation models. Three that she suggested are similar to the CSE model. She provided four criteria for evaluation models: range, specificity, rigor, and relevance. These criteria are implied in both the CIPP and CSE models.

Similarly, Michael Q. Patton (1982) described a staff-development evaluation program that encompasses all the elements of the decision-making models.

One point remains foremost in the CSE model: the emphasis is always on improved decision-making capabilities of personnel who are directly affected by or who affect staff-development programs by continuous data collections. In short, the process is a never-ending reappraisal.

There are many similarities between the CIPP and CSE models. The basic difference between them relates to the "intensity of evaluation." The CIPP model requires an extensive evaluation team and specific training. The CSE model is easier to use. But if you desire a thorough examination of virtually all elements of an in-service project, then CIPP certainly achieves that goal.

Formative and Summative Evaluations

The basic objectives of any evaluation system are to determine (1) the extent to which the project objectives are being achieved and (2) the impact that the project is having on the participants. To accomplish these objectives, staff developers can choose two additional evaluation methodologies: Formative and Summative. Michael C. Scriven (1967) and others have suggested these models.

Formative evaluation. Formative evaluation is designed to provide on-going feedback as quickly as possible. Formative instruments are specifically designed to monitor the activities or components of a program as they take place, to determine where problems are emerging. Using a Formative evaluation means problems will be speedily identified and rectified. For example, if some complex methodology is being presented that teachers find difficult to use with their classes, it will be through Formative evaluation that trouble-shooting takes place. If teachers attend workshops but are not given feedback until the conclusion of the project, then the feedback comes too late. By continuously checking the "small steps," an in-service project leader can identify potentially unsatisfactory learning or even instructional problems. Evaluators should initiate Formative evaluation so that they can observe many different perspectives of the program or course while it is in operation.

Only a few selected items need to be checked at any one Formative evaluation. These are all based on the stated learning objectives for the project. The important point is to collect feedback while enough time remains to make adjustments to the project plans.

Leonard Bickman (1987) noted that the rationale for Formative evaluation is to provide on-going data by which to make correctives. When students and program staff members alike realize that they are being monitored and helped, they tend to become more responsible and more productive. The instructional climate and total program environment become positive and supportive. Conversely, in-service projects have "gone on the rocks" because the project director was not evaluating activities over short periods of time, but rather waited until the very end of the project to accomplish a one-shot final evaluation.

Using Formative evaluation is much more subtle than simply specifying performance objectives. Formative evaluation requires that the project director carefully observe a selected set of experiences for all participants. For example, in most instructionally related programs, some form of activity is used to build a cluster of specific or generic skills. A project director subscribing to Formative evaluation would monitor the skills and, when an in-service teacher did poorly, provide a new set of experiences. *Correctives* are an integral part of the Formative evaluation model.

The essential characteristic of Formative evaluation is that "hard data" are collected so as to add a more "objective" evaluation to what are usually considered "soft data." Evaluation is thereby built into the scheme, so that feedback is used when it is needed most—not stored for the future.

Summative evaluation. This is an evaluation that is conducted as the final assessment of a project (or part of a project). Summative evaluation might be the final Formative evaluation of a project. Summative evaluations can take several forms, as long as they are consistent with the prescribed objectives of the program. Summative data can be tabulated into absolute responses and then given as a percentage for each item. Comparisons among participants can be made on summative data (but not on the formative measures). Summative evaluations are placed at logical points in the project, such as at the end of a unit, learning activity, or program element. Most important, one Summative evaluation is inadequate. The Summative sets are arranged in profiles to illustrate the sum of evaluation activities.

Most projects fail because the evaluation is a one-shot postevaluation. Such an evaluation strategy can never aid an in-service project. It's too late for any modifications; the project is over. Of course, it can be argued that Formative and Summative techniques cause the direction of the project to change. Yes, this is true;

and I submit that, if necessary, the objectives of the project might even be altered. Ultimate success is the underlying goal of this technique. If a project needs to be modified because of unrealistic expectations (objectives), then why not alter it?

Perhaps the most compelling reason for adopting a Formative and Summative model is that there really are no "surprises" at the end of the project. With early feedback systems built into the system, all elements converge toward success.

TRANSACTION MODELS

These are models that focus on process. Two distinct models are presented: the Temporary Systems approach and the Concerns-Based Adoption Model (CBAM). The latter is typically a model to describe the implementation of innovations. However, it has had extensive use as an in-service evaluation model, thus it is described here.

Temporary Systems Approach

As a social system, the school is marked with a high degree of stability and permanence. Matthew B. Miles (1964) made the above observation and then asked the question: "How do permanent organizations change?" One apparent solution is through the establishment of temporary systems within the permanent ones. Temporary systems, noted Miles, operate for only short durations, have well-established goals, and are expected to end after brief periods of time.

Workshops, conferences, clinics, seminars, and training sessions are all part of the typical educator's yearly repertoire of activities. In these sessions, small numbers of people meet for defined periods of time to achieve specified sets of goals or objectives; that is, they operate as temporary systems.

While involved in a temporary system, participants temporarily drop most of their usual roles and responsibilities and concentrate on a few short-term objectives, knowing that they will be in the temporary system for only a brief period. During the temporary-system phase of a training project, participants are free to try out new ideas, practice a new technique without the usual penalties for mistakes, and work in a generally supportive and noncompetitive climate removed from back-home interruptions.

To install a temporary system into the evaluation paradigm of any in-service project, staff developers must consider five rather simple phases: (1) planning or preparing for the project, (2) organizing the project's "start-up," (3) operating the project, (4) closing the system (that is, preparing the participants for their back-home roles), and (5) implementing the strategies learned in the project.

In temporary systems, informality is the norm. Individuals are encouraged to react without inhibitions or to "test the water," as might later be required in the permanent organization.

In addition, temporary systems afford an opportunity for immediate feedback, which tends to have a prompt effect on behavior. The feedback mechanisms of a temporary system help establish social behaviors and norms that govern the system. Contributory attitudes of participants in a temporary system are continuously reinforced. Feedback is obtained by systematically asking participants to complete forms that evaluate the processes.

The feedback is tabulated quickly, summarized, and shared with the staff. Corrective actions or adjustments should be made in those areas not received well by the participants. Feedback should be provided to *everyone* associated with the temporary system. Participants are also given a report on the tabulated results. After all, they should share fully in the system's decision making and learn how they are reacting as a group. Where possible, return the individual rating sheets so that each member can compare his or her own rating with that of the entire group. (This can be done by having each member place a code or symbol on his or her instrument.)

When this technique is used, dissidents frequently show behavior changes and fall in line with the group. These changes are especially helpful when one or two grousing individuals become disruptive and negatively influence the project's intended outcome. If the staff uses temporary-systems management strategies, the minority will be shown to be just that: a minority. The majority then rejects the inappropriate minority behavior.

For example, Figure 4-2 could be used to obtain feedback concerning individ-

FIGURE 4-2.

QUICKIE FEEDBACK

Directions: Place an X on each line above the category that best describes your reactions.

1. How has the project progressed to date?

Moving very slowly   Could move faster   Moving along nicely

2. What is your participation in the project?

Not with it at all   Could be more involved   Really involved with it

3. Are the organization and conduct of the project meeting your expectations?

Not at all   Meeting some and   Meeting and then some
                    not meeting others

4. Are the project sessions informative enough?

Very informative   Informative   Uninformative   Very uninformative

5. To what extent is the material presented relevant to your classroom instruction?

Very relevant   Relevant   Irrelevant   Very irrelevant

6. Any suggestions or comments:

FIGURE 4-3.

SUMMATIVE PERCEPTION

You are having a variety of experiences during this project and, of course, these experiences affect what you learn. The experiences and your subsequent learning will help the program director improve the project.

For each item below, circle the number showing how well you think the management tasks have been done by the director and the staff.

Frequencies

Low   *High*

1. Project goals were not specified clearly.   1 2 3 4 5 6 7   Project goals were specified very clearly.

2. Climate of this project was poor.   1 2 3 4 5 6 7   Climate of this project was good.

3. The "wrong" people came to this project.   1 2 3 4 5 6 7   The "right" people came to this project.

4. Overall design of this project was ineffective.   1 2 3 4 5 6 7   Overall design of this project was quite effective.

5. Project did not get off to a good start.   1 2 3 4 5 6 7   Project got off to a very good start.

6. This project will have no influence on how I teach.   1 2 3 4 5 6 7   This project will strongly influence how I teach.

7. Staff resources were poorly used in this project.   1 2 3 4 5 6 7   Staff resources were well used in this project.

8. No "experiential" or hands-on learning activities were used in this project.   1 2 3 4 5 6 7   "Experiential" or hands-on activities have been frequently used in this project.

9. I would definitely *not* recommend this project for others.   1 2 3 4 5 6 7   I would definitely recommend this project for others.

---

ual participation. Recall that adults prefer to be engaged in active rather than passive roles. This figure provides a profile for the director.

Figure 4-3 is a model that provides information on overall conduct of the temporary system. I (1987) collected data on thirteen different in-service projects from 1972 to 1986, and found a high degree of relationship among the various groups. Further, Marion E. Hannaford and I (1987) found that four elements of the Temporary Systems approach—goals, design, climate, and staff utilization—are the critical elements in conducting in-service projects labeled as successful by participants six months after they completed them.

The Temporary Systems approach combines elements of the decision-making model, but the emphasis is on *process*. The transactions of a project are the critical traits. Using this technique provides adults with a chance to help shape the project's vision and virtually ensure its success.

Concerns-Based Adoption Model (CBAM)

The CBAM was developed at the Texas Research and Development Center for Teacher Education to find out what happens to individuals when they try out new practices or implement innovations (Hall, Loucks, Rutherford and Newlove 1975). The basis for CBAM is that (1) change (that is, implementation of new programs) is viewed as a process, not an event and (2) people are most concerned about how changes affect them personally. These two tenets are implied in nearly all staff-development programs. Thus you find participants in major staff-development programs involved both experientially and emotionally.

The CBAM is designed to measure how teachers' concerns about a program change during the period of implementation and at what levels teachers actually use the new project in the classroom. These measurements have direct implications for evaluating in-service projects (Hall and Loucks 1981).

There are seven "stages of concern" in the CBAM:

Stage

6   Refocusing: I have a better idea.

5   Collaboration: How can I relate this to others?

4   Consequence: How does this affect my students?

3   Management: I spend my time just getting ready.

2   Personal: How does this affect me?

1   Informational: I need to know more.

0   Awareness: I am not concerned.

These seven stages can be used as an evaluation tool. For example, you can ascertain where individuals are in a project by the manner in which they respond to questions about the project.

Simultaneously, the eight "levels of use" can be applied to groups being studied:

Level

VI   Renewal: Alternatives are incorporated.

V   Integration: Deliberate efforts are made to coordinate with others.

IVB   Refinement: Positive changes are made.

IVA   Routine: A pattern is established.

III   Mechanical: User makes some changes.

II   Preparation: There are preparations for use.

I   Orientation: More information is sought.

0   Nonuse: No action.

Sample profiles can be prepared to show the extent of personal concern and the degree to which individuals apply their new skills or techniques. (Of course, an assumption is made that in-service projects are implementing something new.)

Profiles can be prepared at the school site to illustrate the building level of implementation.

The CBAM has been tested extensively with in-service education projects. Scores of published studies support its use as an evaluation tool. Susan F. Loucks and Marge Melle (1982) discussed its positive use in the Jefferson County Public Schools, Colorado.

Using the CBAM requires specific training, since the model is complex. Instruments have been developed to determine program efficacy. The model should be considered as one evaluation technique for long-range in-service education programs that implement innovations in curriculum or instructional techniques.

PROCEDURES FOR DEVISING YOUR OWN EVALUATION SYSTEM

When a long-range evaluation system (one that is more comprehensive than an ad hoc system) is designed for the first time, several tasks need to be carried out prior to collecting data. The first task is to write the objectives for the evaluation system. After writing the objectives, you need to prepare a set of procedures that are convergent with the stated evaluation objectives. Finally, you identify the audience to whom the evaluation results will be disseminated and by whom they will be used. The initial evaluation design should identify the evaluation model that is appropriate to the local situation.

Using Evaluation Questions

Once these tasks have been accomplished, it then becomes a simpler task to identify the specific evaluation activities that the system will address. Typically, evaluators make a list of questions to aid in preparing specific evaluation objectives. The following short list is typical of the specific questions that staff developers ask when designing an evaluation system:

1. To what extent did participants in the Computer Training Program achieve the course objectives?
2. To what extent is the equipment in the Science Program being used to implement the new science curriculum?
3. To what extent are the objectives of Teacher Expectations and Student Achievement (TESA) convergent with those needed to help our students?
4. To what extent do we need to extend the professional competence of our instructional staff in the Wellness Program?

Other Aids

These questions are examples of those appropriate for further investigation through an evaluation system. Then, of course, you would proceed with collect-

TABLE 4-1.

THIRTEEN EVALUATION METHODS
FOR IN-SERVICE PROJECTS

METHOD	REPORTED SCORE	MEASURE
Single group pretest-posttest	Percentages	Increase or decline
Control and experimental pretest-posttest	Analysis of variance Mean scores Standard deviation	Dependent variable level of significance
Periodic Likert-type feedback	Summary sheets Raw scores	Objectives Impact Adjustments
Classroom observations	Percent of implementation Narrative Case study	Specific criteria
Weekly journals	Narrative	Implementation
Random pretest and sessions of study and control group	Summary	Attitude or support
Single survey workshop questionnaire	Percentages	Immediate reaction to presentation
Sign-up sheet for future commitment	Raw score	Future need
Annual follow-up study	Percentages	School improvement
Teacher or student attitude survey	Group means by item Percentages	Positive attitude
Standardized tests	Percentile ranks	Achievement gains
Anecdotal records	Percent increase or decrease of incidence	Implementation Behavior change
Teacher observations	Raw scores	Behavior change

Source: William Jordan (1987). *Thirteen Evaluation Methods for In-Service Education Projects.* Pullman, Washington State University, unpublished paper. Used with permission.

ing the data to determine the answers to the questions. As you collect data, you could consult the matrix in Table 4-1, designed by William Jordan (1987), to determine specific sources of information for preparing staff-development evaluations.

Observe that Jordan illustrated how to locate the most appropriate evaluation methodology for a specific in-service education. Note, too, how each method and its matching score and measure are convergent, logical, and appropriate. Jordan's grid can be used as a handy evaluation-planning tool by staff-development directors.

OVERVIEW OF OTHER MODELS

Initially, this chapter indicated that Systems Analysis, Goal Free, Art Criticism, Accreditation, and Adversary models would not be expanded. However, they are briefly discussed here so that those interested can determine their value for staff-development programs.

The Systems Analysis model is an outgrowth of the planning-programming-budgeting system initiated by then-Secretary of Defense Robert McNamara. Users of the Systems Analysis approach assume that quantitative measures are the essence of evaluation. "Inputs" and "outputs" are carefully calculated. Thus an evaluator quantifies the staff-development efforts and seeks quantifiable measures of the outputs.

The Systems Analysis model is useful when there are direct, causal relationships between training and outcome. Be cautioned, as Thomas R. Guskey (1986) concluded, that the assumptions associated with linear designs for in-service education may be invalid. If a project meets a linear assumption (cause-effect), then Systems Analysis is appropriate.

The Goal Free model was described by Michael Scriven (1972) as a means of reducing evaluator bias. He suggested that an evaluator *not* be informed about the project's goals and objectives. Instead, an evaluator probes and searches for project outcomes. Scriven viewed Goal Free evaluation as similar to the Consumer Union's approach to testing products: the effects of the probe are observed and reported.

Applying the Goal Free model to staff development requires an outside evaluator who can probe those who have been involved in the project. Can the evaluator observe any differences between the participants and nonparticipants? Obviously, evaluators must spend much time on site to determine the consequences.

The Art Criticism model has been proposed by Elliot W. Eisner (1985), who viewed evaluation as similar to art or literary criticism. Conduct is somewhat similar to Goal Free, except that a general framework is constructed from professional experience, selected standards of practice, and specific contexts.

As evaluation methods, both the Art Criticism and Goal Free models tend to be highly subjective—akin to judging figure skaters. Reproduction of results is unimportant. Using the Art Criticism model could lead to conflicting opinions, depending on the evaluators' perspectives and experiences.

The Accreditation model represents one of the oldest evaluation approaches. It uses "expert observers" who emphasize processes or means. Accreditation standards are prescribed, which guide the observers. Implicit in this approach is the assumption that selected quantitative units reflect the quality of the program. Tabulating institutional artifacts is a common technique used to accredit institutions of all types.

An Accreditation model can be applied to staff development if an agency establishes a set of standards. The criteria presented in Chapter 1 could easily be converted into staff-development standards. Evaluators would then apply those criteria to the projects being observed.

The Adversary evaluation is often described as an "advocate-adversary" model. Selected individuals or teams give presentations for and against a program. A "jury" then makes a decision about the program. The model could be used during the planning phase of a major project or to determine opinions about suggested policy changes. Applied in this manner, the model identifies strengths and weaknesses for possible reconciliation.

These five models can be applied to evaluate staff-development programs. However, a search of published in-service and staff-development evaluation studies has yielded no explicit mention of these. Perhaps staff developers need to be made aware of their potential.

CONCLUSION

The objectives of the in-service project drive the choice of evaluation model. If an in-service project is to change some selected student behavior, then you evaluate the resulting impact on the specific student behavior. By carefully selecting a model and a set of specific concerns, you can attain a high probability that the evaluation components will be convergent with the training components.

Small school districts need to compile evaluations of their projects, as do larger districts. Classified staff members need to receive in-service training relating to evaluation. Equity agendas must be evaluated to determine if results are perceived. The goal here is to encourage the planning of appropriate and simple systems of evaluation: to evaluate the findings and trends.

In essence, we evaluate to find out how well we do, so as to make more rational future decisions. One evaluation is interesting, but a dozen or twenty show patterns of who is successful and what works best (Hackman 1982).

"Gee, all I wanted to know were a few tricks for evaluating our workshop. . . ." Do not be alarmed if that statement is running through your mind at this point. The intent is to illustrate many available methods of systematically evaluating staff-development programs. You seek the evaluation models that best fit the goals of your specific set of in-service projects. Once that task has been accomplished, the rest should be rather straightforward.

AN EVALUATION CHECKLIST

_____ 1. A written goal exists for the in-service activity or project.
_____ 2. Objectives of the project are stated.
_____ 3. The goals and objectives are the basis for evaluative questions.
_____ 4. The evaluation model is convergent with the goals and objectives.
_____ 5. Evaluations will be synthesized and used for future actions.
_____ 6. The evaluation provides feedback to the instructor.

_____ **7.** Short- or long-range evaluations are specified.

_____ **8.** Feedback to all presenters is made in time to make adjustments to meet participants' needs.

_____ **9.** Appropriate concluding reports are prepared that summarize the various staff-development evaluations.

_____ **10.** Temporary-Systems Management training is provided to all evaluation team members.

_____ **11.** Every in-service project (no matter how simple) is evaluated.

_____ **12.** The evaluations are used in future decision making.

_____ **13.** Data from evaluations and needs assessments are examined for congruency.

CHAPTER 5

INCENTIVES FOR STAFF DEVELOPMENT

I've been teaching in this school for six years, and I've never heard my principal ever tell anyone that a good job was being done.

Classroom teacher to a project researcher

What motivates a teacher to continue education beyond college preservice? Is it enough for the teacher to attain self-satisfaction, having achieved another college credit and one advancement on the salary schedule? Are there any other incentives for teachers to continue to expand their skills?

One issue central to in-service education is largely ignored: that of providing incentives to encourage and reward staff development. Emerging statewide trends require mandatory continuing education for all staff members (Flakus-Mosqueda 1983). It may seem relatively simple to pass a state law requiring more staff development. Yet more important, school board members and administrators need to devise more humane ways of motivating *all* staff members to continue their education and to acknowledge staff members for their efforts in improving their skills.

REWARDS FOUND IN TEACHING

Educators may find a clue by reviewing the traditional incentives and rewards of teaching. Dan C. Lortie (1975) classified work rewards into three groups: First there are *extrinsic* rewards, such as the money and prestige associated with particular roles. Second, there are *ancillary* rewards; that is, rewards that remain constant and are considered "part of the job," such as unpaid summer vacations, professional conferences, and tenure. Third, there are *intrinsic* rewards, which are subjective and valued differently from person to person, such as compliments and self-satisfaction. These reward classifications can be applied to discover incentive systems for teacher- and staff-development programs. That is, policymakers can select incentives that embrace the continuum of extrinsic, ancillary, and intrinsic rewards.

Reporting on a twenty-year follow-up study in Dade County, Florida (Miami),

Robert B. Kottkamp and colleagues (1986) observed a slight shift in teacher attitudes toward ancillary rewards. Intrinsic rewards, such as seeing students learn, remained very high, while the values attached to extrinsic rewards declined. However, teachers reported having little influence on their extrinsic rewards, which could affect the last finding. Dan C. Lortie (1986) concluded that these teachers showed some disenchantment with teaching. The collection of studies edited by Carole Ames and Russell Ames (1985) supported and extended the Dade County findings.

Intrinsic rewards vary in importance, depending on the individual teacher. For some teachers, the subjective rewards are enough to motivate them to continue their education. These incentives include pride in one's work and increased self-esteem, achieved by becoming a more effective teacher for the ultimate client, the student. Joseph J. Blase, Marlene I. Strahe, and Edward J. Pajak (1986) concluded that teachers perceive rewards as primarily psychic and student oriented. These writers suggested that teacher motivation and rewards come basically through the students. Incentives become even more important to support the intrinsic-value orientation held by teachers.

It seems reasonable to assume that educators who are satisfied with their jobs are more likely to involve themselves in staff-development activities. Robert E. Yager, Eddy M. Hidayat, and John E. Penick (1985) provided some interesting evidence to support this notion. They reported that science teachers who were identified as most effective have one very important trait in common. They all participate significantly more in voluntary staff-development activities than do teachers who were judged least effective. Being judged effective implies job satisfaction. As Frederick Herzberg (1976) showed, factors related to doing the job (motivation) led to job satisfaction. Factors surrounding the job (hygienes; that is, environment or conditions) led to job dissatisfaction. He also reported that motivation factors play a small part in producing job dissatisfaction, and hygiene factors play a small part in producing job satisfaction.

To apply Herzberg's theory, Jeri L. Engleking (1986) sampled teachers in two large northwestern U.S. school districts (as part of a research study conducted by Everett V. Samuelson and this author, and funded by the U.S. Department of Education). Engleking found that the major categories of *satisfiers* in rank order were:

- Recognition
- Achievement
- Relations with students and parents
- Evaluation or supervision by superiors
- Communication with administrators
- Interpersonal communications with peers
- The job itself
- Responsibility

The source of teacher *dissatisfiers* in rank order were:

* Relations with students and parents
* Lack of achievement
* District policy and administrative practice
* Communications with administrators
* Lack of recognition
* Lack of time
* Salary

The findings can be directly related to staff development because these teachers placed much value on achievement and were highly achievement oriented. Their job dissatisfaction related to the difficulty of establishing good relations with students and parents, and the lack of student achievement. One finding of critical importance revealed that salary was among the lowest items on the dissatisfier list. Actually, only 11 of the 442 sampled teachers even identified salary as relevant in this study. To be sure, salary is very important for achieving an acceptable standard of living; but as a motivational factor, it is not significant in and of itself.

Michael Kane and Cheryl Chase (1983), of the Education Commission of the States, concluded that: (1) intrinsic satisfiers are more likely to motivate teacher improvement than is money alone, and (2) recognizing talented teachers by giving them staff-development responsibilities increases the power of intrinsic rewards and lessens the likelihood of their leaving teaching.

If staff developers and administrators are to attain a vision that enhances the human potential of their organizations, then they must systematically incorporate job satisfiers into the reward system. More important, job satisfiers create a comprehensive incentives program for all employees.

Beyond Traditional Inducements

Even if limited by contracts and budgets, school districts can offer more to their teaching staff intrinsically. Bruce Joyce and Beverly Showers (1987) wrote that in-service education programs need to demonstrate some immediate payoff in the classroom. They asserted that a powerful incentive for pursuing any staff-development activity is the clear understanding that it produces success. James R. Ezell (1975) and I illustrated the value of an immediate payoff in our study of science in-service programs in two school districts. Teachers immediately observed the value of a relevant curriculum-oriented, in-service project. Their new skills and knowledge were sufficient rewards in themselves. And those skills and knowledge were immediately applied in the classroom.

Intrinsic rewards are more likely to be found when teachers are included in the planning and implementation of in-service programs. Earlier chapters on criteria (Chapter 1) and planning (Chapter 2) indicated that needs assessments and inclusion of teachers in the planning process are vital to the success of in-service projects. Teachers are inclined to choose those options most relevant to their needs and classroom situations; guiding their own self-improvement, they are rewarded with feelings of self-worth. These points were clearly expressed by Albert Bandura (1982), a world authority on modeling behaviors, and by Patricia Ashton's (1985) research studies on motivation and teacher sense of efficacy.

The feelings of self-worth and efficacy are directly related to Abraham Maslow's classic hierarchy of needs (listed from lowest to highest): (1) physiology, (2) safety, (3) affiliation, (4) esteem, and (5) self-actualization. We continuously seek self-actualizing teachers. Yet a rewards or incentive program must focus on self-esteem as the prerequisite for self-actualization. Teachers who feel positive about staff-development activities reflect those positive traits through better self-esteem and efficacy; ultimately, they show behaviors related to self-actualization. In other words, more care is needed to design needs-driven in-service projects that will have positive effects in the classroom.

University or College Credit

School districts must also provide extrinsic rewards. As previously stated, credit for advancement on the salary schedule and released time are the two prevalent incentives used to encourage teachers to participate in in-service programs. Yet two problems related to these rewards are apparent. First, as teachers acquire more credits, they begin to look for even greater rewards, and those payoffs can take them right out of the teaching field, for example, into administrative or supervisory positions. Therefore, if a teacher takes more courses, earns more credits, and leaves the classroom, the students lose a valuable resource.

A second problem, closely related to the credit incentive, is the apparent "stability" of the teaching field. Teachers are remaining in the classroom longer and are advancing further along the salary scale, both vertically (in years of experience) and horizontally (in number of earned credits) (Kottkamp et al. 1986). There is a point at which a teacher can no longer move any further on the salary schedule. What then are that teacher's alternatives? To remain in teaching with no hope of advancement, or to leave the classroom?

One technique used by school boards and administrators is to offer extra days at full pay for teachers and classified staff attending staff-development programs. Glenys Hill (1987) discovered that school districts allow from two to ten days of extra compensation directly attached to in-service education projects. Of course, the extrinsic value of these days may be in doubt. As Paul Berman and Milbrey W. McLaughlin (1978) reported in the classic Rand studies, pay for attending in-service sessions was inversely related to implementation of the skills in the respective classrooms.

BROADENING THE SPECTRUM OF RECOGNITION

Status as a Reward

School board members, administrators, and bargaining unit personnel must seek alternatives to the traditional extrinsic incentives to encourage greater teacher participation in staff-development activities. New incentives may require some restructuring of scheduling and methods of assigning duties. Enhancing the status of teachers seems to be the most viable possibility for rewarding them, and the incentives can be both extrinsic and intrinsic. One method of providing such status is rotating the department chairperson position biennially among those who participate in staff-development programs. The intrinsic value of this reward, of course, depends on whether teachers value this post. In addition, the chairperson usually receives both a stipend and an extra released period (depending upon the bargaining agreement and the number of teachers in the department), to add an extrinsic incentive.

A second possibility for enhancing the status of teachers who participate in in-service programs is to appoint master teachers. These teachers could be asked to aid first-year teachers in the classroom. The master teachers can offer suggestions for classroom management and methods of teaching, all without the threat of negative reports in teachers' files, as often occurs when an administrator attempts such an assessment. The master teachers, of course, require released time to observe and confer with these first-year teachers. As an additional benefit, mentoring by the experienced teachers makes the new teachers feel more comfortable in an unfamiliar setting and narrows the gap that often occurs between the older and newer staff members.

A third incentive is to use local teachers to provide workshops, conferences, and other incentive programs. Instead of hiring outside consultants, some school districts now make use of teachers who have themselves participated in workshops. Those teachers return to the schools and conduct similar workshops, putting to work the skills and knowledge they have acquired. This not only provides increased status for the teachers (who in turn feel their participation in the workshops has useful applications) but also saves the school district the fees it would spend for outside consultants. In effect, the teachers become a cadre of trained consultants, always available for additional advice. The money thus saved can be used for workshop materials and stipends for teachers who conduct the workshops (Heath et al. 1987).

Released-Time Options

School boards should consider some of the options for releasing teachers for in-service activities. Team teaching is one that provides released time. By teaming, teachers can plan a course of classroom activities that will release one of them periodically, and at the same time they can plan their own course of study.

TABLE 5-1.

INCENTIVES FOR STAFF-DEVELOPMENT ACCOMPLISHMENTS

Extrinsic Rewards
Incentives That Cost Money
Salary increase
Promotion
An extended contract
A reduced teaching load for one year
Added fringe benefits
Released time
Extra planning time
Travel to paid selected professional meetings
Continuing Education Units (CEU)
Ticket to cultural activities
Magazine subscription for teacher's classroom
Beginning-teacher mentoring projects

Intrinsic Rewards
Responsibilities as Incentive
Recognize as role model
Appoint as committee chair
Ask to perform as a consultant
Have teacher's class perform a task they do well
Ask teacher to serve on accreditation committee
Institute a responsible "career ladder" program
Recognition as Incentive
Recognize in newspaper (media) and/or by school board
Grant professional-development allowance
Provide extra classroom materials to exceptional teachers
Extend a compliment for job well done
Recognize at school board dinner
Award credential of appreciation
Present teacher at professional meeting
Name hallways, rooms, offices after staff
Award family pass to athletic events of school district
Take teacher to lunch

Team teaching provides the teacher with the additional benefits of sharing ideas with a peer, trying out new methods with students, and evaluating the results through the reactions of students and team members.

Another option for providing released time is to engage a team of regular substitutes—teachers known to be dependable and capable in the class. The substitute group might consist of teachers who prefer working part time or who know the routine of a specific school or classroom group. Obviously, it might be efficacious to simply ask teachers, administrators, and classified staff what types of incentives they prefer, then reinforce those selected (within reason).

Table 5-1 illustrates twenty-eight incentives or rewards that can be used to recognize personnel who complete staff-development activities sanctioned by the school district.

BEGINNING-TEACHER ASSISTANCE PROJECTS

The twenty-eight incentives listed in Table 5-1 could all be expanded. Owing to space limitations, only one topic is discussed further: beginning-teacher assistance projects. The implications for school improvement and staff development are almost limitless when viewed from a teacher-induction perspective. All members of a school are affected by teacher-induction practices, thus the inclusion in the discussion here.

The so-called educational reform movements of the 1980s made at least one genuine contribution to staff development: the initiation of beginning-teacher, mentor, or induction programs. As of this writing, about twenty states have some formalized beginning-teacher assistance program. Considering that in 1980, Frederick McDonald reported only *one* state had an active in-service program for beginning teachers, the growth to twenty states represents a remarkable rate of acceptance.

The mentor teacher program gained national visibility when the state of California implemented a program to help new or beginning teachers make the transition from student to teacher (Lowney 1986). New teachers typically are assigned to an experienced teacher who is recognized for his or her instructional excellence. The teacher receives recognition and extra pay for the service, and moves along a career ladder, if one is in place. The beginning teacher receives support, guidance, and coaching from the mentor. The mentor is neither a supervisor nor an evaluator. It has long been known that beginning teachers have very high dropout rates. Nearly one out of six new teachers drops out of teaching within the first year. Almost half leave teaching within the first seven years (Huling-Austin 1986). The mentor program recognizes the unique needs of new teachers, strengthens their fragile commitment to the profession, and simultaneously provides recognition to committed and experienced teachers.

Beginning teachers often have major problems adjusting their instruction to the level of their students, pacing their lessons, managing their classrooms effectively, interacting with students from a different socioeconomic status, and establishing nitty-gritty classroom routines. Through the mentor system, these troublesome problems can be identified and quickly resolved. Quite frankly, these programs help make the first year of teaching a positive rather than an aversive experience.

The Jefferson County (Colorado) Schools' project is a staff-development program that links the school district with preservice university clinical experiences. The project yields great benefits for everyone: the support teachers, inductees, and most important, the students (Schiff, Irwin and McBride 1987). Collectively, beginning-teacher programs are investments in human capital and reflect visions of confidence.

RESPONSIBILITIES AS INCENTIVES

The responsibilities assigned to a first-year teacher are almost identical to those assigned to a veteran who has taught for thirty years. Such a condition is unfortunate, since it fails to show distinctions that are experience-referenced (see Philip W. Jackson 1986). Teachers enjoy getting recognition for a job well done, and they also enjoy assuming greater responsibilities for instructionally related concerns. In fact, career teachers welcome additional responsibilities as long as they do not impinge on their primary function of teaching (Samuelson and Orlich 1985). In Table 5-1, six different responsibilities are listed, which could be used as incentives. Only two are briefly discussed: committee chairs and career ladders. These two were selected because the former costs the district virtually nothing, while the latter either might be costly or could be implemented with a minimum of cost. Career-ladder plans have been studied in every state or province in North America, and the concept has been applied in many school districts.

Committee Chairs

Regardless of the size of the district, committees are needed to do the job of educating youth. These committees range from those dealing with teacher negotiations to an array of textbook curriculum or textbook-adoption matters. Through a functional committee structure, teachers practice true professionalism: making decisions that affect their work. Teachers should constitute the vast majority of any curriculum or instructionally related committee. And all committees should have a carefully selected mix of new and experienced faculty members. Serving on a curriculum or a textbook-adoption committee is an excellent learning experience. The novice observes the politics of textbook selection, participates in evaluating print and nonprint materials, discusses the philosophy espoused by the materials, and becomes a key player in decision making that directly affects students.

Career Ladders

As an actor would say in a John Wayne western, "Them there's 'fightin' words!" The concept of career ladders has become confused with merit pay, yet this need not be the case. Forty-two states (Bell 1984) have mandated career-ladder programs of some type. It is most obvious that merit pay is *not* provided in forty-two states! What then is a basic definition of the concept? A career ladder is a process by which a teacher can be rewarded financially for professional stature that requires added learning and greater instructional responsibility.

Career-ladder programs foster professional growth for teachers. The concept implies that professionals be given increased responsibility, status, and pay as they acquire more experience and more skills. It has long been known that people need new job challenges periodically if they are to remain highly motivated.

Career ladders can provide recognition for meritorious service *without* merit pay. The underlying concept of a career ladder is that competent teachers become collaborative partners and share in selected leadership functions with their administrators. Typically, these functions include: making curriculum decisions, serving as mentors, selecting textbooks, piloting new programs, supervising student teachers, designing new instructional programs, serving as instructional role models, conducting in-service programs, and evaluating school district programs or curricula.

These functions are not necessarily related to merit pay. If merit pay can objectively be tied into the career ladder, then so be it. A career ladder can be tailor-made for any school district that genuinely wants collaborative decision making and truly shared educational governance. The current set of career ladders simply focuses on skills and minor job distinctions, wrote Samuel B. Bacharach et al. (1986).

Functioning as part of staff-development efforts, a career-ladder program recognizes people for their individual excellence and provides formal acknowledgment for doing some important, but often thankless, tasks. In the last analysis, a career-ladder program shows concern for human potential and enhances teacher efficacy (Patricia Ashton, 1985).

RECOGNITION AS INCENTIVE

The quotation from a school teacher that opens this chapter illustrates part of the crisis in the schools. Responsibility, status, and recognition are extremely powerful motivators. To find salary near the bottom of a long list of teacher dissatisfiers is nothing novel, for Paul Hersey and Kenneth H. Blanchard (1982) and other management writers have long suggested that leaders acknowledge intrinsic motivators and use them in a humane and positive manner to improve the organization. Schools have been slow to use the relatively simple reward of recognition as an incentive for staff development. Jeri L. Engleking's (1986) findings of teachers in two major school districts illustrated the need for individual recognition as a supportive incentive.

Recognition is so effortless that one must wonder why it is not used more frequently. Ten different means for recognition are presented in Table 5-1, three of which are discussed briefly here: recognizing teachers' efforts in the media, establishing a professional-development allowance, and providing extra classroom materials. These recognitions were selected because they all can be implemented practically.

Media Recognition

Patrons of any school district should be informed that local teachers, administrators, and classified personnel are improving their competence to offer better service. Support for the school district staff-development program can be generated easily with a well-organized and well-coordinated media plan. To do it takes only a bit of extra effort.

Initially, you release a story to the media about each staff-training project that takes place. The release should acknowledge the participants, explain their involvement in the project, and describe how the project benefits the schools.

Media coverage is not sought simply for public relations or publicity but to inform the public that their tax dollars are being invested wisely to help improve their schools.

Professional Development Mini-Grants

One of the innovative ideas that became a part of the staff-development programs at Boise, Idaho, and Teacher Center of Broome-Tioga Counties, New York, is a professional development mini-grant. The Boise district sponsored a small-grant competition among the schools to enhance the workplace. The major criterion for the allowance was that the enhancement represent the efforts of the entire school staff. Teachers were very excited about the chance to make their workplace better, as a consequence of staff development. Collaboration could be observed, as teachers and principals tried to improve some problem area in their building. In some cases, it actually helped to develop a school esprit de corps. Many local school districts and intermediate school units sponsor mini-grant competitions that encourage teachers to participate in in-service education as individuals; the Boise plan encouraged a group enterprise.

Additional Incentives

Since most staff-development activities are oriented toward instructional or curricular improvements, it is logical to conclude that participants should also receive a professional award for extra classroom materials, so that they can implement the skills even more successfully. For example, those teachers who have performed exceptionally well during in-service projects could be provided with some incentive fund allowing them to purchase items for their classroom or to improve the environment or working conditions. This would be a no-strings-attached grant. The incentive plan bestows well-deserved public recognition for instructional excellence or commitment to a long-range staff-development program.

In some cases, teachers learn about programs that have been developed and tested elsewhere. If one of these projects is appropriate to a school and the teachers are willing to undertake the in-service training, then the district should purchase the program for the adoptees in behalf of the group. That is, the group gets recognized for its efforts, while the district underwrites the expense for adoption.

Outside innovations are made workable by mutual adaptation (Berman and McLaughlin 1978a). In plain English, this means that teachers adapt the curriculum materials developed elsewhere to fit the needs of their specific students or situations. The adaptation is simply a stamping of one's own imprint on the project, or "taking ownership." With strong ownership developed in the schools, programs are truly implemented, not briefly adopted and later abandoned. Ownership emerges as a powerful incentive.

THE MARYSVILLE RECOGNITION PROGRAM*

Each school district can develop or adopt its own incentives, but let us examine one school district's comprehensive incentive plan. The city of Marysville, Washington, lies north of Seattle and is a blue-collar, working-class town. It has a total enrollment (K–12) of 7,000 students. Eleven school sites constitute the physical plant of the district. The school district instituted an employee-recognition program when Superintendent Richard L. Huselton and his administrative team concluded that staff development required a total district commitment. In introducing the formalized program, the superintendent stated:

> Human resources are vital to the process of educating youth and we in the Marysville School District are deeply aware of the knowledge, talent, and dedication of our employees. Our employee recognition program is an attempt to show appreciation to our employees and at the same time have others become aware of the vast amount of exceptional expertise which is enthusiastically given by so many people.
>
> Although our jobs are greatly varied and our roles in the educational process different, we are truly equal human beings. No employee works for this school district who is not a worthy person.
>
> None of the activities carried out by the school district are mandatory programs and employees are involved because they want to improve their job skills and people-relationship skills in order to do a better job for children.

The superintendent's introduction is supported by a similar message signed by the five-member school board.

How does the program work? Sixteen different types of incentives make up this recognition program. Table 5-2 lists the specific components.

The Marysville School Board and superintendent subscribe to the concept of overall staff development as described in Chapter 1 by E. Lawrence Dale. Their vision of staff development is the enhancement of all human potential in the school district. All employees are eligible to participate in the program, but par-

*Used by permission of Richard L. Huselton.

TABLE 5-2.
COMPONENTS OF THE MARYSVILLE
RECOGNITION PROGRAM

1. Business card recognition
2. Teacher of the Year
3. Audiotapes about human effectiveness and motivation
4. Foundation donations
5. Service pin
6. Superintendent's pin
7. "Win" breakfasts
8. Human effectiveness course
9. MJHS Teacher of the Month
10. Thunderbird Award
11. Transportation Awards
12. Special Education Aide Award
13. Special Educator of the Year
14. Name cards/folders
15. Achievement Plus Award
16. Curriculum Quill Award

Note: These components are very localized, for example, MJHS, Thunderbird, Curriculum Quill awards.

ticipation is voluntary. To plan for staff development, the district conducts needs assessments and sponsors various in-service projects. In this regard, Bob Tomsich and Barbara Pond (1986) reported that such a collaborative effort of planning and participating by teachers, administrators, and classified staff yielded a quality program.

In 1985, the National School Public Relations Association (NSPRA) prepared a packet on the topic of employee recognition—*"Staff Recognition . . . Unlocking The Potential for Success."* The NSPRA materials contain a booklet about related information and some research on the topic. Identifying fears, reducing jealousy and competition, and giving ideas by which recognition can be initiated are all discussed. Two model folders include program samples of certificates and other items being used throughout Canada and the United States. The packet is an ideal starter for a district or a school embarking on a staff-development recognition program.

PROMOTING LEADERSHIP THROUGH STAFF DEVELOPMENT

More than any other measure, the quality of the staff determines the quality of service offered to the children and patrons of a school district. School districts that maintain a competitive edge over other districts can often outrecruit less-competitive districts. But even the most desirable school districts must promote leadership development if they are to remain high-quality organizations.

During the 1970s, most educators became aware that many specific groups, including women, minorities, and the handicapped, were not represented in leadership areas. For the most part, males dominated the school leadership roles. To encourage under-represented groups, staff developers and administrators—especially principals—began identifying a pool of capable women, minority members, and the handicapped so these people could participate in special leadership-development projects. Their activities included: attendance at special leadership seminars and institutes, internships at various levels in the school district, appointment to major committees and committee chairs, and some mentoring. In time, some of these people received appropriate administrative credentials through higher education and promotion to administrative and staff positions. It appears that many people now holding the title of Director of Staff Development are women or members of minorities (Wenz 1987).

If the superintendent of schools, administrative cabinet, and school board make a commitment to develop leadership potential, they must plan and implement a staff-development program that provides for under-represented groups. This should not be construed to mean that every woman or minority person will be interested or should be "groomed," nor does it imply that men should be omitted from the process. Effective schools *are* effective because all people have the opportunity to grow in the highest professional spirit. A vision, indeed.

STAFF DEVELOPMENT FOR CLASSIFIED PERSONNEL

The recognition programs showcased by the NSPRA (1985) also encourage classified personnel to be a vital part of staff-development efforts. This approach requires needs assessments for the various job categories: secretaries, janitors, bus drivers, nurses, cafeteria workers, and shop personnel. The larger the school district, the greater the number of job categories.

These individuals also need staff-development programs to fit their needs. They require opportunities for job advancement, just as do teachers and administrators (Blackwell 1987). In very small school districts, the superintendent manages this aspect of the program. In larger school districts, the director of personnel administers the classified staff-development program.

The same high-quality standards should be established for these programs as for the professional staff. When every school district employee has an opportunity to grow on the job, service improves in every area. Administrators can tell how good their staff-development program is when their personnel are offered promotions or better jobs in neighboring districts. Yes, that is a mark of a very successful program.

SPECIAL CONSIDERATIONS FOR STAFF DEVELOPMENT

In-service education can also focus on special circumstances requiring attention within the school district, such as *safety and health*. For example, safety programs are now an absolute must. New chemical safety standards require every employee to know what chemicals are dangerous and how to handle or dispose of them. Science, shop, home economics, and art teachers must be given systematic safety training. Coaches must receive special training on athletic injuries and safety-related concerns. A school district must offer such programs if it is to avoid liability law suits!

Wellness programs have also been incorporated into staff-development efforts (Davis and Morgan 1986). These programs offer a wide variety of activities, all related to being healthy and experiencing less stress on the job. "Anti-stress" workshops are in vogue as of this writing. A total wellness program requires a collaborative effort.

A wellness program can also aid in reducing *absenteeism,* a problem for some individuals. However, specific programs must be designed to reduce this unproductive trait. In some cases, it is related to other causes, such as alcoholism or drug use. Quite obviously, AIDS education will be a topic in staff development as the disease reaches pandemic proportions.

Two areas now becoming more openly discussed as well as taken more seriously in all sectors of our society are *alcoholism and drug abuse.* Yes, educators are among those who have alcohol problems or succumb to drug abuse. Staff-development programs must use qualified professionals to help staff members who have these problems.

Child-abuse identification programs have also become an essential part of staff development. In most states, child abuse must be reported by school officials. Teachers and administrators must receive in-service education about recognizing this antisocial menace.

You may wonder how these special considerations can be classified under the rubric of incentives. The rationale is that positive incentive programs and job satisfaction can reduce, if not eliminate, many of these debilitating morale and personal health problems.

Salaries are obviously an incentive. As will be illustrated in Chapter 6, a substantial proportion of a salary schedule in the public schools is allocated to educators who participate in various staff-development programs. It is most common for school districts to acknowledge a teacher's participation in workshops, institutes, and college courses by granting a small stipend as a salary raise that continues to be paid as long as the teacher remains with the district.

School district administrators miss a great opportunity if they fail to inform their personnel about the impact such activities have on an individual's salary.

For example, once a year a short note could be enclosed with the pay warrant, indicating the percentage of the total salary obtained through salary recognition of in-service education credits. Estimates show that the contribution could easily range from 20 to 30 percent of a teacher's total salary (Cole 1987; Valiant 1984). Salary alone is not a primary incentive for participating in a staff-development program, but it can be shown to be an investment that has a long-term payoff. And that becomes an incentive.

CONCLUSION

Staff development has progressed a long way since the first certificates were awarded to those attending that original workshop sponsored by the Progressive Education Association in the 1930s. With a well-organized incentives program, participants become advocates for in-service education. Incentives can be an important facet for building morale. A positive incentives program helps reduce personal stress and relieve health problems, and prevents them from becoming major issues. The vision is reflected in a positive attitude about the job, the workplace, and—most important—the students.

CHECKLIST FOR INCENTIVES

____ **1.** The school district uses a wide variety of incentives to reward completion of district-sponsored staff-development activities.

____ **2.** Incentives are awarded on systematic and objective bases.

____ **3.** The incentives for staff development are authorized through school district policy.

____ **4.** Incentives are identified by a set of written and officially adopted administrative regulations.

____ **5.** The school district publicly acknowledges outstanding performances through professionally relevant events.

____ **6.** Incentive programs are collaboratively identified and adopted by all staff members.

____ **7.** Administrators are also provided with incentives for participating in staff-development activities.

____ **8.** Incentives for staff development are identified for all classified employees.

____ **9.** A leadership training program is in place, particularly for women, minorities, and the handicapped.

____ **10.** The incentive policy is reviewed periodically.

CHAPTER 6

FUNDING STAFF DEVELOPMENT INITIATIVES

Energy is neither created nor destroyed.
Law of Conservation of Mass, Energy, and Momentum

Perhaps you are puzzled why a general law of physics is used as an introductory device for a chapter on staff-development costs? My rationale is simple: it takes energy (money) to drive any staff-development program (mass), and that energy is usually shifted or allocated among competing needs (momentum).

We have little reliable data that provide an accurate estimate of the money invested in the United States in staff-development or in-service programs for elementary and secondary school personnel. One of the problems in determining such costs is the various definitions of staff-development or in-service education, a problem discussed in Chapter 1. Some people use the definition of in-service education as "anything that you can get away with."

The need for effective staff development has emerged from the concept that encourages investment in human resources, so eloquently described by Theodore W. Schultz, 1979 Nobel Laureate for Economics. Schultz's concept (1960 and 1963) of developing human capital—that is, the importance of investing in humans rather than in machinery—still stands out as a landmark concept. How does Schultz's theory relate to staff development? Staff development means that a school district invests in its total staff to perform education services at a high level of quality. And to ensure that quality in this age of knowledge explosion and declining resources, staff development has become a necessity.

STAFF DEVELOPMENT AT THE NATIONAL AND INTERNATIONAL LEVELS

An ERIC (Educational Resources Information Center) computer search conducted in 1987 yielded fifty-nine entries purportedly related to the amounts

The author thanks Larry D. LaBolle, Robert J. Valiant, and Richard D. Cole for allowing generous use of their studies and data in this chapter.

invested in staff-development or teacher in-service programs, nationally and internationally. Of those total entries, only a few are germane to our topic. Thus we acknowledge a paucity of published studies and encourage staff developers to meet that need by publishing local or state-related cost data.

National Indicators

There are, however, some indicators by which we can infer the costs of staff-development programs at the federal level. C. Emily Feistritzer and Rhonda J. McMillion (1979) identified nineteen discretionary and two state formula programs funded at the federal level with components exclusively for educational personnel development. Their analyses of data revealed that in fiscal year 1978, approximately $222 million was spent at the federal level on activities, programs, and projects involving personnel development. For fiscal year (FY) 1979, the amount appropriated at the federal level was $356,312,000; for 1980, $340,475,000.

Feistritzer and McMillion assumed that the entire budget for such programs was properly classified as staff development. Such an assumption may be somewhat valid, but not all of the suggested sums were spent directly or indirectly on in-service, per se. Most of these funds were concentrated in categorical grant programs. Only the Teacher Corps and Teachers Centers were entirely committed to general staff development. These two former components accounted for less than 3 percent of the U.S. Department of Education budget of $12 billion (Gudridge 1980).

Two federal projects are indicative of the national involvement in staff development. Data obtained from the *Annual Education Reports* of the U.S. Department of Education for FY 1983 and FY 1984 showed that during the early 1980s, over 275,000 educators received in-service training under Chapter 1 of the Education Consolidation and Improvement Act (ECIA), Education of Disadvantaged Program. The Training Program for Special Program Staff and Leadership Personnel yielded data that 1,019 participants were trained at a cost of $942 per person (*Annual Evaluation Report* FY 1984, pages 513-1 and 513-2). Using $942 per person as a reasonable base, the calculated in-service efforts of ECIA, Chapter 1, ranged between $211 million and $257 million per year.

From the same source (pages 104-1 and 104-2), the federal appropriation for staff development from Chapter 2, State Block Grants, ECIA ranges from $220 million to $250 million for the early 1980s.

Surprisingly, investments in staff development under federal review for in-service training for education of handicapped youth is 5 percent of the over $50 million annual appropriations. Ninety-five percent is allocated for preservice training (*Annual Evaluation Report*, FY 1984, page 309-1).

Another source of both awareness training and implementation training is the National Diffusion Network (NDN) of the U.S. Department of Education. It supported 124 national curriculum projects in 1981. Reporting on the NDN for that year, Shirley Boes Neill estimated that the NDN projects cost $66 million. Costs of the projects ranged from $2,000 to $12 million, with the median cost of a project at $248,642. The estimated cost of installing an NDN project in a local school in 1981 ranged from $4,000 to $5,000. The costs dropped to $545 per school in FY 1984. These costs included NDN administrative costs, state NDN facilitators, and local project directors. The cost figures did not include local school district costs for released time for teachers attending the in-service training, costs for travel and lodging, or costs for materials. In FY 1984, the NDN appropriation was $10 million, with more than 64,000 educators receiving in-service training to use exemplary projects being supported by NDN (*Annual Evaluation Report*, FY 1984, pages 119-3 and 119-7).

The NDN projects are evaluated through a rigorous system. Each project in NDN actually works in classrooms. As these projects are disseminated, some implementation and in-service funds are available to local adopting districts. Susan F. Loucks (1983) reported that NDN projects tended to have a 75 percent rate of adoption and implementation.

Another major provider of federal funds for staff development is the National Science Foundation (NSF). According to budget data published by the National Science Foundation, through its Directorate for Science Education, $84.7 million was appropriated for all science education activities for FY 1980 (*Science Education Databook*). Of that amount, approximately $11,860,000 (14 percent) could be classified as directly related to staff development. Thus the two major federal agencies that provide the bulk of the nation's staff development (U.S. Department of Education and NSF) invested about $425.2 million during FY 1980 in staff development or in-service education projects.

The current shortage of science and mathematics teachers has led to the need

TABLE 6-1.

**NATIONAL SCIENCE FOUNDATION
PRECOLLEGE APPROPRIATIONS FOR
SCIENCE EDUCATION STAFF DEVELOPMENT**

FISCAL YEAR	APPROPRIATION	ESTIMATED AMOUNT FOR STAFF DEVELOPMENT[c]
1982	$16,745,000	$15,000,000
1983	1,108,000 (16,087,000)[a]	1,000,000
1984	37,132,000 (31,450,000)[a]	35,000,000
1985	25,188,000 (31,450,000)[a]	25,188,000

Notes: [c]Estimates reflect staff-development projects only.
[a]Unobligated funds. Owing to pressure or restrictions from the White House or Office of Management and Budget, these amounts were not allowed for the authorized purposes.
Source: National Science Foundation Annual Report, 1982, 1983, 1984 and 1985, (Washington, D.C.: NSF) NS1.1, Appendix B, Financial Reports.

for training—and retraining—classroom teachers for the public schools. The National Science Teachers Association estimates as much as $1 billion may be needed to retrain teachers in a program of summer institutes and short seminars during the coming school years.

Table 6-1 shows expenditures for science- and mathematics-related staff-development activities for elementary and secondary teachers by the National Science Foundation. The erratic funding pattern shown in this table is not at all what one observes with U.S. Department of Education's major legislative pieces. The White House became very angry at the NSF and tried to eliminate the entire science education section during 1980–81. Only through explicit congressional mandates did science education receive monetary support in FY 1984. However, the executive branch still had its agenda served by not allowing the agency to spend its full appropriation, hence "unobligated" funds for three consecutive fiscal years.

NSF congressional appropriations for science education were increased to $156 million for fiscal year 1989 (Aldridge 1988). From virtually no budget in 1983 to $156 million in 1989 illustrates how politics impact staff development activities at the national level. Strategic planning (the current enthusiasm of educational consultants) is hardly worthwhile under such fluctuating fiscal commitments.

Assuming that the average NSF project spent a high of $1,000 per participant, then the number of teachers involved during the early 1980s ranged between 25,000 and 35,000. Those are not small numbers.

While not directly related to the NSF efforts, congressional legislation for FY 1986, FY 1987, and FY 1988 from Title II, PL 98–337, Education for Economic Security Act, also appropriated $100 million, $45 million, and $80 million for in-service teacher training collectively in mathematics, science, foreign languages, and computer sciences. However, these amounts do not approach the efforts made by the U.S. Department of Education to conduct preservice or in-service programs in special education.

The U.S. Department of Education and the National Science Foundation are but two federal agencies that sponsor major thrusts in school-based staff development. The Department of Energy sponsors a multimillion-dollar teacher in-service education program, and the National Institute of Education has had budgets in excess of $50 million. A rather small proportion of their budgets supports staff development in the schools. The Department of Health and Human Services provides specific in-service teacher training. The Department of Defense supports a worldwide effort for staff development associated with its overseas dependent schools, grades K–12, which are staffed by civilian educators. No questions about it; the federal contribution to educator staff development easily approaches $1 billion, or about $470 per teacher in the United States.

Among the various staff-development activities supported by the federal government, the amounts appropriated per program vary widely, as one might assume. For example, I recently directed an NSF training project in which approximately eighty teachers each received one full week of in-service training. The total cost of the project was $62,000; the per teacher cost was $775. That latter figure is somewhat higher than the $470 amount derived earlier.

Others in the field have tried to determine the various costs of in-service education. For example, Jay C. Thompson, Jr., and Van E. Cooley (1986) conducted a survey of selected exemplary staff-development programs at 267 school districts in the United States. They reported direct costs for staff development based on *per pupil* allocations: about one-fourth budgeted under $1.50, while 45 percent budgeted from $1.51 to $8; about one-third budgeted more than $8.01 per pupil.

James M. Banner, Jr. (1985), described the Council for Basic Education cosponsored mathematics and science institutes for secondary school teachers. Eleven institutes were held nationally for 325 participants. Derived data would indicate about a $600 per participant cost shared by federal grants, college sources, and several private businesses.

Data do not "prove" anything. But comparable data do provide baselines by which to compare relative "direct" in-service costs. The national indicators cited previously illustrate a wide variation in staff-development costs. One problem lies in the fact that several researchers use different bases, thus comparisons must be made with great care. However, a school district coud use one or more techniques to establish its own data. Now let us examine some international data.

International Indicators

Philip Kaplan (1980) attempted to make international comparisons of the costs of in-service teacher education. He examined direct costs in England, Australia, United States, Denmark, Sweden, and France. Kaplan found the task difficult, since there is no standard methodology for collecting such records. These studies showed the need for comparative monetary indexing of conversion tables to draw meaningful conclusions.

One published study provides a model by which staff-development costs can be computed and reported internationally, nationally, or locally. This comprehensive study was carried out by B. H. Fennell and associates (1980) for the province of Alberta, Canada. The purpose was to assess the costs of teacher professional development and in-service training related to the implementation of new instructional programs. The group computed expenditures by local school boards and the costs to the province's budget for in-service training during the 1977–79 school years. Four kinds of expenditures on teacher professional development for in-service education were reviewed.

The first was direct expenditure by school authorities. During the 1977–79 school years, $7.8 million was invested for all school jurisdictions in Alberta as direct costs. The second type, indirect costs (discussed in a following section), accounted for $24,361,000 during the 1978–79 school years. Expenditures of the Alberta Education Department, the third kind of expenditure, amounted to $1,176,000 for the same period. Expenditures by teachers in the Alberta Teachers Association, amounting to $7,622,000, constituted the fourth kind. The total costs for the 1977–79 school years were estimated at $40,948,000.

Since there were 23,867 teachers included in this study, the per-teacher total cost was $1,715 for in-service training and professional development. As will be apparent, this sum far exceeds estimates that are reported later in the chapter, as well as those reported earlier. With Fennell's data, the direct amount invested per teacher in Alberta was $375 per year for the 1977–79 academic years, with indirect costs adding $1,340 more.

Direct costs included advanced study and bursaries, training, travel and subsistence, and dues and fees. The indirect costs included convention and professional development days, attendance at in-service seminars and institutes, released-time pay for substitutes, program implementation, and estimates of allocations by individual teachers for in-service activities.

Quite obviously other comparative data are needed to determine a relative percentage by which to compare Canadian and United States in-service costs. But the Fennell study is the only one of its kind in the ERIC system!

COST REPORTS ON SPECIFIC STAFF-DEVELOPMENT PROGRAMS

Funding levels for teacher in-service education vary widely across the country, and there are no agreed-upon reporting standards. In Chicago, the school board has allocated approximately 1 percent of its educational fund to in-service education each year (Conran and Chase 1982), while in Lake Washington (a school district in the state of Washington), more than $500,000 was allocated in 1982 to its staff-development program with the amount approaching $1 million in 1987 (Youngs and Hager 1982; Costello 1986).

Gail V. Bass (1978) reported that 15 percent of a $6.6 million alternative-school federal grant to Minneapolis was spent on in-service training. She, however, reported a similar federal project involving the city of Alum Rock that spent 5 percent on in-service *and* curriculum development. The Minneapolis schools distributed a memo stressing the importance of in-service to make the project successful. Bass's study offers both empirical and inferential evidence that the support for staff development is an administrative value decision. As Margaret A. Thomas (1978) observed, with funded projects, the principal especially is the critical decision maker on in-service expenditures.

Phillip J. Runkel et al. (1980) provided one of the more detailed examples of a cost analysis for a staff-development program, but again it covered a project with a limited scope. His analysis was based on the cost of maintaining a cadre of specialists to assist only with an organizational development (OD) model of teacher in-service training. Runkel's example of a detailed assessment of staff-development costs was for a district with 1,000 to 1,500 professional staff and a student body of 20,000 to 30,000. The estimated costs of maintaining the cadre of organizational specialists for one year amounted to $27,900. This included salaries for a part-time coordinator and part-time secretary, fringe benefits, substitute costs, consultants, supplies, and materials.

Patrick McIntyre (1976) examined costs, benefits, and liabilities associated with an in-service education program designed by the Teacher Corps. In terms of dollar costs to the local school districts, he reported that the average teacher contract for an in-service project was $2,521. In five schools, approximately 100 contracts had been negotiated, resulting in a total cost approaching $250,000. The bulk of these costs were "indirect" in nature, since none of the schools had budgeted any sum approximating that expenditure.

Michael Kane and Cheryl Chase (1983) reported data on three projects, one of which was an industry–school district in-service project in Rochester, New York that cost about $200,000 per year. This project focused on science staff development. Similarly, Houston, Texas, offered bonuses and incentive pay for science and mathematics teachers. One such project for thirty-four teachers cost $68,500, or about $2,000 per teacher. The San Diego Public Schools and Underhill, Vermont, Independent School District reported costs on a classroom problem-solving project: direct costs were $99,317 and $88,153, respectively; a total of seventeen classrooms were involved for a unit cost of $11,027.

Lillian V. Cady and Mark Johnson (1981) reported that in the state of Washington, during the 1979–80 academic year, school personnel who were enrolled in off-campus courses paid approximately one-third of the total cost. Approximately $992,998 was paid in tuition charges by school personnel for all off-campus courses in the field of education. The state expenditure for credit-related salary increases during the 1979–80 year was approximately $3 million. Cady and Johnson noted that, although the teachers enrolled in the off-campus courses paid almost $1 million, there was in fact a $3 million, credit-related salary increase during the same time.

If those who enroll in off-campus education courses pay only approximately one-third of the cost, who pays the other two-thirds? In the state of Washington, the cost was subsidized by a state appropriation to the respective institutions. Interestingly, the teachers enrolled in these courses did not know this, nor were they told about it later. When they enrolled in an off-campus course, they assumed that their fee was paying for the total cost of the course. If the state was paying for two-thirds of these courses, then the responsible state agencies were negligent in not informing their clientele (in this case, teachers) that fees and tuition accounted for only one-third of the total costs. Taxpayers were not getting credit for their very substantial contribution to in-service education when they were subsidizing the off-campus courses. (The actual cost for on-campus courses had a 70 percent subsidy: students paid 30 percent through tuition, taxpayers subsidized the remainder.)

Do universities and school districts enter into formal agreements to provide in-service education? Cady and Johnson reported that forty-one out of sixty-three school districts *had no* formal arrangements with any college or university to provide training to their personnel. This finding may be similar to what occurs in the nation as a whole—with the exception of Florida, where school district teacher-education centers must collaborate with universities.

In a cost analysis of the Bay Area Writing Project (BAWP), Jim Stahlecker (1979) described the structure and cost of the program. The advantage of his study is that he examined a program that had evolved over a five-year period and was relatively stable. For the one year examined, the annual BAWP budget was $650,000. Of that amount, $150,000 was spent for professional staff salaries. The standard type of in-service program provided by the project was generally ten weeks in length and utilized a different sector for each of the ten 3-hour sessions. School districts were charged $1,750 per participant for this standard type of in-service program. Stahlecker's analysis of the indirect costs of such a program suggests that the total school district costs ranged somewhere between $2,632 and $3,051 per participant.

Districts using BAWP in-service programs provided them at no cost to the participating teachers. In most cases, teachers were not given released time to attend class. However, most participants earned credit from the University of California at substantially reduced tuition. Thus, while BAWP teachers were involved in district-sponsored in-service education, they were at the same time advancing themselves along the district's salary schedule. The ultimate cost of these pay increases was not determined in the calculation of indirect costs to school districts, but the indirect cost for districts did include administrative time and time spent by support staff in planning and carrying out the in-service programs. The $1,750 district fee covered the teacher consultant fees and coordinator's fee, but not the costs incurred by the BAWP central staff. Unfortunately, Stahlecker did not provide any subdivisions of these costs. Districts absorbed approximately 61 to 69 percent of the cost of a project, while BAWP absorbed approximately 31 to 39 percent of the cost.

In the computation of indirect costs, the average substitute-teacher salary was estimated at $35 per day and the average number of teachers per session was fifteen. Stahlecker did not expand upon these data, but the implication is that a district that released its teachers for ten half-day sessions might expend as much as $2,625 for substitute-teacher salaries. The indirect cost would be substantially higher than Stahlecker's estimate, since his high estimate only allowed $525 for substitute-teacher expenses.

Stahlecker stressed the importance of college credit as a motivator for teacher participation in in-service education.

In Chapter 3, we discussed the Florida Teacher Education Centers. The funding for these operational units of the state government is from a variety of sources. The state legislature first provides an appropriation that supports the operation of the centers. Each school district can budget $6 per full-time student, which is used to support its beginning-teacher project. Colleges and universities in Florida can augment from their own budgets the amount budgeted by the state for staff development. In fact, they receive a legislative line-item appropriation providing them with a specific number of faculty positions to work directly with the teacher centers.

The state of Florida has increased the amount budgeted for staff development from $9,397,288 during the 1975–76 academic year to over $22 million during the 1986–87 academic year. (Recall that in 1987, the state of New York invested $10 million alone in its teacher center program.)

Program elements supported by the teacher education center concept include: (1) teacher education improvement; (2) beginning-teacher assistance; and (3) summer institutes in critical shortage areas such as science, mathematics, computer education, and foreign languages. No question about it, the state of Florida is a leader in the staff-development movement.

AN EXTENSIVE ANALYSIS OF IN-SERVICE COSTS

The most comprehensive study of in-service costs was conducted by Donald R. Moore and Arthur A. Hyde and is the basis for three publications: *Rethinking Staff Development: A Handbook for Analyzing Your Program and Its Costs* (1978), *An Analysis of Staff Development Programs and Their Costs in Three Urban School Districts* (1980), and *Making Sense of Staff Development Programs: An Analysis of Staff Development Programs and Their Costs in Three Urban School Districts* (1981). All deal with the same study, but each differs in emphasis. For our purposes, we use the first publication (1978) as the primary source and supplement the ideas and comments from the two later publications.*

Rationale for Studying Costs

Moore and Hyde identified four reasons for studying and analyzing staff-development costs. First, in-service education must be better defined and understood because it is now used more extensively to bring about instructional improvement within the schools. Teacher turnover has declined sharply with the reduction of the school-age population. Second, fiscal analysis of staff development in a district often produces some unexpected results. Third, to plan for the future, those programs and routines presently in place must be identified and analyzed. Fourth, costs must be reviewed as priorities and clearly established for future planning. As the fiscal resources available to school districts decline, budget proposals have to be better supported by cost information.

Educators who seek increased funding for staff development need to prepare graphic analyses of program costs, proposed accomplishments, and past results. Such cost analyses should compare both efficient and inefficient uses of resources. They should provide management with information that will result in reallocations, which in turn will support more productive staff development. (These are hints of systems analysis.)

Moore and Hyde identified a broad range of activities associated with staff

---

*Data from Moore and Hyde study used with permission of Donald R. Moore and Arthur A. Hyde.

development. They argued that a reasonable basis for planning cannot be established unless the full range of activities used to conduct staff development is examined. For example, when a principal observes a teacher, it may not lead to staff improvement, but Moore and Hyde assumed that it is an activity intended to achieve such a purpose and should therefore be identified as a cost of staff development.

They assumed that much of staff development was embedded in the *routines* of a school district. Identifying those routines results in a better understanding of the contrast between what is actually occurring and the perception of what is occurring. That is, many assumptions are made about staff development that may be invalid. It is important to study routines because they define trainer roles and establish what is appropriate or inappropriate to calculate as a cost. Routines can be difficult to identify and study because they are dispersed throughout the school district. They are rarely labeled as staff development, and school districts do not usually keep financial records on them, but they reflect the way people spend their time.

Some routines at the school-building level that are often overlooked as part of staff development are staff meetings, department meetings, work days associated with the opening and closing of school, early release for curriculum development, preparation periods for training projects, and on-site in-service that utilizes the school's own staff. Some routines on the district level that are equally overlooked as part of staff development are program reviews of specifically funded programs and participation on district committees (such as facility planning committees, curriculum planning committees, and program planning committees).

The Moore and Hyde sample was limited to three cities with populations ranging from 500,000 to 750,000. The districts were rated as either high, medium, or low in in-service activity. Their sample included "Seaside," a district selected from the upper one-third, "Riverview," selected from the middle one-third, and "Union," selected from the lower one-third.

After the extent of teacher in-service activity was identified in each district, the amount of teacher time spent in each of the activities was estimated through interviews. Administrative staff were also asked to estimate the percentage of their time spent in their various staff-development activities. The financial administrators of each district were interviewed to determine how the expenses and salaries of teachers and administrative personnel involved in staff development were charged for the identifiable costs.

How Staff Development Was Conducted

Each district had a department called Staff Development or In-Service Education, but in none of the districts was this department the single best indicator of the scope of staff development. Staff-development responsibilities were dispersed among several departments and a large number of people. The offices designated to coordinate staff development often played a minor role in this swirl of activity. A close analysis revealed why this rather startling situation existed. For a large number of people, staff development was often only a minor responsibility, which had to be carried out to accomplish the objectives of their department or program. Yet the need for accomplishing these important objectives elevated staff development to an important—and sometimes predominant—position in those districts. Thus Moore and Hyde found wide involvement in staff development, but generally a lack of coordination. They concluded that staff development evolved largely out of the needs of a particular program, with the end results an unarticulated staff-development program.

Middle-level leaders—such as department chairs, coordinators, curriculum specialists, and principals—carry out staff development with great personal autonomy and with little planning, coordination, or communication. Efforts are not clearly centralized or responsive to the school or school–community concerns.

Even though they observed many similarities among the three districts, Moore and Hyde (1980) found that the major thrust of staff development was very different in each district. To encourage teachers to participate in courses and workshops, one district spent heavily on substitute teachers, stipends, sabbaticals, and salary increases for those taking courses and workshops. Another district relied more heavily on salary increases; the third depended a great deal on stipends.

All three districts distributed salary increases to teachers for completing course work. As teachers finished certain district-specified educational requirements, they gained an additional salary increase plus those gained for longevity. The long-range cost of this type of staff-development incentive becomes substantial where school staffs are stable and where teachers stay on the job longer. For example, over a twelve-year period, a $1,000 per-year raise for one individual reflects $12,000, not including other substantial associated employment costs.

Moore and Hyde found that salary increases awarded for increased education in the year under study amounted to $870,000 for Seaside, $205,000 for Riverside, and $199,000 for Union. It was obvious that the structure of the salary schedule had an impact on encouraging teachers to further their education. In Seaside, a teacher with a bachelor's degree could earn an additional $1,842 for taking courses without earning a master's degree. In Union, the same teacher could earn an additional $362. In Riverview, there was no provision for an increase until a master's degree was earned. By earning a master's degree, a teacher in Seaside could earn an additional pay increase of $3,069. In Riverview, a teacher could earn an additional increase of $2,000. And in Union, a teacher could earn an additional pay increase of $1,641. The difference these salary increases provided in terms of motivation was at least in part confirmed. In Riverview, a substantial number of teachers employed in the district for more than twenty years were still on their ending salary step.

In-Service Expenditures

In all three districts studied, the majority of staff-development opportunities were job-embedded—done during the teacher's regular working day. Special funding played only a minor role in staff development. The areas of greatest cost were staff salaries and benefits, teacher salaries and benefits, substitute-teacher costs, consultant fees, teacher stipends, sabbaticals, and salary increases.

These unbudgeted costs were relatively substantial when compared to the amounts of money budgeted for direct support of in-service education. Seaside spent $9,363,000 on in-service education, which amounted to 5.72 percent of its total budget. Riverview spent $4,607,000, which amounted to 3.76 percent of its budget. And Union spent $4,069,000, which amounted to 3.28 percent of its budget.

A substantial portion of the staff-development financing came from local funds. Although the percentages varied slightly in the three different Moore and Hyde publications, it is relatively safe to conclude that at least 90 percent of Seaside's in-service expenditures, at least 50 percent of Riverview's, and at least 80 percent of Union's were from local funds.

When all three districts were asked to estimate their total investment in staff development, the actual cost of staff development was *fifty times more* than most local school staffs had estimated. The significant difference came partly from what Moore and Hyde identified as "hidden cost." (We call these *indirect* costs.) This is not to imply that costs were deliberately being disguised. It is more a matter of recognizing the true breadth of in-service education and of identifying related costs. These findings provide a sharp contrast to those of W. Robert Houston and H. Jerome Frieberg (1979), who concluded that the school district with more than 1 percent of its budget devoted to staff development is rare indeed.

REPLICATION STUDIES

Larry D. LaBolle (1983) used the Moore and Hyde model to study four rural Alaskan school districts and their total investment in staff development. Robert J. Valiant (1985) used the model to study three moderate-size school districts in the state of Washington. Richard D. Cole (1987) studied four smaller districts (1,000 to 5,000 pupils). All investigators corroborated Moore and Hyde's findings, with similarities.

Tables 6-2 and 6-3 provide data by which elements of the four independent studies can be compared. Note in Table 6-2 that the *total* computed staff-development expenditures (as a percentage of the total operating expenditures) ranged from 2.77 to 11.81 percent. The median percentage falls between 3.76 and 5.70 percent. These data are far in excess of the widely published figure of 1 percent.

Table 6-3 shows the average total cost per participant for ten districts. The low was $969 and the high $9,934, with the median about $3,178 per participant. Again, these figures are higher than earlier reported data, with the lower end comparing closely to data computed by B. H. Fennell et al. (1980) for Alberta.

Observe how the ratio of direct to indirect costs ranges from 1:1, to 1:10. These ratios reflect why staff-development costs are vastly underestimated.

TABLE 6-2.

TOTAL STAFF-DEVELOPMENT COSTS AS A PERCENTAGE OF TOTAL OPERATING EXPENDITURES FOR REPORTED YEARS

DISTRICT	FISCAL YEAR STUDIED	TOTAL BUDGETED EXPENDITURES	STAFF-DEVELOPMENT COSTS	PERCENT OF TOTAL EXPENDITURES
Seaside[M]	1977	$163,656,000	$9,368,000	5.72
Riverview[M]	1978	122,429,000	4,607,000	3.76
Union[M]	1978	123,943,000	3,953,000	3.28
Baleen[L]	1982	4,666,572	551,328	11.81
Beluga[L]	1982	7,562,071	701,508	9.28
Scrimshaw[L]	1982	4,485,726	280,693	6.26
Ptarmigan[L]	1982	6,748,070	384,944	5.70
Fruitland[V]	1983	14,961,300	526,461	3.10
Orchard[V]	1983	19,005,800	526,461	2.77
Vineyard[V]	1983	26,826,400	1,014,038	3.78
Capital[C]	1985	4,938,634	320,032	6.48
Newton[C]	1985	16,631,887	943,144	5.67
Lake Shore[C]	1985	10,681,618	613,433	5.74
Long Creek[C]	1985	8,675,265	481,286	5.54

[M]Districts from Moore and Hyde Study (1978).
[L]Districts from LaBolle Study (1983).
[V]Districts from Valiant Study (1984).
[C]Districts from Cole Study (1987).

Further, it should be noted that the percentage of federal funds for staff development in these studies ranged from 0 to 37.7 percent. Riverview had 37.7 percent federally funded. But the second highest percentage was 13.6 percent, at Fruitland. The median was 4.6 percent for federal support. Surprisingly, other sources had a median ranging between 89.8 and 95.8 percent. So while there is a very substantial federal outlay for staff development, this sample shows that it is really quite minimal at the local school district level.

Valiant and Cole provided the most definitive estimates showing the impact of providing salary adjustments for staff-development course credits. Both observed that the districts' salary schedules rewarded earned educational credits. To determine salary costs, they computed salaries without any educational increments for all persons at each step on the salary schedules for each district. For Vineyard, the sum of the salaries was the theoretical cost if all persons were denied their educational increments: $10,241,983 for the 1982–83 school year, compared to the actual cost of salaries for all 547 persons represented on the schedule ($12,234,327). It was found that educational credits accounted for $1,992,334 in the Vineyard School District during the year studied. This amounted to about 20 percent of the salary budget.

Costs for educational increments earned during 1982–83 were available for all three districts. Vineyard teachers earned an average educational increment of

TABLE 6-3.

AVERAGE NUMBER OF HOURS AND COSTS PER PARTICIPANT FOR STAFF-DEVELOPMENT ACTIVITIES

DISTRICT	FISCAL YEAR STUDIED	HOURS SPENT PER PARTICIPANT	AVERAGE COST PER PARTICIPANT FOR ALL STAFF PARTICIPANT	RATIO OF DIRECT COSTS TO INDIRECT COSTS
Seaside[M]	1977	101.71	$1,768	1:6
Riverview[M]	1978	33.45	1,124	1:1
Union[M]	1978	45.67	969	1:3
Baleen[L]	1982	253.40	9,934	1:1
Beluga[L]	1982	189.00	7,625	1:2
Scrimshaw[L]	1982	133.50	4,968	1:2
Ptarmigan[L]	1982	127.90	4,873	1:2
Fruitland[V]	1983	25.52	1,246	1:3
Orchard[V]	1983	40.55	1,235	1:10
Vineyard[V]	1983	53.05	1,701	1:1
Capital[C]	1985	105.10	3,596	1:4
Newton[C]	1985	67.50	3,286	1:3
Lake Shore[C]	1985	57.10	3,178	1:2
Long Creek[C]	1985	54.10	3,230	1:2

[M]Districts from Moore and Hyde (1978).
[L]Districts from LaBolle (1983).
[V]Districts from Valiant (1984).
[C]Districts from Cole (1987).

$309, followed by Orchard teachers at $220 and Fruitland at $202. Liberal local credit provisions in Vineyard account for much of the difference, with several options leading to in-service credit. Vineyard teachers remained in the district an average of nine years each. Thus the $309 earned during 1982–83 could produce an average additional income of $2,781 over the course of the nine years. For only one year, 1,198 teachers accrued $307,799 in salary increases owing to staff-development incentives. The average gain per teacher was $266.

Cole calculated that for one year alone teachers averaged $872 more salary because of educational increases, to a high of $1,902 per teacher per year. He illustrated that a teacher who received the maximum educational and staff-development allocation would have a pay increase of $5,100 over just a five-year period.

Local salary incentives have an accumulative effect on the operating budgets of school districts. These effects are, in fact, similar to compound interest. Cole and I estimated that nearly half the salary increments for teachers at the top of the salary schedule could be attributed to staff-development credits—either district authorized or university courses! These are *indirect* costs and are seldom classified as a longitudinal cost of in-service education.

With the academic year of 1985–86 as a baseline and the estimated current expenditures for public schools of $125 billion (*Statistical Abstract, 1986,* Table 233, page 142), and applying only the 3.76 percent figure, the total invested nationally for staff development exceeds $4.5 billion.

IMPLICATIONS

The concept of computing direct and indirect costs of staff development is a relatively recent phenomenon. As a cost-analysis tool, these two elements can help district decision-makers interpret more appropriately any cost data for school- or district-based staff-development activities. For planners, the financing of any legislated or mandated in-service education must be the initial question addressed. A state that considers legal prescriptions to increase (or change) teacher competencies ultimately has to pay for them. Since only some general aspects of financing have been addressed in this chapter, several additional questions need to be considered by policymakers:

1. In a time of scarcity (money or taxes), how will policymakers reallocate resources for staff development? If such reallocations are to be made, where will budget reductions or shifts be made?
2. If teachers must pay the fees for in-service education, will policymakers seek a uniform financial reward, such as a salary scale adjustment? Or will policymakers seek a wider range of incentives to encourage participation?
3. To what extent will policymakers assume that staff development financed at the local level is similar to American business and industry?
4. Will "tight" national and local fiscal policies force school districts to coordinate their previously independent staff-development efforts with other districts?
5. Will local policymakers seek agreements with institutions of higher education to conduct local in-service programs?
6. Will university policymakers be willing to (a) provide in-service education to local schools, (b) allow graduate credit for courses typically "free of intellectual content" (that is, workshops without study), and (c) reward professors for conducting a service-oriented mission?
7. Will policymakers seek alternative delivery systems over the current labor-intensive model?
8. Will teacher bargaining units become more assertive to influence policymakers on staff-development issues?
9. Will state and local policymakers study and jointly implement new field-tested methods in the current structure of in-service education?

Since most in-service education is conducted at local school or district levels, a problem of fiscal equity emerges. The poorer school districts may be most in need of in-service yet not able to support the financial burden. It seems well established that the districts with poorest financial resources pay teachers relatively poor salaries. Shifting the financial burden to poorer local districts simply means few or no systematic in-service programs where they may be badly needed.

Affecting any of these nine questions is the problem of defining in-service. School districts should not be expected to pay directly—or even indirectly—for courses, workshops, or institutes that have no clear in-service or job-related application.

Finally, criteria and techniques by which to conduct effective in-service programs need widespread dissemination, especially by state departments of education.

Each of the nine policy implications has its own bottom line. Policymakers have a difficult agenda concerning in-service teacher education. University researchers can make a genuine contribution by conducting meaningful research on these items, and particularly in providing empirical and objective data to aid in this otherwise value-laden task.

Now let us examine some comparable data from nonschool studies that have reported about staff training.

NONSCHOOL STUDIES

While not directly related to teacher in-service, Carl R. Puuri and Raymond G. Weinmann (1981) reported cost data on in-service education for silviculturists in the U.S. Department of Agriculture's Forest Service. They reported that in 1979, in five national regions with formal programs in continuing education and training, the cost per participant ranged from $1,750 to $11,380. Their estimates included the actual cost of instruction, books, school supplies, room and board, travel, incidentals, per diem allowances, and salary estimates for workdays away from the duty station (direct and indirect costs).

Puuri and Weinmann then asked the question, "Why train?" They responded:

> It may be asked why an investment should be made to further the education of a silviculturist who already has a college degree: The reason is that a forestry school, no matter what its emphasis or standards, simply cannot fit into a four-year course all that a silviculturist needs to know to write workable prescriptions for timber stands on public lands. Perhaps that was not always true, but it is certainly true today.*

This rationale is most applicable to America's teacher corps! The "good old days" of some knowledge stability are gone. The knowledge explosion requires frequent and systematic staff renewal—just to "stay up with the kids."

Beverly McQuigg (1980) provided data showing how the nation's business and industrial corporations are investing in human resources development through corporate-sponsored training. In a study of 191 organizations, she reported that

---

*From "Continuing Education and Certification of Silviculturalists on the USDA Forest Service," *Journal of Forestry* 79, page 206.

55 percent had formal in-service programs. As early as 1976, American industry invested $1.2 billion in combined management and development. Of that amount, 62 percent was allocated to salary and administrative costs, with 11 percent spent on outside seminars and workshops. The balance was divided among other costs: books, instructional equipment and materials, facilities, tuition refunds, consultants, and other training costs. McQuigg predicted management-development expenditures to rise to at least $2.2 billion in 1982.

Anthony E. Schwaller (1980) reported that a Conference Board of New York City survey of 610 firms employing 500 or more employees revealed over $2 billion spent in 1974–75 on employee education and training. He also reported that 3.7 million employees participated in in-house courses taught during the workday. About 700,000 employees were enrolled in company-sponsored courses after working hours. Schwaller estimated that over $4 billion was being spent annually by the private sector for education and training of employees.

According to a 1983 study by the American Society for Training and Development, employee training in the nation's largest companies costs between $20 and $30 billion annually. This is equal to more than half of the cost of higher education in the United States ("Employers Lead . . ." 1983). McQuigg and Schwaller were obviously too conservative in their estimates.

San Diego, California, conducted an organizational development project for people responsible for selected electrical and radio service. According to Albert C. Gross (1978), costs were cut by $130,000 and customer satisfaction increased. The direct costs to conduct this staff-development project were not available.

Jack Gordon (1986) and Chris Lee (1986) reported data from surveys conducted of U.S. organizations with fifty or more employees. Collectively, their data revealed that private industry invests about $29 billion per year in formal staff training and development. Gordon listed thirty-eight specific types of training activities; the top seven were new-employee orientation, performance appraisals, new-equipment orientation, leadership, time management, train-the-trainer, and word processing. (These are similar to school in-service topics!)

Lee prepares a monthly Training Profile for the journal *Training*. In October 1986 (page 68), she listed forty-one different private and nonprofit organizations that had a profile published between 1983 and 1986. These companies, to name just a few, included AT&T Communications, Bay Area Rapid Transit District, Florida Power, the Good Samaritan Hospital, Hewlett-Packard, Life of Virginia, Motorola, Inc., and the U.S. Postal Service. Table 6-4 lists some pertinent data.

In *Mirrors of Excellence,* W. Robert Houston and collaborators (1986) presented short case studies describing ten large corporate and federal agency staff-development programs. A sample of those included are the Boeing Company (aerospace), Arthur Anderson and Company (accounting), M. D. Anderson Hospital (health care), Walt Disney World (entertainment), and Southern Company Services (utility). This short monograph is most appropriate reading for school board members who might be reluctant to budget school district funds for needed

TABLE 6-4.

SELECTED TRAINING COSTS FROM PRIVATE INDUSTRIES

COMPANY	NUMBER OF EMPLOYEES	FULL-TIME TRAINERS	TRAINING BUDGET
AT&T Communications (Marketing)	16,270	160	$20,100,000
Bay Area Rapid Transit District	2,002	17	2,112,124
Florida Power Company (Technical Group)	2,220	25	1,625,000
Good Samaritan Hospital	1,858	0	19,360
Hewlett-Packard (Computer Sales Force)	3,649	9	1,687,000
Life of Virginia (Sales Agents and Managers)	1,000	2	378,000
Motorola, Inc.	100,000	803	44,500,000
U.S. Postal Service	744,490	1,366	75,500,000

Source: Data used with permission of *Training,* The Magazine of Human Resources Development. Copyright Lakewood Publications, Inc., Minneapolis, MN (612) 333-0471. All rights reserved.

in-service projects. Staff developers should examine the piece for tips on organizing large and comprehensive programs.

This brief treatment of nonschool staff development is important to public school teachers and administrators for four reasons. First, by knowing the companies that conduct staff training, school personnel can more easily convince lay school boards of the importance of staff development. (I recommend that each school district subscribe to *Training* magazine so policymakers can have private-sector data readily available to them.) Could a manager of an AT&T plant think that school in-service is a "frill" if he or she were a school board member?

Second, many similarities can be observed between the training programs of schools and industries. School district staff developers should attempt to find successful models from industry that can be applied to the context of the schools.

Third, comparative cost analyses can be studied so that baseline data for various organizations can be used to determine relative cost-effectiveness.

Fourth, it is critical to know what private industry is doing in the field, since certain industrial models are at times inappropriately suggested for use in the school sector.

CONCLUSION

The concepts of direct and indirect costs are the key to determining cost-effective in-service education and staff development. As Margo Johnson (1980) indicated, in-service education has become one of *the* major political issues for educators.

Thus, staff development must be studied in a policy-budget-resource allocation context.

Administrators and school board members do not have the option of *not* funding staff-development efforts. The demographics right now show how essential it is for school districts to invest in developing their human potential or they will suffer the consequences of knowledge gaps, inadequately prepared staff, and a system not fully committed to the twenty-first century. The funding of quality in-service programs is the very least that policymakers can do to improve the schools. Perhaps it is the most.

CHECKLIST FOR FUNDING STAFF DEVELOPMENT

____ **1.** A school district policy exists regarding the funding of staff development.

____ **2.** The school district takes advantage of federally funded initiatives.

____ **3.** The school district cooperates with institutions of higher education to obtain grants for quality staff-development programs.

____ **4.** The school district keeps an accurate accounting of staff-development costs.

____ **5.** The *direct* and *indirect* costs are either computed or reasonably estimated for school district and school-based staff-development activities.

____ **6.** Staff-development policies are analyzed to determine their impact on salary distributions.

____ **7.** Funding sources for staff development are summarized each year.

____ **8.** Funding priorities are established each year, based on systematic needs assessments.

____ **9.** Local industries are surveyed to determine their staff-development investments.

____ **10.** A central resource file (including the journal *Training*) is maintained.

CHAPTER 7

A PARADIGM FOR STAFF DEVELOPMENT

The trouble with American educators is that they seek one grand theory to address all problems.

Anonymous

Establishing a set of criteria for a school district's staff-development program (as described in Chapter 1) and then conducting appropriate needs assessments (as described in Chapter 2) will automatically improve the vast majority of in-service projects conducted each year. By detailing both criteria and needs, you begin to set a planning style that requires staff developers and administrators to conceptualize the process. Such conceptualization changes the thinking and acting processes from *atheoretical* thinking to *pretheoretical* thinking. You then seek patterns of effective practices, identify similarities and differences in projects that work or fail, and view change as a long-range process. More important, you begin to think in a conceptual manner. Staff development and in-service education become integral parts of curriculum development and instructional improvement. Unfortunately, staff development and in-service education now are for the most part considered separate entities of administration, rather than part of curriculum development. As the planning process evolves, planners begin to realize that there are many in-service projects that ought to take place, not just the in-service project for this year.

To work toward a vision, administrators, principals, staff developers, and members of the staff-development advisory committee (teachers) need to understand systematic planning and data collecting. Systematic planning at all levels of education—elementary to graduate education—tends to be intuitive, personalized, and rather arbitrary in nature: "We planned last year" is a common mindset. Planning should instead be a process—a continuous and reflective journey, not an event. If staff-development committees are to plan and think systematically, they need models. In this chapter, we explore several models that are subsumed under one major paradigm.

In Chapter 2, I reviewed several methods of conducting assessments, particularly as they form data sets that can directly affect decision making. The data, per se, need to be placed in a frame of reference that allows a holistic view of the organization's staff-development efforts. In other words, the data are used to validate and establish a comprehensive picture of needs. Data always need interpretation, but when decision making is based on the collected data, personal biases are held to a minimum. As data begin to drive in-service projects, there is a tendency for recipients of the training to evaluate their experiences in a highly positive manner. There is also a mounting body of studies that report positive effects of in-service training. Either explicitly or implicitly, successful programs tend to rely on a conceptual model, whether it be competency based, organizational development, social system, concerns based, developmental, or AAIM (explained later).

My basic assumption is that if school district staff-development directors rely on an explicit planning paradigm, they thereby increase the probability that their in-service education efforts will be successful.

THEORY AND PARADIGMS FOR STAFF-DEVELOPMENT PROGRAMS

The absence of theory associated with the bulk of in-service training programs at all levels is amplified by Donald R. Cruickshank, Christopher Lorish, and Linda Thompson (1979), who reported the apparent lack of theoretically based in-service programs and the attending problems that emerge. Sharon Feiman (1981) also observed how little theory was called upon by in-service program designers.

Gary D. Fenstermacher and David C. Berliner (1983) prepared *A Conceptual Framework for the Analysis of Staff Development*, one of the few attempts to establish a workable model. They identified four critical determinants for staff development: (1) initiation, (2) purpose, (3) participation, and (4) motivation. These are expanded into three dimensions—worth, merit, and success—with an accompanying twelve enhancing conditions. However, their framework is basically an evaluation model (Accreditation) and not a theoretical paradigm. Further, their framework is not needs driven, and it can be used to prepare personally rationalized in-service programs.

Likewise, Meredith D. Gall and Ronald S. Renchler (1985) wrote *Effective Staff Development for Teachers: A Research-Based Model*, in which twenty-seven criteria were listed by which to conduct in-service projects or to plan an effective staff-development program. Their criteria, while having some empirical basis, are very similar to those of Gordon Lawrence (1982), Roy Edelfelt (1977), and Evelyn Craven (1978). The twenty-seven criteria, if followed, would improve the general nature of staff development, but Gall and Renchler did not organize their extensive list into a usable paradigm.

Sally Glassberg and Sharon N. Oja (1981) presented a model derived from the major conclusions of the developmental psychologists, particularly Jean Piaget (1970) and Lawrence Kohlberg (1971). Shirley M. Hord and associates (1987) suggested the Concerns-Based Adoption Model, or CBAM. Ann Lieberman (1986) collected several major statements and research findings, as did Gary A.

Griffin (1983), Bruce Joyce and Beverly Showers (1988), and Susan Loucks-Horsley, Catherine K. Harding, et al. (1987).

However, the above models and statements can be categorized as model specific and not adequately comprehensive. Several models will be synthesized here into a meaningful and useful paradigm that can be applied or tested in the schools. The use of the paradigm, the predictions that one makes from its application, and its testing interact in a cyclical manner. Thus there is an inquiry model that allows for continuous testing and revising. In short, the paradigm predicts practice, and practice will validate or negate the paradigm.

Characteristics of a Paradigm

N. L. Gage wrote: "Paradigms are not theories; they are rather ways of thinking or patterns for research that, when carried out, can lead to the development of theory" (1963, page 95). Two major characteristics of a paradigm were then identified by Gage. First, a paradigm is generalizable to a class of events or processes. Second, a paradigm may represent variables and their relationships in graphic form. Thus, a paradigm represents a pretheoretical statement that attempts to establish order in a class of events and to provide a means by which that order can be communicated.

The ultimate end of building a paradigm is to describe and predict practices or consequences that will probably follow when identified concepts or models are applied in the most appropriate manner and then to observe those predictable results. This is the process of *validation*.

In 1986, Lee S. Shulman again commented on the need for educational paradigms as they relate to teaching. Shulman argued that research programs grow from specific perspectives that focus on some part of the educational field while ignoring the other parts. The paradigm suggested here certainly meets that criterion.

This discussion on the construction of a paradigm applicable to in-service education is most essential, for as Richard Hofstadter (1963) observed, educators for the most part, especially administrators, have a great distrust of and disdain for theory. And that includes paradigms!

In this paradigm, staff development subsumes in-service education. The connotation tends to be critical. Some educators describe staff development and in-service education as distinct *processes,* while others consider them as *acts.* How you implement a staff-development program depends greatly on which emphasis—process or act?—you adopt.

Throughout, the vision in this book views in-service education as leading to changes in teacher behavior, in the classroom, and in the individual building or district operations. Thus you should be aware of various theories concerning change strategies, a topic that is addressed in Chapter 9. Further, a staff-development and in-service paradigm is of great use to program designers, for it causes them to analyze their assumptions, assertions, and definitions before they even begin planning projects.

The Paradigm in General

For several years I have attempted in my classes and in the field to describe the various theories, paradigms, classifications, and models for in-service education. There appear to be currently described in the literature four general classifications, which subsume at least fifteen different in-service models: (1) organization based, (2) individual based, (3) role-based, and (4) trainer based.

As an advance organizer, Table 7-1 illustrates the essential elements of the paradigm. It shows how easy it is to select the most appropriate model. Each

TABLE 7-1.

PARADIGM OF IN-SERVICE MODELS

ELEMENTS OF THE PARADIGM			
CLASSES (FOCUS)	MODELS (OPERATION)	CHARACTERISTICS (VARIABLES)	DELIVERY SYSTEMS (MECHANISMS)
I. Organization	• AAIM	Major systems	
	• School-Based	Individual subsystems	
	• Organization-Development	Systems and subsystems	
	• Social-System	Superordinate and subordinate dimensions	
II. Individual	• Behavioral	Single-subject designs	
	• Humanistic	Relationships and interactions	Decision makers select most appropriate delivery system for conducting in-service education; refer to Table 3-2 for listing
	• Concerns-Based Adoption	Individual needs	
	• Developmental	Experiential orientation	
III. Roles	• Independent-Study	Transmission of knowledge	
	• Competency	Demonstration of skills or processes	
	• Education-Center	Special focal groups	
IV. Trainer	• Exchange	Modeling and interchanges	
	• Linking-Agent	External interventions	
	• Peer-Coaching	Internal feedback	
	• Advocacy	Credentialing of clientele	

major class is then introduced and followed by a detailed description of the selected model.

By selecting a testable model from the paradigm, in-service program directors can predict more accurately the logical consequences of their decisions. That predictability is one of the powerful advantages of using an explicit paradigm. Further, the more closely that the elements of the paradigm converge, the higher the probability that the in-service project will be successful. A valid paradigm generates predictable and successful results.

Figure 7-1 is a dichotomous key, which can be used to classify any in-service project model or determine the most likely model for the success of a specific project. This key is analogous to plant or animal classification schemes. The taxonomy establishes hierarchical relationships among the various models and can be expanded to accommodate other models as their operations are described in the literature.

For example, if a school district's needs assessment identifies a need to improve some institutional dimension of a selected school, then the in-service pro-

FIGURE 7.1.

A DICHOTOMOUS KEY FOR STAFF DEVELOPMENT

Prior to designing any staff-development program, select the one major focus, or goal, of the intended project, then proceed through the key. The Goal or Focus is to:
Further the organization. *Go to 1.*
Promote individual competence. *Go to 4.*
Change an individual's role. *Go to 7.*
Develop a cadre of specialized trainers. *Go to 9.*

1. The goal of the project is to develop a systematic plan for the organization. *Use the AAIM model.*

1a. The goal for the project is to develop some subsytem within the organization. *Go to 2.*

2. The goal of the project is to focus on one school or one unit in the organization. *Use the School-Based model.*

2a. The goal of the project is not focused on any one specific unit. *Go to 3.*

3. The goal of the project is to increase the organization's problem-solving capacity. *Use the Organization-Development model.*

3a. The goal of the project is to promote a social hierarchy. *Use the Social-Systems model. (If no, go to 4.)*

4. The project will emphasize the concept of "reinforcement." *Use the Behavioral model.*

4a. The project will not emphasize "reinforcement" techniques. *Go to 5.*

5. The project will place a premium on individualism. *Use the Humanistic model.*

FIGURE 7.1 (continued)

5a. The project will not stress individualism per se. *Go to 6.*

6. Individual concerns about change will be the prime focus of the project. *Use the CBAM model.*

6a. The project will stress individual growth and development. *Use the Developmental model.* (If no, go to 7.)

7. The goal of the project is to promote individualized training materials. *Use the Independent-Study model.*

7a. The goal of the project is not to focus on individualized training materials. *Go to 8.*

8. The goal of the project is to utilize carefully prescribed competencies or objectives. *Use the Competency-Based model.*

8a. The goal of the project is to establish a common learning site. *Use the Educator-Center model.* (If no, go to 9.)

9. The goal of the project is to develop trainers by allowing individuals to trade roles. *Use the Exchange model.*

9a. The goal of the project is to use other means to develop trainers. *Go to 10.*

10. The goal of the project is to establish agents for change within the system. *Use the Linking-Agent model.*

10a. The goal of the project is to use peers or colleagues as much as possible. *Use the Peer-Coaching model.* (If no, go to 11.)

11. The goal of the project is to create a pool of staunch program supporters. *Use the Advocacy model.*

---

gram director would seek an appropriate class and model to focus on institutional context—that is, an organizational classification. From among the different models, the one that is ultimately selected best coincides with the identified need and goals. Compatibility of training, focus, and delivery converge through explicit planning and by following the rules of the paradigm. If the paradigm is applied properly, efficacious in-service projects and staff-development programs evolve more scientifically and not simply as random events. Figure 7-1 and Table 7-1 illustrate how the paradigm can be applied. Of critical importance here are the decision-making processes employed to select the model.

CLASS 1: ORGANIZATION-BASED MODELS

The common characteristic of organization-based in-service models is their focus on the institution, agency, or school building. To be sure, individuals are not wholly overlooked in this classification. Organizational problems are identified, usually by needs assessments. The primary emphasis is on solving problems or providing new skills in the system or in a related subsystem. At least four organization-based models have been described in the literature:

1. AAIM
2. School-Based
3. Organization-Development
4. Social-System

AAIM Model*

In 1979, I published a six-step model for conducting in-service programs, which began with needs assessment and was followed by five other logical steps. The six steps are (1) needs assessment, (2) awareness, (3) application, (4) implementation, (5) maintenance, and (6) evaluation (which is conducted concurrently with the other steps).

Needs assessment. Chapter 2 provides detailed treatment of identifying needs, and by now it should be clear that needs assessments are fundamental to any in-service project. My own experiences in directing major, funded projects have led me to conclude that the identified needs in all school districts are multiple in nature. Therefore, a wide variety of activities must be anticipated. Information-gathering activities are often required, which leads us to the next step.

Awareness. Training projects or activities designed to provide information about new concepts, developments, skills, equipment, curricula, or teaching or administrative techniques are classified as awareness sessions. These activities are essential to keep all staff personnel up to date and informed about professional skills.

Awareness sessions usually take place through conferences, institutes, multimedia presentations, promotions from sales representatives, lectures, or visitations. In most cases, university courses and seminars are awareness-level in-service activities. The information obtained at this level makes the recipient aware that something "exists" or is available for use. Visiting speakers often provide enthusiastic presentations, promoting some new product or skill. The listeners learn about these processes or products often for the first time.

In most cases, in-service programs are centered on one awareness project after another. Thus the staff becomes exposed to something new, but that is it—only exposed!

*Donald C. Orlich (1979). "Establishing Effective In-Service Programs by Taking . . . AAIM." *The Clearing House,* 53(1), 53–55. Used with permission of Heldref Publications, Washington, D.C., Copyright 1979.

While the awareness session is critical for calling attention to innovations, it is totally inadequate to serve as an in-service model. Thus, if a district desires to incorporate important innovations into its on-going instructional or administrative practices, additional steps must be taken. Participants need to practice the innovative activities, and the need for practice leads directly to the next element of the model.

Application. An administrator may be aware of Program Evaluation Review Techniques (PERT), and a teacher may know about inquiry-oriented teaching, but if neither has a chance to apply these concepts in some supportive environment, then there is a high probability that the innovation will not be put to use. The term *application* connotes that something is used, practiced, or tried out in a context different from that in which it was learned.

One of the tested methods of application is microteaching (see Appendix D). A teacher selects only a few peers or students, and tries the technique in a way that focuses on the procedure—without the penalty for failure that there is in the classroom. This same technique can be used by administrators. Gaining practice or experience is the essence of the application phase. By incorporating the application phase into a school district's in-service model, you meet unanticipated events and deal with them. The decision for a full-scale in-service activity can be supported or aborted, depending on the outcome of this phase. Assuming a successful third stage, the in-service activity moves to the total assimilation stage—implementation.

Implementation. Full commitment to in-service activities becomes apparent during the implementation step, the most intensive period of a project. All appropriate teachers or administrators are involved in a full spectrum of in-service activities that relate to the objectives of the program. During the fourth stage of my model, the most intensive work and full-scale application take place. Further, during this phase, responsible supervisory personnel focus on helping the involved staff perfect the skills and procedures—teaching or administering new behaviors. And during this step, the so-called full effort reaches its peak.

The word *appropriate* was carefully used in the previous paragraph because it has been often assumed that "everyone" ought to be involved in most district in-service activities. Such full-scale involvement is seldom, if ever, warranted in any school district. Systematic needs assessments pinpoint desirable in-service activities and designate specific personnel as the recipients.

In the vast majority of instances, district in-service projects are terminated upon completion of a successful (or even unsuccessful) implementation stage. To be sure, the new behaviors are incorporated into the educator's repertoire of skills after implementation, and the organizational efforts required by the project begin to decline quickly. After all, the program is over. But there is yet a much-needed, final phase.

Maintenance. The final phase of the AAIM model encourages a continued, low-visibility set of in-service activities that should follow any major implementation effort. The term *maintenance* implies that some kind of service is required after assimilation. New staff will be hired in the district, people will change grade levels or switch buildings, and some personnel simply will need additional training to perfect their skills. To address these on-going needs, a school district must develop a set of internal mechanisms by which to maintain in-service activities.

One successful method is to select (and reward with pay) teachers or administrators who are proficient in the new behaviors or skills to conduct short-term clinics or projects. A second method is to use the principal or a central-office resource person (if either has the time) as the training agent. Yet another technique is to use multimedia instructional systems. The essential point is to provide all appropriate individuals with the preparation required for the continued success of the program.

Evaluation. Throughout the application of the AAIM model, formative evaluation (as described in Chapter 4) is systematically applied. During each phase, some type of evaluation is conducted. The director of staff development continuously obtains data or feedback on each specific phase. Decisions are regularly made on how much progress has been achieved. Formative-evaluation techniques allow adjustments to be made that will have an immediate impact on the project. Used in this manner, evaluation is viewed as a constructive element rather than a subjective grading given the project when completed. If you evaluate only when a project is concluded, then you only know whether it was a failure or a success. If the latter, then congratulations! If it is the former, what can you do about it now? The point of formative-evaluation procedures is to make adjustments while the project is in progress. To ensure success is the major impetus for using evaluation in this model.

School-Based Model

This model has great application to in-service activities, since the individual school becomes responsible for its own programs. As far back as 1955, John I. Goodlad proposed that the school be a basic unit for change, and he implied that in-service education was the means to accomplish curriculum change. After thirty years, we have barely understood the potentials of this model. Euan S. Henderson (1979); John I. Goodlad (1978); Kenneth R. Howey, R. Bents, and Dean Corrigan (1981), and Georgea Sparks et al. (1985), and Kenneth A. Sirotnik and Richard W. Clark (1988) have collectively supported school-based models. Goodlad viewed the school as a basic unit of change and of study. Staff development becomes but one technique to effect change in schools.

Henderson's notion was that the needs of the individual school become the staff-development focal point. To implement the model, you initially conduct a school-based needs assessment. From the needs analysis, areas of necessary staff growth are identified, followed by development of programs and delivery systems. Henderson urged the use of a variety of in- and out-of-school resource people to conduct the programs.

The school-based model certainly uses components of the AAIM model. However, the school-based model requires great personal commitment by all employed in the specific building. It is mandatory to train for team building when using this model. Simultaneously, the school-based focus must also accommodate the school district's staff-development efforts. Under these circumstances, interorganizational conflict may arise if the goals of the system and subsystems are not carefully articulated and coordinated. For example, if the school staff is committed to an activity-oriented science in-service project and the school district simultaneously institutes a writing-across-the-curriculum program, a conflict for time emerges. Teachers will not have time to participate in both programs with equal vigor. The major point is to allow adequate time for teachers and nonteachers who are participating in one or more in-service projects. Coordination requires a sensitive and communication-minded principal.

Because decision making and resource allocations ultimately reside with the person in authority, the *principal* is responsible for administrating successful school-level efforts. The principal can do a great deal to support the staff's desires to improve a school. And the principal can allocate precious time and resources to the staff and encourage them to participate fully in the change process. James M. Lipham (1981), synthesizing several research studies, found that it is the building principal who sets the goals and coordinates the efforts of the staff in achieving them.

Nicki King (1980) described how principals in one district studied were given the budgets for staff-development programs and the freedom to develop them. At three of six schools in the district, *no* staff-development programs were conducted for two academic years! At the other three schools, the amount of staff development and its intensity varied with the interest and commitment of the principal. The most successful in-service programs, wrote King, were those in which teachers and administrators participated jointly in staff-development programs. Judith Warren Little (1982) and Milbrey W. McLaughlin and David D. Marsh's (1978) findings corroborate those of King.

Implementing a school-based model requires detailed planning and organization. As the "effective schools movement" becomes institutionalized as a change strategy, a school-based staff-development model will certainly emerge as one of the favored mechanisms for change.

Organization-Development Model

Many researchers collectively described the major elements of the Organization-Development (OD) model for staff development. Proponents of OD have stressed that most school systems are reactive—that is, they react to criticism—and that by incorporating the major techniques of OD, organizations may become proactive—that is, they will anticipate problems and solve them before they interfere with organizational efficiency. (See Richard A. Schmuck and Matthew B. Miles 1971; Phillip J. Runkel, Spencer H. Wyant, Warren E. Bell, and Margaret Runkel 1980; Michael Fullen, Matthew B. Miles, and Gib Taylor 1980; Betty Dillon-Peterson 1981; and Richard A. Schmuck 1987.)

The Organization-Development model encompasses a series of processes and strategies to develop an organization's capacity to attain optimal performance. Since the focus is on the organization and its members, it is important that all members of the system (including the various subsystems) identify, study, diagnose, and analyze the strengths, weaknesses, and potentials of the organization. Personnel assigned to particular units in the organization determine the needed changes and suggest implementation strategies.

There are at least six basic steps, or processes, in the OD model: (1) developing working teams within the organization, (2) determining the organizational climate and the barriers to change, (3) specifying organizational goals and objectives, (4) planning an implementation strategy to achieve the objectives, (5) conducting the implementation strategies, and (6) evaluating each step of the process, with feedback openly provided to all members.

As you may imagine, this model requires a high degree of trust and frankness. The relationships that emerge link people together to achieve the specified organizational goals. Line and staff relationships tend to be less structured than those found in traditional school districts.

Implementing this model requires a great deal of administrator and teacher collaboration. Time is spent clarifying organizational goals, meeting in various groups, having intensive discussions, and providing frank analyses of the organization, with consistent and systematic feedback. Evidence from business use of OD is very positive, and an excellent review of its application to schools was written by Michael Fullen, Matthew B. Miles, and Gib Taylor (1980).

You might conclude that OD is the ultimate in self-renewal mechanisms. However, I suggest that the OD model always be used in conjunction with the School-Based model. Phillip J. Runkel et al. (1980) noted that only sixteen hours of OD training were needed to implement the model in a school.

Organizational development, per se, does not purport to develop self-actualized persons or good humans. Even though the model focuses on units, subsystems, or systems, the positive end result of this model is an organization fostering humans who can work more efficiently, solve problems more rapidly, and create changes in the organization with minimal stress. Technological changes have taken place in our society with terrifying speed. These changes are just beginning to be felt in the schools. As technological innovations become incorporated in the schools, there is a need for planned, purposeful, and sustained effort to accommodate change. Organization-Development may be the model to help schools attain the dynamic quality observed in self-renewing organizations. As a staff-development model, it is vastly under utilized in the schools.

Social-System Model

Jacob W. Getzels (1959) provided an early theoretical model that is applicable to staff development. People who conduct in-service programs as a function of administration, with subordinate and superordinate relationships, either implicitly or explicitly subscribe to the Social-System model. The model consists of two dimensions: *nomothetic,* consisting of the attributes of the organization—that is, the institution, role, and expectation; and *idiographic,* consisting of the individuals within the institution, their personalities, and their needs dispositions. Roles, role expectations, and status tend to be obvious in the system. Getzels assumed that stress would generate from role-personality conflict, role conflict, and personality conflict. These conflicts lead to incongruence of nomothetic and idiographic dimensions and ultimately result in loss of productivity for individuals and the organization.

In-service programs that are administrator planned and dominated correspond with this theory. Especially fitting are one-shot projects generally rated by teachers as irrelevant and not addressing either institutional or personal needs.

Why would I even suggest using the Social-System model for staff development? On first thought, this model should be rejected, since it is the epitome of the defect view. To be sure, those who subscribe to the model tend to be authoritarian in their conduct of organizational affairs. Perhaps the prime reason that this model is so important is that many schools are yet administered in an authoritarian manner. Clearly, described line and staff relationships are prevalent in larger school districts. One common complaint from teachers who work in metropolitan schools is that the bureaucracy is "impossible to break through." This is probably an accurate description of metropolitan systems, since they are rather inflexibly organized. Nomothetic and idiographic conflicts occur because the nomothetic dimension takes precedence over the idiographic. You may assume that line administrators are unaware of this model, and do not perceive their actions as falling under it. The primary reason for incorporating it into the paradigm is to make educators conscious that this model operates in many schools.

Line and staff organizations do not have to be authoritarian or inflexible. There are many administrative techniques that help open the lines of communication between those in superordinate and subordinate positions. For example, if the superordinates simply initiated a system of needs assessments and a collaborative staff-development council, authoritarianism would begin to diminish.

Collaboration is a growth process to which authoritarian organizations may evolve. The initial steps might be prompted by state laws or collective-bargaining agreements. These steps increase collaborative decision making and limit superordinate control. If the AAIM model were adopted in a tightly run district, you might even begin to observe a shift from nomothetic emphases to a more balanced approach, whereby the defect view is replaced with a growth approach. In the evolutionary sequence of staff-development models, the Social-System model stabilizes the status quo. But it also is one that, given more enlightened administrators, can evolve toward a less authoritarian system. Let us assume that individuals now subscribing to the model are capable of changing their authoritarian styles through their own in-service "growth."

CLASS 2: INDIVIDUAL-BASED MODELS

The basic premise of all individual-based models is that the individual involved makes the difference between an effective and an ineffective organization. The amount of freedom given to the individual varies with each of the four identified models, from little freedom in the behavioral model to nearly absolute freedom in the humanistic model. The documented models are:

1. Behavioral
2. Humanistic
3. Concerns-Based Adoption
4. Developmental

Behavioral Model

The Behavioral model stems from the pioneering work of B. F. Skinner (1969). However, for in-service application, the model is more precisely described by Jerry P. Litzenberger (1979). Litzenberger adapted single-subject or time-series design to incorporate both a research and evaluation basis for programs that focus on just one person or one subsystem. The Behavioral model requires that (1) a problem be identified, (2) baseline behaviors be charted, (3) a contingency be introduced, (4) new behaviors be charted, and (5) evaluation be continuous.

Problem identification means that a specific behavior is precisely identified; for instance, the teacher would like to use a wider variety of questioning techniques during class recitation periods. Once the problem is stated, baseline behaviors are observed and charted. What kinds of questioning behaviors are already being used by the teacher and at what frequency? These data are then carefully analyzed to determine what contingency is to be introduced. In this case, the contingency might be to specify a different questioning technique to add to those the teacher is perhaps overemphasizing.

The teacher's behaviors in using questioning techniques are again charted, as they were to determine the baseline behavior. The teacher is then shown the data after each day or each period, so that the evaluation of the contingency is continuous.

The Behavioral model is a powerful mechanism for in-service education. I suggest that it be an alternative to the "clinical model of supervision." The clinical model tends to be defect oriented and, in the last analysis, administrator dominated and somewhat authoritarian (Garman and Hazi 1988). The Behavioral model allows the teacher to select components of his or her own personal behavior to be changed. Teachers are always pleased to observe the trend line on the data chart going in the direction desired. In some cases, teachers have distracting verbal behaviors, "uh huhs," "ahhs," and the like. In such instances, a contingency would be added to reduce the incidence of these behaviors.

This model is easily converted into a contingency contract: the individual agrees to add or change some observable behavior, by way of a written in-service contract designed "for one." The model has much potential, especially in schools where the number of participants is often rather small. One could well argue that the Behavioral model is the epitome of self-direction and individualism.

Humanistic Model

Arthur W. Combs (1962) and Carl Rogers (1969) are the early architects of the Humanistic model for in-service education. However, William Beck (1978) carefully illustrated how the model could be applied directly to in-service programs. This model is proposed as an alternative to the so-called product-based or competency-based teacher education that was virtually the only model for educators from about 1967 to 1982.

The underlying basis of the model is Third Force Psychology, which is humanistic or growth oriented. The model stresses the affective domain and encourages the expression of emotions and feelings. Human relations skills are emphasized, thus training in these skills is a prerequisite for using the humanistic model. Motivation is based on Abraham Maslow's hierarchy of needs, with each person satisfying his or her own higher needs for esteem or self-actualization. Finally, the teacher in the project is perceived as a learning facilitator.

In applying this model to in-service education, Beck states that the teacher is the "hub" of the in-service process. Each individual designs a personal agenda for growth. The goals of in-service education and the organizational structure must all emphasize the growth of the individuals who participate.

This model requires varied leadership styles and much collaboration on an individualized basis between principal and teacher. The climate for such an effort must be teacher centered and nonthreatening. Evaluation is formative in nature. The Humanistic model acknowledges that individuals are the key to identifying their own growth goals. Ultimately, the organization grows or changes because of individual growth.

Implementing the model requires an administrator who respects the concept of thoughtful individualization of staff development, to the point that it could conflict with school or district goals. The Humanistic model requires an investment of sufficient time to enable all parties to discuss their ideas and plans openly. The entire process tends to proceed in an "unscheduled" manner, with flexibility being the critical planning concept.

Concerns-Based Adoption Model

Gene E. Hall and Susan F. Loucks (1978), Loucks and Hall (1977), and Shirley M. Hord et al. (1987) have described the Concerns-Based Adoption model (CBAM). The basis of CBAM is that change is a process involving people both experientially and emotionally. In-service education is the mechanism to initiate desired change. Through systematic data collection, individual perspectives and concerns about impending changes can be assessed. Concerns are the feelings, attitudes, thoughts, or reactions that an individual experiences in relation to some new idea, practice, program, or process. In CBAM there are seven "stages of concern" at ascending levels: awareness, information, personal, management, consequence, collaboration, and refocusing. The model identifies eight "levels of use" for an innovation: nonuse, orientation, preparation, mechanical use, routine, refinement, integration, and renewal. The CBAM model requires longitudinal commitment; one-shot projects cannot suffice. Let us examine this model at length.

Assumptions. Underlying the CBAM model are seven assumptions that establish a frame of reference for viewing change. According to Gene E. Hall and Susan F. Loucks (1978), the assumptions are:

1. Change in schools and colleges is a process, not an event.
2. The individual teacher needs to be the primary focus of intervention for change in the classroom.
3. Change is a highly personal experience.
4. Full description of the innovation in operation is critical to its success.
5. Individuals experience the process of change in identifiable stages and levels.
6. In-service training can be best facilitated for the individual by use of a client-centered diagnostic-prescriptive model.
7. A change facilitator needs to work in an adaptive or systematic way.

Since in-service projects focus on adapting new ideas, practices, programs, or processes to the classroom, the CBAM model meets all the necessary conditions for my general paradigm.

Using CBAM for in-service education. Implementing the CBAM model requires collecting data via a questionnaire titled "Stages of Concern About the Innovation." This Likert-type instrument contains thirty-five statements related to an individual's "stages of concern" about an intended innovation. After collecting data from those involved in the project, the researcher prepares a profile that illustrates the stages of concern for the cohort—the group involved in the process. Once the in-service project is initiated, a staff developer determines the "levels of use" of the innovation: eight distinct levels of behavior to indicate how well the innovation is or is not being used by the cohort.

The developers of the CBAM model recognized that change is a dynamic process, a comment that holds true for all successful in-service projects. The model acknowledges the critical position that teachers play in the successful implementation of an in-service project. Those who reflect CBAM's higher "levels of use" of the new skills or behaviors have truly mastered them. This model can also be used as one element of a school-based staff-development program.

Developmental Model

Malcolm S. Knowles (1984) expresses the major assumptions of the Developmental model. However, Sharon N. Oja (1980), Sally Glassberg and Sharon N. Oja (1981); Theodore E. Andrews; W. Robert Houston and Brenda L. Bryant (1981); and Kathryn M. Tallerico (1987) collectively have described how the model is applied. The Developmental model assumes that adults have a great accumulation of valuable experiences on which to draw, that they are self-directed, and that they enjoy problem-oriented learning rather than subject-centered learning alone. (Obviously, there are situations when subject material is critical to adults, especially in the professions where information and skills change so rapidly.) When these adult attributes are used to plan in-service projects, the plans are focused on broadly stated goals rather than on narrowly specified objectives.

Collectively, those subscribing to the developmental model also subscribe to the growth approach espoused by Philip W. Jackson in Chapter 1. The concepts of growth and development may or may not be synonymous: the exact definition depends on one's theory of growth or development. But there are many similar elements. For example, adults are usually characterized as self-directed, self-rewarding, and seeking job-related and relevant experiences. Alan B. Knox (1986) cautioned that there is a wide spectrum of adult learners and that they require a great deal of individualization if educators are to meet each person's needs.

Sharon N. Oja (1980) summarized the many developmental theories as they relate to adult learners and in-service education. She concluded with four common elements from the various theoretical statements on staff development. First, in-service projects should allow for concrete experiences, followed by reflective periods so that new learning can be assimilated. As the new behaviors or skills are applied in the classroom, feedback and support from colleagues must be provided. (This step is introduced in Chapter 3, where peer coaching is discussed.)

Second, adults participating in in-service activities need continuous supervising and advising. (This element is implied in the AAIM model previously presented.)

Third, teachers or administrators who are participating in the staff-development program need to be encouraged to assume more responsibilities and more complex roles in the in-service project. These roles vary, but include that of discussion leader, group observer, peer teacher, or resource person.

Fourth, Oja suggested the need to provide longitudinal support during the period when new techniques are being practiced. During this time the adult learner often feels anxious and frustrated. The leader's personal regard is needed to help reduce these potentially negative feelings. Kathryn M. Tallerico (1987) described the four points in the Adams County, Colorado, staff-development program.

Theodore E. Andrews (1981), summarized yet another adult model, consisting of five steps: (1) exploration, (2) interaction, (3) active participation, (4) reflection and articulation, and (5) synthesis or integration. Again, note how these five elements focus on active participation during the in-service learning experiences. Perhaps the lesson to be learned from the developmentalists is that in-service projects require dynamism, relevance, and emotional support.

CLASS 3: ROLE-BASED MODELS

Role-based models have as a common characteristic their emphasis on the educator's role as determined by the institution and as modified by the individual. Role-based models focus on the individual's self-determination of needs—but in an institutional context. Three models fitting this classification have been used in staff development:

1. Independent-Study
2. Competency-Based
3. Educator-Center

Independent Study Model

This model focuses on the individual and supports the assumption that the *individual* knows best what he or she truly needs for staff development.

The correspondence course has been available for most of the twentieth century and may be the most popular form of independent study. The National Education Association (1971) is an important contributor to this model, since it has prepared several sets of materials for independent-teacher use with in-service programs—materials designed for individual or small-group utilization. Maureen A. Sullivan (1987) described how individual professional reading evolved into a powerful staff-development model. In a similar vein, Heidi Watts (1985) discussed how individuals could study their own classrooms and determine how to solve self-identified problems.

The Association of California School Administrators developed a training model called Project Leadership (William Kipp, Arthur N. Thayer, and James L. Olivero 1981). Project Leadership is one of the few in-service programs designed specifically for school administrators, allowing them to identify their own high-priority goals for continued learning. The project utilizes a peer network and a workshop format for some training.

Project Leadership is based somewhat on the anthropological finding that administrators rely on the oral tradition to further their professional training. The implications are that school administrators tend to listen to each other. There is a collective feeling that people in job-alike positions are the best sources of professional information. Departments of educational administration have long known that without a former superintendent or principal on their staff, their collective professional opinions are suspect. Project Leadership (as do administrator assessment centers) legitimizes the power of the oral tradition in its training format: job-alike individuals learn (both fact and fiction) from peers.

Competency-Based Model

The Competency-Based model for in-service education is an adaptation of the Behavioral model, and attempts to extend or develop very specific professional skills. One of the early teacher-training programs was Science: A Process Approach, produced by the American Association for the Advancement of Science.

Walter R. Borg, Marjorie L. Kelley, Phillip Langer and Meredith Gall (1970), then of the Far West Laboratory for Educational Research and Development, produced a series of mini-courses to develop teacher skills. These courses used (1) printed materials, (2) training and modeling films, and (3) microteaching focus on specific sets of teaching behaviors or strategies, such as questioning, tutoring mathematics, or developing independent learners. Each mini-course is self-organized and specifies learner behaviors or competencies. Each has handbooks for participants and leaders, model and practice films that explicitly illustrate each competency, and self-evaluation forms.

Through microteaching, the teacher practices new competencies until they are easily assimilated. To be sure, this model overlaps with the individual-based models, but it must be considered as separate because of its theoretical positioning with modeling and the competency approach to teaching.

The Basic Skills Articulation Plan in Ohio stresses the application of a competency-based training program. Shirley S. Scholl and Phyllis McQueen (1985) described the project as a small group process, but it can be adapted to be an "in-service project for one."

Educator-Center Model

As mentioned earlier in the book, the teacher center (or educator center) was imported to the United States by American teachers who visited British schools. Centers are administered by teachers to meet their own perceived needs (Wentz 1987).

The rationale for teacher centers rests on three premises: (1) fundamental reform comes only through the teachers who must implement such changes; (2) teachers are unlikely to change how they teach simply because they are told to do so; and (3) teachers take reform seriously only when they themselves define their problems, determine their needs, and voluntarily seek help.

The Maryland Professional Development Academy (Huddle and Hammond 1987) and the Maine Principals' Academy (Donaldson 1987) are adaptations of the teacher-center concept to the needs of administrators. These academies are excellent examples of professional education centers that focus on critical concerns of principals.

As Sarah L. Levine (1986) concluded, the teacher center, administrator-assessment center, and the administrator academy will play a broad role in future staff development. During the late 1970s and early 1980s, the federal government funded several dozen teacher centers. When the federal funding was withdrawn, most of the centers simply folded. But many others were absorbed into he on-going programs of school districts, consortia of school districts, and universities. In some cases, state regional service districts assumed their responsibilities, but without the federal funding, as was the case in New York and Florida.

Teacher centers need not be elaborate or highly structured. Some centers display the essence of simplicity while others are very elaborate in organization and function. Proponents of the educator-center concept suggest that the center is "a frame of reference," "an ideal," or "a way of treating everyone as an equal and a professional who can contribute to anyone's growth." As a model for staff development, the educator center has yet to reach its full potential.

CLASS 4: TRAINER-BASED MODELS

Trainer-based models are a special subset of the role-based models. The basic difference is one of specialization. One could argue that trainers simply play a more *dynamic* role, and thus should be included in the role-based classification. However, one could also argue that training roles emerge as a consequence of being "certified" to conduct in-service education. That certification comes from one's "technical esteem," not from any licensing agency.

Four trainer-based models have been described in the literature:

1. Exchange
2. Linking-Agent
3. Peer-Coaching
4. Advocacy

Exchange Model

The Exchange model establishes a mechanism for individuals to exchange positions for the purpose of job-embedded training. This is an adaptation of the very successful practice of international teacher exchanges. As a staff-development practice, professionals change positions to gain new insights, knowledge, or skills. In reality, the model could be classified as an "externship."

Laurence B. Carlson and Robert E. Potter (1972) described a project that they called Behaviorally Engineered Classroom for Rural Areas (BECRA). The objective of BECRA was to provide special-education services. The exchange aspect stemmed from preparing preservice students to apply a special-education classroom model. Students first worked as aides in a selected rural school, as part of their orientation to get to know teachers and children in specific classes. The inexperienced teachers then replaced their respective experienced teachers in those rural schools. The experienced teachers were subsequently brought to the university campus to receive the same training that preservice teachers had received.

The Exchange model is most effective when it allows teachers to be trained during the regular school day (job-embedded), but with no loss to the children or school district. Further, it permits intensive instruction rather than awareness training sessions, and it is applicable to almost all areas of the school curriculum. James Franco and Donald Zundel (1986) described an adaptation of this model in Sitka and Juneau, Alaska. Eight instructional modules constituted the instructional aspects of Project IMPACT. Evaluation of the project has been very favorable.

Linking-Agent Model

The Linking-Agent model is an adaptation of the very successful agricultural extension agent. Land-grant universities have long used extension agents as disseminators of new farming techniques and as in-service trainers. The Linking-Agent model uses a person designated as a linking- or change-agent who has the responsibility of helping institute specific curricula practices. For example, I directed a series of in-service projects whereby we provided extensive training on inquiry-oriented teaching processes to selected elementary school teachers and principals. These individuals acted as internal linking- or change-agents in their schools, working with their colleagues on a daily basis. (See Orlich et al., 1972, 1973 for details. I've also used this model successfully in a series of National Science Foundation projects from 1972 to 1987.)

Richard O. Carlson (1965) suggested using internal change-agents to aid schools in making needed changes. He stated that without such people the schools faced a "barrier to change." Ronald G. Havelock (1967) and Robert B. Howsam (1967) were early proponents of the Linking-Agent model as a means of disseminating research data from the generators of the knowledge to the transmitters of the knowledge—the practitioners. Sam D. Sieber, Daren S. Louis, and Loya Metzger (1972) reported an extensive national project that utilized educational linkers, identified as dissemination agents. A staff-development model using linking-agents solved the problem of inadequate follow-up in long-range programs in the Fall River, Massachusetts, public schools writing project, wrote Joseph J. Caruso (1985).

Peer-Coaching Model

The Peer-Coaching model has emerged as one of the major innovations in staff development. The basic concept is rather simple: train a group of teachers or administrators to be proficient in selected instructional or managerial techniques, and then allow them to act as coaches for their colleagues. While the concept is simple, the time needed to implement the model is extensive. The Peer-Coaching model is a special application of the Linking-Agent model. Since peer coaching is well discussed in Chapter 3, the topic will be only briefly discussed here.

Beverly Showers (1983, 1985) and Bruce Joyce and Beverly Showers (1988) have been the major developers and proponents of the model. They have designed it into a very effective job-embedded training mechanism. The model recognizes in-house staff as the providers of in-service education. Feedback and positive reinforcement help those being trained to extend or improve new skills. With the advent of locally negotiated staff-development contracts and provisions, peer coaching will become a household word with school board members and administrators. Peer coaching truly enhances the human potential in any school system.

Advocacy Model

James Gray and Miles Myers (1978) described the Bay Area Writing Project (BAWP), an in-service program that teaches teachers how to teach writing more effectively. Gray and his associates established an in-service system that builds by a "multiplier effect." While the emphasis is on assisting English teachers, the BAWP has had an impact on writing instruction in all areas of the school. The cadre of trained teachers thus becomes an advocate for writing, not just for improved English instruction. Barbara Berman and Fredda J. Friederwitzer (1985) described a similar "multiplier strategy" for a mathematics project.

Madeline Hunter's (1985) Theory into Practice model is an excellent example of the Advocacy model. Her program has four main elements: (1) teaching to an objective; (2) teaching at an appropriate level of difficulty for the learners; (3) monitoring and adjusting instruction; and (4) increasing motivation, learning, retention, and transfer. The Advocacy component comes not from the four basic elements of the program but from the delivery and indoctrination systems built into the presentation of the elements by "certifying" clientele. That is, the teacher attends a series of workshops arranged in some hierarchical manner. After attending several of these, the teacher can advocate or teach the lower-level workshops. By the "assumed credentialing" of trainers, through a pyramiding principle the model automatically builds a huge corps of advocates. (See Garman and Hazi, 1988.)

CONCLUSION

In this chapter I have attempted to describe a comprehensive paradigm for staff development and attendant in-service programs and projects. To state that one has, indeed, identified *the* major planning paradigm and established classifications and models for the profession may be naïve and optimistic, if not arrogant. Yet my hope is that this proposal will be a major step in providing a comprehensive system for identifying and implementing effective, consistent, and concept-oriented in-service programs. When directors, administrators, designers, and planners become aware of internally consistent in-service classifications and models, they may begin to view in-service education as a valuable activity, not something conducted by the organization in a perfunctory manner.

Educators will certainly examine and evaluate this paradigm, and predictably changes and improvements will be made; classifications and models will be created, merged, and deleted. That process, of course, is in keeping with scholarly and scientific tradition. The vision is that in-service education will be positively affected by the acceptance and implementation of a testable, comprehensive planning paradigm.

CHECKLIST FOR PARADIGM USE

_____ 1. The focus of the staff-development effort is clearly known in advance; that is, organization, individual, role, or trainer.

_____ 2. A specific model is identified from the dichotomous key.

_____ 3. The selected model is operationally defined.

_____ 4. Assumptions of the selected model are identified.

_____ 5. Consequences are predicted to test the model's efficacy.

_____ 6. Direct and indirect costs of each model are calculated and compared.

_____ 7. User reactions to the models are obtained.

_____ 8. The paradigm is expanded to meet emerging models or models adapted locally.

_____ 9. Predicted results are compared to the actual results.

_____ 10. Results of the process are disseminated locally and nationally.

CHAPTER 8

STAFF DEVELOPMENT FOR ADMINISTRATORS

The leader is like the follower; only more so.

Paul Pigors

There is a need to describe staff-development efforts for specific client groups who deliver services to the schools. Included in these client groups are classroom teachers, counselors, special educators, teachers of the gifted, support staff, and administrators. Targeted staff-development projects are strongly supported in the literature and in practice. The latter is obvious when you examine the many papers, sessions, and workshops presented at the annual conferences of the National Staff Development Council and the National Council of States on Inservice Education. However, to provide a detailed treatment for such diverse groups truly requires a separate volume, with each section edited by a knowledgeable professional in the respective client arena.

This chapter addresses one critical client group—administrators—and delimits treatment of others. The rationale is that administrators work in a broad educational context. Their collective decisions and actions can affect every member of the organization. More important, the area is now emerging with great intensity. We share in the excitement evolving from these developments.

School administrators play a critical role in a staff-development program or in-service education project. Administrators are responsible for the functions of planning, organizing, staffing, directing, coordinating, and budgeting. These functions, in addition to the more personally interactive ones, are part of any staff-development activity. Administrators know that in-service education can be an effective tool by which to extend teacher and staff knowledge and skills and to change attitudes. But how do school leaders determine their own staff-development needs?

The school administration ranges from line officers (superintendent, principal) to staff positions (curriculum directors, specialists). The organizational charts of school districts vary owing to their relative size and complexity. From the totality of administrative roles have evolved conditions, problems, and novel circumstances that require continued in-service education or professional development.

Planning for administrative staff development includes assessing needs, developing training objectives, determining activities, preparing evaluation plans, and developing budgets to accomplish the various components of a program.

Staff-development programs designed for administrators appear to have six commonalities:

- Developing new skills
- Acquiring current information
- Learning about new programs
- Solving problems that tend to recur
- Expanding a knowledge of administrative theory and practice
- Preparing for new challenges, jobs, or positions

This is not an inclusive list of reasons why administrators attend in-service projects, but the items are illustrative of processes that are similar to those used by teachers. Content for administrator training is obviously very different from that of teacher in-service education. The many suggestions already made in this book are also applicable to in-service programs oriented to administrators.

GENERAL REVIEW OF PROGRAMS

What types of programs are available to school administrators? Joseph Murphy and Philip Hallinger (1986) identified eleven different administrator in-service training practices, consisting of state, professional association, and university programs. Table 8-1 is adapted from their paper and illustrates the differences between traditional preparatory offerings and emerging in-service projects.

Perhaps the greatest difference between administrator certification or graduate training programs and the emerging trends of administrator staff development is the focus on practitioner-related problems and issues, as opposed to the theoretical and administrative principles that characterize university programs. Thus the vision to be inferred from Murphy and Hallinger's synthesis is that a novel era may be here. What seems to be emerging is that administrators are becoming more involved in *their* staff development and as a consequence, all staff development will be enhanced. We have long known that administrators play a "gatekeeper" role in the change process. With their increased involvement in the human enhancement process, it is valid to assume that changes for the better will be instituted in staff development for all persons working in the schools.

John C. Daresh and James C. LaPlant (1985) explored the research agendas that can be inferred from published literature about administrator in-service offerings. They concluded that the typical study was descriptive and primarily focused on the principal's role.

Two findings of Daresh and LaPlant that reinforce what was developed earlier in Chapter 2 is that administrators desire in-service education content based on

TABLE 8-1.

COMPARISON OF EMERGING PROGRAMS WITH TRADITIONAL TRAINING PRACTICES

FOCUS	PAST PRACTICE	EMERGING PROGRAMS
Goals	Accumulation of knowledge	Empowerment for change/implementation focus
Program base	Certification	Identified needs of participants
Organizational perspective	Organizational-environmental interchange	Internal focus
Mode of operation	Independent work	Professional socialization and mutual work arrangements
Professionalization	Limited emphasis	Important component
Content		
Paradigm	Science	Craft
Knowledge base	Social science framework	Teacher effects and school improvement
Theoretical structure	Deductive (from theory)	Inductive (from practice)
Program Delivery		
Model	Unitary, university-based	Variety of approaches and deliverers
Instruction	Professor-driven, homogeneous	Professor and practitioner-driven, varied
Professional control	Limited	Stronger role in agenda setting, delivery, postprogram implementation and governance
Learning theory	Pedagogy	Andragogy
Principles of quality Staff development	Limited emphasis	Important component

Source: Joseph Murphy and Philip Hallinger, "Some Encouraging Signs in Staff Development for School Administrators," *Journal of Staff Development,* 7 (2), 15. Used with permission of the authors and the *Journal.*

their needs and that they desire topics of immediate concern. Recall the strong pleas for "relevance" in teacher in-service education projects. That same plea is empirically supported for administrators.

Daresh and LaPlant further reported that administrators want to be involved in project planning, prefer active participation, support long-term or short-range projects, and desire some control of decision making. Again, these findings corroborate earlier ones about teacher in-service projects. The processes of effective staff-development programs are applicable to training programs for any group.

What are some of the issues in which administrators are interested? A study by Samuel E. Gerla (1987) reported that in-service needs of administrators serving smaller school districts—that is, those having 2,000 or fewer students—were:

1. Staff motivation
2. Infusion of thinking skills in the curriculum
3. Strategies for effective teaching
4. Problem-solving techniques relating to administrative issues
5. Utilization of effective practices by successful administrators
6. Implementation of "effective schools" research
7. Climates for staff supervision
8. Strategies of instructional leadership

This list illustrates the desire for contemporary topics as a basis for administrator in-service education.

As was noted previously, Murphy and Hallinger described various institutes or programs currently available for administrators. In 1982, the National Institute of Education published a directory of training programs for principals. On closer inspection, however, it showed that these models cover the entire spectrum of administrative roles. Descriptions of six sponsors of such programs are listed in Table 8-2. As you examine the various descriptions, note their commonalities: management and problem-solving skills, "hot" topics, cultural perspectives, in-

TABLE 8-2.
SELECTED MODELS OF ADMINISTRATOR STAFF DEVELOPMENT

SPONSOR	FOCUS	CONTENT/STRUCTURE
Georgia Academy of School Executives	Instructional management	Skills and problem solving, contemporary topics, short-term seminars
San Diego Leadership Development Center	Leadership awareness	Legislatively prescribed areas; short-term courses
Wayne County Educational Leadership Impact Program (Michigan)	Leadership experiences	Needs-related topics; short-term seminars and workshops
Denver Public Schools Staff Academy	Resource assistance	Needs-driven, stressing growth and renewal; classes of various duration
New York City Supervisory Training Program	Principal development	Needs-driven for aspiring, new, and incumbent principals; programs vary in length
Danforth Foundation School Administrators Fellowship Program	High school principal development	Individualized, with networking techniques; one-day a week for one year

Source: Directory of Inservice Training Program for Principals, (Washington, D.C.: National Institute of Education, Program on Educational Policy and Organization, 1982).

dividual development, technological implications for leadership, school-climate issues, and effective schooling practices. The selected in-service education models illustrate that administrators are, in fact, leading their own staff-development efforts. To be sure, there is some university involvement. But the majority of projects are self-directed.

Project LEAD, or Leadership in Educational Administration Development is a program founded in 1987. This project is a U.S. Department of Education initiative that establishes technical assistance centers in each state to promote development of leadership skills in school administrators. The LEAD assistance centers will provide eight functions:

1. Collect information on leadership skills
2. Assess leadership skills
3. Conduct training programs for new and experienced administrators
4. Maintain consulting programs on site and at the center
5. Establish training curricula and materials that draw from industry, business, military, and civilian agencies
6. Include a broad range of personnel in the training
7. Disseminate information about "effective school" administration practices
8. Establish model projects for leadership development

These functions provide a busy agenda. Project LEAD will undoubtedly play a major role in shaping the future of administrator staff development for the remainder of the twentieth century.

SUPERINTENDENT STAFF DEVELOPMENT

We should discuss school board and superintendent staff-development programs as a single option. However, the focus of this book is on professional and classified personnel. School board members tend to receive specific in-service training from their respective state associations and the National School Boards Association. For the most part, these programs are one-shot and informational. There's no question that school board members would benefit from the canons being developed in this book. So we shall delimit the "real" policymakers from discussion and focus on their chief executives.

Administrator professional organizations provide the bulk of staff development for superintendents. This is not to negate their own efforts, especially since superintendents enroll in university courses or workshops. The bulk of the administrator training relates to legislated issues. State departments of education and regional educational districts hold numerous briefings regarding laws, policies, rules, and regulations affecting the management of the schools. Obviously, these briefings are critical to superintendents, since they are responsible for getting many jobs done. The delegation of authority takes place, but the superintendent needs to have a vast array of information to delegate properly.

National Academy for School Executives

Because the problems of a superintendency tend to be practical (on a continuum of practical to theoretical), it is not surprising that their training projects are oriented toward the very useful, if not mundane (Murphy and Hallinger 1986). The American Association of School Administrators (AASA) realized this situation in the late 1960s and early 1970s, with the establishment of the National Academy for School Executives (NASE). The general objective of NASE is to provide school executives with opportunities to expand, enhance, and enrich their professional competence. The basic client group of NASE is practicing school superintendents. However, administrators aspiring to the superintendency, nonline administrators, and school board members all participate in NASE activities.

The seminars and workshops tend to last as long as a week, while institutes range from two to three days. Seminars focus on emerging educational issues or programs. For example, NASE conducted a six-day seminar that focused entirely on strategic planning. No question; after six days of intensive instruction, activities, simulations, and discussion, an attendee knows the topic. The academy has always assumed that its offerings complement, stimulate, and extend the existing graduate, professional, and certification programs offered by universities. With almost one activity scheduled per week, NASE draws its "professors" from universities, school districts, federal agencies, and the private sector. Practicing superintendents and other administrators tend to be "professors" in the academy.

All NASE programs and presenters are evaluated by the participants, with feedback provided to planning staff at NASE and to the presenter. Distinguished NASE Professors are honored by AASA for their instructional skills. Those who are rated average or below average are seldom asked to present again.

Project Leadership

Project Leadership was introduced briefly in Chapter 7 as an exemplary role-based model that focused on the individual, and it was classified as an Independent-Study model. This program is superintendent oriented, but it encourages all school administrators to participate in the many different activities. The program is conducted under the auspices of the Association of California School Administrators.

The objectives of Project Leadership are to:

1. Provide administrators with an opportunity for both initial and renewal education in essential basic skills.
2. Provide districts with leaders who can educate other administrators within the district.
3. Provide individually selected options for the improvement of personal skills or skills to meet the needs of other administrators in the district.
4. Create a climate for learning that offers planned procedures for attaining high-priority goals, particularly goals in areas that will enhance the administrator's impact on teachers and students.

5. Create a collegial sense among participants.
6. Review relevant research and successful practices for possible transfer to Project Leadership participants.
7. Disseminate the latest concepts and successful programs in school management and curriculum leadership.
8. Provide field-tested learning materials for participants to use in their districts.

Each participant initially prepares a detailed assessment instrument to determine areas of greatest need. All persons typically complete a prescribed set of instructional guides. There are three basic organizational mechanisms in Project Leadership: (1) statewide workshops lasting two or three days, (2) satellite sessions having representatives from three to six school districts, and (3) local district networks. Project Leadership materials cover about forty different topics ranging from time management to conflict resolution. It takes about three years to complete the entire repertoire.

A state participating in Project Leadership is subdivided into satellites by the state director. Each satellite has a liaison administrator who coordinates the training efforts of the enrolled districts. The satellites usually engage participants in follow-up activities to the statewide workshops. The liaison administrator helps each participant develop and complete a personal growth plan for the year. Participants are expected to make presentations at the satellite and at local networks using one of the prepared Presenter Guides.

Project Leadership activities allow each participant to become a human resource. The training network maintains the oral tradition. Individuals can easily call any network member for help or information. Further, local school districts develop the potential for additional in-service projects at almost no cost. As with NASE, Project Leadership assumes that professional education programs are augmented and extended in the field. And both projects support continued, lifelong development of practicing administrators. There is simply no place for an out-of-date administrator.

State and Local Efforts

Although this section focuses on the superintendent, other district administrators take part in various staff-development programs sponsored by professional associations, as do teachers. Nearly all school districts sponsor the annual "administrators' retreat," which functions as a social, in-service, and goal-setting mechanism. Thus local school districts provide awareness sessions that can be classified as in-service education. Topics are developed locally and internal resource persons usually conduct the sessions.

Administrative cabinets are urged to conduct needs assessments among all administrative groups, or if large enough, among job-alike groups. In this manner, a model is followed and a vision of continued growth and development is portrayed. Consider all the line and staff administrators in a typical district; that number provides the magnitude of staff development that ought to be planned at local and state levels.

Now let us focus on the "administrator of the hour": the school principal.

PRINCIPALS AS A SPECIAL CASE

Over the past few years, the spotlight has been on the principal as the key administrator in either making changes or implementing effective schooling practices. Let us sample a few of the published studies relating the principal as chief player in implementing successful schooling practices or innovations.

As chief administrative officers in school buildings, principals tend to initiate or retard change. As Henry M. Brickell (1964, 503) wrote:

> The administrator may promote—or prevent—innovation. He [sic] cannot stand aside or be ignored. He is powerful, not because he has the monopoly on imagination, creativity or interest in change—the opposite is common—but simply because he has the authority to precipitate a decision. Authority is a critical element in innovation, because proposed changes generate mixed reactions which can prevent consensus in peers and results in stagnation.

Brickell's assertion that a line administrator—the principal—plays a critical role in enhancing educational change is supported by several researchers, including Berman and McLaughlin (1978a and 1978b); Ford Foundation (1972); Orlich, May, and Harder (1973); and Thomas (1978).

Principals as Instructional Leaders

Because decision making rests ultimately with the person in authority, the principal is responsible for the successful administration of the school. The principal can support the teachers' desires to improve the school, per se. The principal can allocate precious time and resources to the staff, and can encourage them to participate fully in an improvement process.

Phillip J. Runkel et al. (1980) documented the importance of the principal when using an Organization-Development training model. James M. Lipham (1981) synthesized several research studies, indicating that it is the building principal who sets the goals and *coordinates the efforts* of the staff to achieve them.

Terry E. Deal and Lynn D. Celotti (1980) reported that elementary school principals who used frequent feedback had teachers who implemented project objectives successfully. Deal and Celotti concluded that schools are "loosely coupled" organizations (a term initially described by Weick in 1976) where the teachers tend to act somewhat independently and are not directly affected by others doing similar work in the school. This, the writers noted, tends to reduce the impact of the principal's authority.

Nicki King (1980) provided evidence that the principals in one school district were given budgets for staff-development programs and the freedom to develop them. In three of six schools in the district, *no* staff development programs were conducted for two academic years. The amount and intensity of staff development for the other three schools varied with the interest and time commitment of the principal.

King also reported that in ten of fourteen selected school districts, central administrators controlled all decisions concerning needs assessments and program planning. In these districts, the principals had little or no participation in in-service offerings. With limited contact, such programs were viewed as less effective than those in districts using structured methods to include teachers and principals in preparing and conducting in-service operations. King cautioned about the overuse of administrators as trainers. She observed that teachers often feel some sense of coercion and tend to resent training by principals. She concluded that administrators who facilitate collaboration have programs that are viewed positively by the teachers. The most successful in-service programs, wrote King, are those in which teachers and administrators participate collaboratively in staff-development programs.

The Maryland Department of Education (1978) studied thirty Maryland elementary schools. Eighteen had high-achieving and twelve had low-achieving pupils, as determined by statewide basic skill tests. The writers of the report concluded that the role of the principal as instructional leader tends to account for major differences in student achievement.

Substantiating that finding was an earlier one reported by C. Greer (1970) for a Harlem elementary school. Students in that school attained relatively high reading achievement scores, according to the researcher, because of the principal's direct involvement and development of the school's reading program.

In a comprehensive study of the principal, Margaret A. Thomas (1978) suggested that principals tend to follow three basic types: (1) director—the primary decision maker, (2) administrator—one who separates procedural decisions from substantive decisions, and (3) facilitator—the supportive and collegial decision maker. Thomas's study has many findings and implications, among which are the following:

1. The principal plays a major role in the way a school operates instructionally.
2. The principal is of critical importance in determining a school's climate.
3. Principals who share decision making with their staffs have schools with less tension than those of more authoritarian principals.

Milbrey W. McLaughlin and David D. Marsh (1978, 81) reported that:

> The attitude of the building principal was even more critical to the long-term results of a change-agent project. The support of the school principal for a special project was directly related to the likelihood that staff would continue to use project methods and materials after special funding is withdrawn. Furthermore, principal support positively affected project implementation.

McLaughlin and Marsh noted also that when principals participate in a training program their presence imparts a message that the training is important.

Judith Warren Little (1982, 85) concluded that the building administrator is the "key" in staff-development projects. She stated that there are differences in tactics used by elementary and secondary school principals owing to the characteristics of the institutions. Yet having the principal support and participate in an in-service project is tantamount to success. Further, Little provides evidence that collaboratively planned in-service projects have the greatest probability for successful implementation.

Diane K. Broughton, Mark E. Crouch, and Gary W. Floyd (1978) reported the successful implementation of a complex differentiated staff elementary school. Three longitudinal in-service projects were associated with the collaboratively planned, designed, and implemented school project. By using questionnaires returned by 100 percent of the instructional staff, these researchers reported that the enthusiasm of the principal throughout the program, then in its fifth year (and in 1988 in its fourteenth year), was identified as the most significant and influential factor in maintaining the project.

Principals and School Effectiveness

In 1986, the governor of Arkansas, Bill Clinton, wrote that stronger school leadership is required and the principal is the key to school improvement. Governor Clinton was not speaking alone, but was endorsing the charge of the National Governors' Association. Thus the political climate is supportive of administrative development with an implied result: more effective schools.

The call for strong instructional leadership has international overtones. Peter Mortimore and Pam Sammons (1987) reported that in the United Kingdom (England), the first of twelve key factors for an effective school is "purposeful leadership" exhibited by the principal. Effective principals exert influence, not control, over their respective staffs. The second finding offered by Mortimore and Sammons was that assistant principals play a major role in a school's effectiveness. These two findings certainly support the need for administrative staff team training.

But the most compelling evidence relating the principal's role to student success is that provided by Richard L. Andrews (1987). His research illustrates dramatically how elementary student achievement scores correlate directly with the principal's influence. Effective principals had students from all socioeconomic levels achieving at relatively high rates, with the converse true for ineffective ones. When effective principals took over elementary schools with poor student achievement patterns, there was a dramatic increase in student scores. When ineffective principals were assigned to the effective or better achieving schools, student achievement profiles declined!

Robert E. Blum, Jocelyn A. Butler, and Nancey L. Olson (1987) reported an in-service training program for principals that has produced positive results. Sponsored by the Northwest Regional Educational Laboratory, this project provides training in five stages: (1) vision building, (2) school climate and culture, (3) curriculum implementation, (4) improvement of instruction, and (5) monitoring of school performance. Data are being collected to assess the impact of field tests. The writers predicted a positive impact on the schools and on student achievement.

Other studies supporting the theory of principal impact on student achievement include Maureen McCormack-Larkin's (1985) description of Project RISE in Milwaukee, where increased academic success was observed in eighteen schools. The Jefferson County, Kentucky, project improved mathematics and reading test scores (Miller, Cohen, and Sayre 1985). Georgea Sparks et al. (1985) provided evidence of dramatic student test-score increases when a six-point staff-development model (similar to AAIM, Chapter 7) was implemented.

With thousands of articles written about the principal as instructional leader, Samuel B. Bacharach and Sharon C. Conley (1986) voiced concern. They wrote that reforms cannot truly take place under current management practices and with organizational patterns found in the schools. Larry Cuban (1982 and 1986) observed that, over the past 100 years, there has been a tendency for teacher-centered instructional practices to persist. Thus while there is mounting evidence that principals are the critical persons who encourage the staff, we must not forget that the basic organization of the schools is not entirely under principals' power to change significantly. (The general discussion of innovation reform is continued in Chapter 9.) Of course, appropriate staff development provides some needed skills to principals. That is the essence of the assessment movement, discussed next.

ADMINISTRATOR ASSESSMENT CENTERS

The National Association of Secondary School Principals (NASSP) adapted an in-service practice from the military and the private sector in creating administrator assessment centers. This program was initiated in 1975 with the first operational center established in Prince William County, Virginia, in 1976. About 100 such centers existed by 1988.

Paul W. Hersey (1986) described twelve basic skills that receive emphasis in these centers. They are:

- Problem analysis
- Judgment
- Organizational ability
- Decisiveness
- Leadership
- Sensibility
- Stress tolerance
- Range of interests

- Personal motivation
- Educational values
- Speaking
- Writing

One of the main training elements in the NASSP centers is the use of the Springfield Simulation. Modeling skills and behaviors can be practiced with true-to-life models. Feedback and discussion about decisions help novice administrators improve or extend skills.

Herman R. Goldberg (1986) calculated that 70 percent of the nation's school superintendents will reach retirement age by 1995. That and other compelling reasons for quality in-service prompted the AASA to establish their own assessment center for superintendents. Eight key areas will be developed for initial assessment work:

- Improving school climate
- Building public support for schools
- Developing school curriculum
- Managing instruction
- Evaluating staff
- Developing staff potential
- Allocating resources
- Planning and evaluating educational research

The lists developed by the NASSP and AASA are certainly not inclusive. An examination of preservice administrative training programs shows some overlap with assessment center programs. But as James L. Olivero (1982) reported, school administrators identified 90 percent more competencies as being appropriate for in-service education rather than for initial credentialing. No question about it, implied Olivero, the learning just begins with the award of the administrative degree or credential.

The *NASSP Bulletins* for January 1986 and 1987 featured assessment center projects, showing the organization's commitment to the concept. The ideal assessment center links as many educational agencies and resources as possible. The centers are organized and administered in much the same way as teacher centers. The Harvard Principal's Center even allows practitioners to teach in the graduate school. Roland S. Barth (1987) wrote that the Harvard Center has had a very positive impact on principals working through the center.

In some states—for example, South Carolina—legislative mandates require all school districts to participate in that state's assessment centers. Any candidate for a principalship without prior experience must be "assessed" before appointment to a position. The concepts of modeling, practice, feedback, and coaching (Joyce and Showers 1982) seem to be universal training elements at most assessment centers.

Completing the Springfield Simulation is usually an initial step in the assessment process. After finishing selected activities, candidates are given feedback and a report on the lists of skills noted previously. Having a list of strengths and weaknesses, the candidate prepares a plan for improvement that includes individual and group work.

Georgine Loacker (1986) observed that the Springfield Simulation applies six adult learner concepts:

1. Adults are self directed.
2. Adults learn best with mutual planning.
3. Adults improve when they set specific goals.
4. Adults can learn analytic thinking and interpersonal skills.
5. Adults learn by experiencing, reflecting, forming concepts, and testing them.
6. Adults learn how to learn.

Larry W. Hughes (1986) observed that the technologies of assessment centers are "old," but are being reapplied in novel ways. Simulation, in-basket episodes, data analyses, and challenge cards all help the centers provide a dimension of reality, which he stated is important. Hughes cautioned that the stressing of discrete competencies can reduce professional decisions to technical tricks. Further, task analyses of administrative jobs and behaviors can develop mechanistic traits that lack collegiality and professional interaction.

John C. Daresh (1986) described two problems faced by novice principals that can be solved in the centers. The first is a lack of technical skills that affects mechanical or procedural issues. These are "how-to-do-it," or immediate job-related, skills or operations. In Alaska, principal internships have helped solve these issues (Hagstron 1987). In some cases, preservice university courses offer some assistance, too. The second problem relates to interpersonal relations. Working *with* teachers and not *on* them requires interactive skills such as conflict management, school community relations, and job assignments, and entails establishing a vision for the school. Interpersonal skills are obviously the more difficult ones to address.

What is interesting about the assessment centers is their planning strategy. First, needs are assessed. From the needs assessment emanates the delivery of services. Sarah DeJarnette Caldwell (1986) cautioned that short-term "executive summaries" for principals are not conducive to effective learning. She urged the development of long-range principal in-service projects that incorporate the elements of practice and coaching.

Writing in a similar vein, James C. LaPlant (1986) described the I/D/E/A Principals' Inservice Program that creates and maintains a principals' collegial support group. The collegial groups meet periodically to plan programs for the team, provide exercises, and support improvement efforts. An individual's commitment to the project is for two years. Initial evaluation of the project by its participants has been very favorable.

The assessment unit is obviously a model that has caused enthusiasm and excitement. Yet Murphy and Hallinger (1986) indicated some reservations. First, the programs collectively stress skills development, with little regard for theory. Second, professional development tends to rely on the experiences of the trainers. Third, the focus on current programs rather than analysis of organizational structures may simply keep the status quo. Fourth, the needs of the individual are overemphasized while organizational development is neglected.

Of course, Murphy and Hallinger applauded the promotion of professional interactions, use of inductive processes and andragogy, personal involvement and activity, emphasis on the school as a unit of change, application of intrinsic rewards, and establishment of a collegial environment.

Obviously, the "last study" is not yet in. Those studies cited here provide compelling empirical evidence that the building principal is a key to successful programs and enhanced student achievement. These efforts are usually accomplished through effective staff-development programs.

It is imperative, therefore, that principals become aware of valid theories and processes associated with change efforts. Trial-and-error attempts at change are counterproductive and intolerable. Principals must use tested theories of change, which predict consequences and aid in designing more effective schools. Educating principals and other administrators about change theory and change processes, and helping them become more effective instructional leaders, should be important goals for professional associations and administrative in-service programs.

IMPLICATIONS

We need to react to some of the literature relating to the principalship. It is very unfortunate that the principal has been targeted as the *only* instructional leader in a school. Principals can encourage, plan, marshal support, evaluate, and supervise various school efforts. But to expect that principals can perform all these jobs is to ignore the reality of the position.

As is noted in Chapter 9, "effective schools" are marked by leaders who share several common traits. The principal is placed in an untenable position if describers of effective programs expect the principal to instruct, supervise, and evaluate the teachers in the building. These functions are not compatible. Supervision requires feedback, support, and modeling. Evaluation, on the other hand, requires judgmental decisions and, in some cases, stern actions. Principals cannot play the role of colleague and then of disciplinarian and expect to maintain high staff morale. Many writers who encourage the principal to provide in-service education may be exhibiting a lack of understanding of the job.

Principals need special staff development apart from those of central-office administrators. If school-based staff development emerges as one of the successful models, then principals need training in organization development, development of interpersonal relations, human relations skills, team building, and problem solving. These processes are seldom found in the graduate programs required for principal credentials. Yet the processes are mandatory for staff development.

Superintendents and other central-office personnel need time for professional reading, reflection, and dialogues with each other on educational issues. These people are pressured for time. Local school boards must authorize periods during the work week when these people can assume a professional orientation. That is, they need time to discuss relevant literature. Yes, it is difficult to provide time. Yet these leaders must be encouraged by local school boards to schedule some job-embedded in-service education for professional development.

Administrators can enter into dialogues with informed teachers and other professionals in the school district. These dialogues would center on issues relating to the improvement of instruction and the work place.

School board members must insist that their selected leaders participate in various professional conferences, institutes, academies, and university-sponsored events. The enhancement of all personnel in the schools ultimately leads to more effective schools at all levels.

CHECKLIST FOR ADMINISTRATORS

_____ 1. The school board policy endorses continued staff development for district administrators.

_____ 2. A wide range of institutes, academies, or projects are examined for relevant administrator staff development.

_____ 3. Principals are given support for their personal staff-development initiatives.

_____ 4. The role functions and conflicts of principals are examined and rectified.

_____ 5. Instructional leadership is shared with colleagues.

_____ 6. Administrator needs assessments are conducted to determine relevant in-service education projects.

_____ 7. The general principles of effective staff development are used for administrative in-service projects.

_____ 8. Time for administrator reflection on educational issues is scheduled.

_____ 9. Incentives are developed for administrators' staff development.

_____ 10. Administrative staff development is evaluated.

CHAPTER 9

STAFF DEVELOPMENT IN A REFORM CLIMATE

We are much beholden to Machiavelli and others, who wrote what men do, and not what they ought to do.

Francis Bacon

If we examine the growth of public education in the United States, it becomes apparent that our culture developed a set of educational traditions valuing not the static but the dynamic. Change is a value so cherished in our system of education that it is prized for itself. William L. Rutherford's paper (1978), "The Madness of Educational Change," summarizes one mood about that tradition and illustrates why educators continuously "reinvent the wheel."

How long has it been this way? What are some of the apparent processes of reform and innovation? What role will staff development play in a major reform? These are the basic questions that will be addressed.

THE INITIAL SET OF REFORMS

One of the first major educational reforms that helped establish our long tradition of change took place with the Massachusetts Law of 1642. That law provided the basic concept leading to our public schools. It also precipitated the famous Olde Deluder Satan Act of 1647. The latter was prescribed by the Massachusetts Bay Colony as a way of thwarting "one chief project of the olde deluder, Satan, to keep men from the knowledge of the Scriptures." The law of 1647 required that towns establish and support schools or face a fine. What is important for this analysis is that the 1647 act marks the first time in human history that the state enforced an obligation on the *people* to establish a school and educate the children: a reform of the greatest magnitude.

To continue support for the public school concept, the Northwest Ordinances of 1785 and 1787 were passed by the Congress of the Confederation. Under these acts, Section 16 of each township in the great Public Domain was reserved for educational purposes.

In the U.S. Constitution, there is no explicit statement about education. This legislative innovation gave the respective states "or to the people" implied control of education via the Tenth Amendment. By not absorbing the institution of public education, the federal government produced yet another major reform: decentralization. There would be no minister of education in the United States. The lack of this official is difficult for educational leaders in other nations to comprehend. Thus the stage was set early in our history for acceptance of varied, decentralized, and innovative educational activities.

To be sure, educational practices tended to develop in local districts. Kenneth V. Lottich (1974) maintained that local school innovations usually began in the New England "cradle" and radiated outward from that focus. Perhaps there is verification for Lottich's theory in the insight of Vermont's Justin Morrill. In 1862, the Morrill Act established the "land grant" colleges. The Morrill Act was an educational reform of intense magnitude. It provided for instruction in subjects not previously considered worthy of university study—for example, engineering and agriculture; it designed an institution to "promote the liberal and practical education of the industrial classes in the several pursuits and professions in life"; and it recognized an institution where the practical, pragmatic, and innovative could be emphasized (Carmichael 1962).

The land-grant college movement is an interesting reform phenomenon, since it was sponsored by forward-looking politicians rather than by forward-looking academicians! University faculties of the mid-nineteenth century were not enthusiastic about their land-grant counterparts. The bitter rivalries which ensued are apparent even today in the control of research, legislative appropriations, or football conference championships, to list but three critical arenas.

The last decade of the nineteenth century witnessed a flurry of committees that studied several aspects of American education, just like in the 1980s. The most famous of these committees was the Committee of Ten. In 1893, this committee issued its report which, for all practical purposes, shaped the American high school for the next full century! And it must be noted that the committee was composed of those not teaching in high schools. While this report viewed the high school as an academic institution, another committee in 1918 tried to reformulate the goals and reforms for high schools with the famous Seven Cardinal Principles of Secondary Education. These principles were discussed widely during World War I. They set the stage for the ever-reformulated goals (reforms) of our schools. The writers of the Seven Cardinal Principles first observed that secondary education had as its overriding goal "a clear conception of the meaning of democracy. It is the ideal of democracy that the individual and society may find fulfillment in the other. . . ." These goals for high school reform were prevalent until the late 1950s.

THE POSTWAR ERA

The period between 1945 and 1970 was marked by the construction of new school plants to accommodate the increasing adolescent and young-adult populations. It was also marked by experimentation with curriculum and by general expansion of and sensitivity toward educational goals. In addition, a "great debate" was held about the function of secondary schools. One position stressed that our schools should look more to their European (French or Russian) counterparts. A more radical position urged the elimination of high schools and compulsory education. The middle position was best illustrated by James B. Conant (1959) in his bestselling book, *The American High School Today: A First Report to Interested Citizens*.

In 1959, Conant defended the goal of a comprehensive high school—one in which, under "one roof," educational objectives would be espoused in relation to vocational education, college preparation, and general education. The result of the Conant Report was to fix, seemingly for the remainder of the twentieth century, the concept of a nonelitist high school system in the United States.

To improve our high schools, Conant presented twenty-one recommendations. A few of these included (1) counseling, (2) required programs of study, (3) programs for the academically talented, (4) an academic supplement to the high school diploma, (5) career education, (6) developmental reading programs, and (7) elimination of small high schools. It is interesting that during these times the elementary schools were the foci of thousands of innovations and widespread experimental practices—for example, the Initial Teaching Alphabet—but the elementary school generally was not criticized by any major reform faction.

In 1961, yet another critic, John W. Gardner, former secretary of the Department of Health, Education, and Welfare (and founder of Common Cause), noted in his outstanding book, *Excellence: Can We Be Equal and Excellent Too?*, that schools act as sorting institutions today just as they have since the nineteenth century. Gardner described the dilemma inherent in any school system that attempts to provide egalitarianism, individualism, and social stratification. He pointed out that it is almost impossible to reach a point of equality in educational opportunity. The children of well-educated, professional, middle-class people will, according to Gardner, assuredly grow up and mature in an atmosphere more conducive to intellectual striving than will children of semiliterate, lower-class laborers. Theoretically, Gardner argued, educational opportunities are equal, but in actuality they are not.

One observation of Gardner's was later verified through tests, questionnaires, and correlational statistics in the monumental Coleman Report (1966) issued by the U.S. Office of Education under the direction of James S. Coleman. The report concluded that, when all factors are considered, the most important variable affecting a child's scholastic performance is the parents' educational background. The next most significant factor is the educational background and social class of the families of the other children in the school. One point that Coleman noted, but which seems to have been ignored, is that the verbal abilities of the teacher have a significant impact on the intellectual skills of students!

The 1970s: Reexamination but No Reforms

The 1970s can be viewed as a period of reexamination of the directions for education. As an institution, the school had been criticized as being not open or truthful with the populace or with the students. *Irrelevant* was the key word of the 1960s, but that concept quickly outlived its usefulness, as *relevance* often also meant shoddy scholarship or irresponsible teaching. While educators in the 1970s stressed the advantages of innovations, the public became alarmed at the declining levels of achievement tests, especially in the basic skills area. Declining test results led to growing criticism on a nationwide scale and to a call for a return to "basics." Numerous groups of citizens and educators reexamined the nature and future direction of education in the United States and released position papers on the subject that implied a needed reform.

In 1978, the U.S. Commissioner of Education, Ernest L. Boyer, stated that our system needed reshaping. He suggested a three-level system built around (1) a basic school (elementary), (2) a middle school (for core or general knowledge that focused on our heritage, institutions, and social issues), and (3) a three-year transitional school (high school).

By now you may have inferred that reform movements tend to be created by individuals, associations, governmental agencies, governing boards, and citizens at large. The last group, citizens, tends to be unique in establishing the reform agenda for schools. In the United States, all our public schools, including universities, are controlled primarily by their respective state legislatures. Each legislature delegates responsibilities to its respective citizens: university boards of regents, state boards of education, and local school boards. All of these groups at some time or another express their ideals for American schools and delight in suggesting reforms, most of which are of a contradictory nature.

What does this very brief orientation about goals have to do with educational reform? The answer is very simple: while there is no consensus on what ought to be done in the schools, there also are concurrent efforts to convert guiding principles into school-reform efforts but without acknowledging the immense political and professional clout that is needed.

The 1980s: More Studies and Maybe Reform

In the United States, we tend to analyze educational problems or crises by way of committee reports. To illustrate the phenomenon of school reports, at least eight major and twenty-one minor national reports were published during 1983 and 1984. I could write at length—even an entire book—on just the eight major reports and their implications. However, I will limit this book to mentioning five important reports in a general overview, and then reflect on their collective implications for reform.

Every good researcher states the limitation of a study. Unfortunately, writers of most reports tend to ignore their major limitations, assumptions, or omissions. Despite the flaws, these reports will cause some change in the schools. States have "tightened up" high school graduation standards and added more academic subjects—even a foreign language. Physics is still being taught in the junior or senior year, without much substantive change. But the new batch of suggested reforms will not prevent some obscure mathematics professor from installing the concept of function at grade 6, where it is totally inappropriate, and science will still be ignored by elementary school teachers and their principals.

A Nation at Risk: The Imperative for Educational Reform (1983), a study sponsored by the U.S. Department of Education, presented the strongest criticism of the schools. It stated, "If an unfriendly foreign power had attempted to impose on America the mediocre instructional performance that exists today, we might well have viewed it as an act of war." Such rhetoric is nonsense. The report, however, has been almost uncritically accepted by school boards, state boards of education, and others who know little of research or of our educational history to "tighten up standards."

A Nation at Risk suggested (1) a tougher set of academic basics for high school graduation, (2) higher standards for universities, (3) a longer school year or school day, (4) merit pay for top teachers, and (5) more citizen participation in the public schools. In actuality, this report called for a two-track high school: college preparatory and vocational. Used as a blueprint, it offered virtually nothing new that had not been urged and discarded during the 1890s and the 1950s. But *A Nation at Risk* did cause states such as Tennessee and Texas to plunge headlong into reform movements. Whether the quality of educational services improves in these two states is not material—the reform is. (Remember: it is invention that is important, not the wheel.)

By the way, C. H. Edson (1983) concluded that *A Nation at Risk* very closely resembles the famous report issued by the Committee of Ten in 1893. Both groups were dominated by nonpublic school personnel. Both reports had recommendations that were intuitive based, rather than based on empirical or evaluation data. Both groups recommended longer school terms. Both reports endorsed a philosophy of social Darwinism—survival of the academic fittest. One difference between the reports is that the Committee of Ten established the concept of academic, general, and vocational education for the high school, whereas *A Nation at Risk* implied that the high school should become an academically elite institution.

Few reformers heeded James B. Conant's advice from 1959 that schools in America can be judged—but only one school at a time. Who ever said that reform was an intellectual enterprise? It's really a public relations one, or one of biased uncommon sense.

A Celebration of Teaching: High Schools in the 1980's (1983) is a national study written by Theodore R. Sizer. Sizer provided a case study of fifteen public and private high schools; he then listed a series of elements for an "essential school." He strongly advocated (1) incentives for learning, (2) emphasis on encouraging quality, (3) more student responsibility, (4) awarding of high school diplomas only when mastery of defined skills is achieved, and (5) inculcation of ethical values. Several of the elements Sizer advocated could be implemented in any high school. His study might be called the "1983 Conant Report."

A Place Called School (1984) is a most comprehensive study in which John I.

Goodlad examined a series of "feeder" schools: elementary, junior high, and senior high schools. He provided detailed case studies and generalizations about the sample of "triples" being studied. He then addressed a series of issues that impinge on the school: teacher preparation, instruction, curriculum, leadership, research, and entry ages of students.

School reform, observed Goodlad, requires great amounts of locally generated data about what is actually taking place in the schools. [Robert E. Blum and Jocelyn A. Butler (1985) refer to that process as "profiling."] A part of that commonplace is a consistent pattern of findings. For example, student satisfaction on how well they are doing academically declines as they move from elementary to junior high to senior high school. The best things that students like about their schools are their friends, sports, other students, nothing, classes, and teachers.

In 1970, Charles E. Silberman labeled the schools of America as exhibiting a "mindlessness." Goodlad, in 1984, described the classrooms as showing a "flatness." Most teachers spend the bulk of their time handling routines with whole-group instruction the predominant form of teaching. Other routines were teachers working alone; teachers controlling the content; little praise, feedback, or teacher correctives to aid instruction; a narrow range of student activities; passive students; and not enough time for students to complete or understand their assignments. This snapshot of classroom instruction is not exactly exciting, dynamic, or innovative.

Of importance to staff development is Goodlad's description of the instructional techniques. As potentials there are lecturing, writing, listening, discussing, preparing for assignments, practicing a performance, taking tests, watching a demonstration, or participating in a simulation or a role-playing episode; and using inquiry, problem solving, or creating a product as a collective set of teaching techniques. At any one time, a teacher has a wide array of methods by which to approach an instructional objective or activity. But Goodlad and his associates found that only elementary teachers tended to use many (but not all) of these, while the observed high school teachers primarily used lectures, written work assignments, testing, and quizzing. Teacher domination of the class was strikingly reinforced by the fact that teachers outtalked the entire class by a ratio of three to one! Such teachers surely are not using interactive or discussion techniques, as described in *Teaching Strategies: A Guide to Better Instruction* (Orlich et al. 1985).

Goodlad's work points to the critical need for data-based in-service education initiatives cr innovations. He recognized the need for school district thrusts on broadly based needs. If his advice is heeded, assessment and evaluations are made, followed by plans for changes.

Much of the current reform energy is derived from state laws and the policies of state boards of education, which employ political or commonsense approaches. Unfortunately, legalistic prescriptions only restrict the options available to local schools. The result simply is more centralized control of the schools by political bodies that may be the least informed about local conditions. Reforms must be relevant to local needs, or they will not be endorsed by the staff.

In 1986, the Task Force on Teaching as a Profession of the Carnegie Forum on Education and the Economy published *A Nation Prepared: Teachers for the 21st Century*. Eight major reforms were proposed. The first was to create a national board to license teachers. The second was that teachers determine what will be taught in the schools, in light of state or local goals. The third was that the teaching profession have ranks or, at least, lead teachers or differentiated staffing. The fourth was that a bachelor's degree in arts and science be the prerequisite for any education courses or certification courses. The fifth was that a new degree, the Master of Teaching, be established. The sixth was that the nation be encouraged to prepare more minority teachers. The seventh suggestion was to establish a merit-pay incentive program whereby student performance on tests would be the basic criterion for judging teacher performance. The eighth suggestion from the group called for an increase in teacher salaries to an average ranging from $20,000 to $56,000 per year, and even suggested a high of $72,000 for annual contracts of "lead" teachers.

A Nation Prepared used an industrial, product model as its blueprint and, in spite of massive lobbying efforts by Carnegie personnel, the report may not be practical. Millions of words have already been written to discuss the pros and cons of this report. Very simply, the writers ignore that fifty states have fifty different school systems. There are contractual agreements between several thousand school districts and their respective teacher bargaining units. Differentiated staffing is an old idea that did not catch on. A six- or seven-year program of higher education leading to a teaching certificate would reduce the entry of students into the profession, not help it. The Master of Teaching would be an anti-intellectual degree; how can someone jump into a graduate study of a field with *no* prerequisite undergraduate work? Further, this master's would be a field degree with emphasis on student teaching and internships. Finally, states would have to raise taxes by 100 to 200 percent just to pay for suggested teacher salaries. The concept of pay for student progress was tried and failed in Gary, Indiana, in the early 1970s (Wilson 1973). A novel experiment at this writing is being tried in Rochester, New York, but the results from Rochester will not be ready for evaluation for at least two to three years hence.

A Carnegie supporter is the Holmes Group, a snobbish club of research universities who have banded together alledgedly to reform education. Their basic report is *Tomorrow's Teachers: A Report of the Holmes Group* (1986). To join, a member must pay $4,000 and all expenses associated with membership. The goals of the group are to make teacher education more intellectual, recognize teacher differentiation, create a national teacher education test, establish a network of cooperating universities, and improve the school as a workplace.

Obviously, these are noble goals. But the group's report does not reflect the research that it praises. It was based on common sense and intuitive generalizations. It suggested differentiated staffing, a concept that proved ineffective in the 1970s. It offered a six-year teacher preparation program for the entering teacher; such a term means that new teachers would lose about $35,000 in salaries, and the program would cost about $15,000 beyond current BA degree requirements. Further, the group suggested a nonintellectual Master in Teaching degree that would be field oriented. They ignored that such courses would be undergraduate level in spite of being labeled for a master's. A somewhat parallel attempt was suggested in the 1967–69 era, when a similar proposal failed with the behavioral and competency-based teacher education projects of the U.S. Office of Education (Blewett 1969).

Politically, the Holmes report showed naïve amateurism. As a plan of action it provided great clichés but no practical ideas that were implementable (Olson 1987).

Now you may ask, "How can this author be so smug to ridicule highly touted reform efforts that are bankrolled by the prestigious Carnegie Corporation and Ford Foundation?" Historical precedents are my reasons. Let us examine some attepts at comprehensive school reforms to gain some insights and to learn why, to quote from Ronald S. Brandt, "the freeway of American education is cluttered with the wrecks of famous bandwagons." *

Federal Legislative Efforts at School Reform
We begin our focus on modern school reform with 1957. On October 4, 1957, the Soviets successfully launched their Sputnik. It was a memorable day for me, since I was teaching junior high school science in Butte, Montana. All that day, for five different class periods, the students discussed nothing but the fact that "we are behind!" These twelve- to fifteen-year-olds truly reflected our national concerns.

The NDEA and ESEA. Congress quickly responded with the now-famous National Defense Education Act (NDEA), which provided schools with hundreds of millions of dollars for in-service education for teachers of science, mathematics, foreign languages, and counseling. NDEA was signed by President Eisenhower in September 1958. The enabling clause stated that the NDEA was designed "to strengthen the national defense and to encourage and assist in the expansion and improvement of educational programs to meet critical national needs . . ." (U.S. Statutes at Large 1958). The main motive was "to meet critical national needs," not to meet school needs or the needs of children or young adolescents. Just as the Carnegie Forum wants the nation better prepared to face the economic challenges from the Orient, not just to teach children well. (Behind every reform is a hidden agenda.)

In 1965, President Lyndon B. Johnson signed into law the historic Elementary and Secondary Education Act (ESEA). This act pumped billions of dollars into

*Quoted by permission of Ronald S. Brandt.

all segments of education, ranging from preschool to graduate school. As the original act was amended, it provided *categorical aid* (aid to specific activities in the school) to help remediate problems.

Billions of dollars were made available under ESEA for the improvement of state departments of education, for educational research and development, for devising and testing innovative practices in the public schools, for installation of educational technology in the schools, and for improving teaching skills. In 1981, the ESEA was changed rather drastically with the passage of President Ronald Reagan's legislation, the Education Consolidation and Improvement Act (ECIA). This act tended to reduce the massive federal aid to education and to allow local school districts greater flexibility and discretion in the use of funds. The ECIA signaled a reduction of specific, categorical aid to public schools.

School reform and attendant social reforms were the agendas of the ESEA. It could be suggested that ECIA was an attempt to eliminate federal aid. What is more important is that both NDEA and ESEA were implemented with glowing press, high expectations, and the hope that massive school reform would some-how take place by infusing federal dollars into the enterprise. But a real test for reform was in the planning phases of the U.S. Office of Education during the late 1960s and early 1970s. It was the Experimental Schools Program.

The ESP. In February 1970, the Department of Education initiated the Experimental Schools Program (ESP), which ultimately absorbed $55 million in tax-payers' money, in eighteen school districts during the period between 1971 and 1977. A hint of the impact of the ESP on school reform is suggested in the frontispiece of Raymond T. Coward's (1977) report about the ESP project: "Experiments that yield light are more worthwhile than experiments that yield fruit," which he quoted from Francis Bacon.

The April 27, 1976, Report to the Congress by the comptroller general of the United States would not delight in either Bacon's quote or Coward's implication, for as the U.S. Government Accounting Office (1976; 10, 28) investigative team wrote about the ESP, "plans were vague and were written in conceptual rather than operational terms." The same investigators concluded by noting, "While, we agree with HEW that much can be learned from the program, we believe that the program's ability to provide information on the impact of comprehensive educational changes will be limited."

Limited indeed! The program was useless, for ESP did not test any of the powerful or then-prevailing educational theories—that is, testable hypotheses—other than some concepts of Individually Guided Education (IGE), a process that was already well established by the University of Wisconsin's R&D Center, and a few vague concepts about "open education." The ESP projects were hailed as a "bridge between basic educational research and actual school practice" (U.S. HEW–OE *Experimental Schools Program* 1971, 1). Actually, they provided no usable information on school reform not already known or known in the 1970s.

The basic strategy of ESP was to support a small number of large-scale, comprehensive experiments focusing on research, demonstration, experimentation, documentation, and evaluation. Tragicomically, no major experimental conclusions can be drawn, save one. There was nothing too insignificant for social engineers in the U.S. Office of Education to fund as long as it was with taxpayers' money.

Mind you, this $55 million educational reform debacle came directly after the associate commissioner for research of the Office of Education wrote that there was "a patchwork of work in all kinds of areas without real focus on any particular need in education" (U.S. Congress, Committee of Education and Labor 1967, 203).

In that same report, the Office of Education's associate commissioner for research established how the patchwork would be straightened out:

> The Bureau of Research seeks to improve education through support of research and related activities conducted outside the Office of Education. Through the Bureau, funds are provided for research projects and programs designed to expand knowledge about the educational process, to develop new curricula and improved education programs and techniques to disseminate the results of these efforts to educators and the public, and to train researchers in the field of education. The Bureau is the central source in the Office of Education for curriculum development and tests and disseminates such curricula and other products of its research. . . . (U.S. Congress, Committee of Education and Labor 1967, 203).

The Office of Education's Bureau of Research, thus, instituted the centralization of research responsibilities to improve programs, plans, and use of "research funds based on office-wide priorities" (U.S. Congress, Committee of Education and Labor 1967, 203).

With the centralization of the research priorities—don't forget that the priorities were established by Office of Education officials—the stage was set to reduce the role of the university and the general research community, and establish "nonprofit" organizations that would play to a federal political agenda.

What is most pathetic about the ESP waste was the total ignoring of institutional roles, expectations, and functions. The public schools, grades K–12, play the major role in the transmission of knowledge. Personnel in these institutions seldom conduct planned research, systematically analyze current trends, or publish critical papers. The universities, to the contrary, have the function of analysis, research, and generation of knowledge—in addition to the transmission of knowledge. Any educational theoretician could have quickly deduced that the ESP program was doomed to fail because the public schools do not have the research capacity to handle the job. And what's more pathetic, Walter R. Borg and his associates (1970) published a similar analysis in a federally funded report! Again, reforms do not tend to be a scholarly approach to identifying problems and reviewing the literature to determine what works and what doesn't. No, this is yet another example of a reform movement that was entirely politically inspired and that subsequently failed.

THE FORD FOUNDATION'S TRY

So, federal efforts at comprehensive school reform are less than successful. Is there any massive nonprofit effort from which we can learn some lessons for reform? The answer is found by reviewing *A Foundation Goes to School* (1972).

During the late 1950s, through the early 1970s, the Ford Foundation supported educational reform efforts in a series of projects conducted in small and large, and rural, urban, and suburban schools. The overall project was labeled the Comprehensive School Improvement Program (CSIP). Approximately $50 million was invested in this project before foundation officials asked, "What are the results?" That question led to an evaluation report and the following ten germane conclusions:

1. Innovations are best implemented in a number of schools with limited objectives and with sharply focused techniques.
2. The policy and governance structures for innovative projects have little to do with their effectiveness, their implementation, or their open acceptance.
3. Change appears to occur on a larger scale when the recipients agree, before the funds are committed, on specific purposes, and on the nature, extent, and limitations of the proposed project. Projects that are granted for broad-purpose ideals—for example, "improving educational opportunity"—tend to have little success.
4. Conspicuous demonstration centers that establish "lighthouse" schools tend *not* to be effective; changes in nearby school systems do not occur because of the neighboring lighthouse. Districtwide influence seems more pronounced and stimulates innovations in schools and classrooms more than do so-called lighthouse districts.
5. The director of the project is of critical importance. When the project leader leaves there is a tendency for the project to terminate.
6. Innovation and change in the schools requires a broad commitment of both intellectual and financial resources.
7. Seldom does the university act as a force for the improvement of educational quality in elementary or secondary schools. Individual professors tend to promote new ideas, but cannot aid as true change-agents.
8. The less complex the school system's structure, the more easily are innovations introduced and accepted. Smaller schools change faster than larger schools.
9. The more lasting innovations tend to occur in middle-size suburbs. Money alone seems *not* to be the decisive factor for an innovative program.

10. Communities that have crises and other school confrontations tend to waste the innovation funds.

The bottom line of the Ford Foundation's massive efforts was that comprehensive school reform is not economically feasible. It is interesting that in 1987, the Ford Foundation contributed $300,000 to the Holmes Group for teacher education reform. Looks like nobody learns from mistakes. (For a detailed historical account, see Diane Ravitch's *The Troubled Crusade: American Education, 1945–1980* (1983).

ENTER THE "EFFECTIVE SCHOOLS MOVEMENT"

During the 1980s, the many "publics" of public education became concerned that the schools were declining in quality at an unprecedented rate. The "decline," of course, referred to the decline in standardized test scores.

What caused those declines? Studies were conducted to investigate test score decline by high school students. A plethora of such studies yielded only one useful finding: if students did not attend school regularly or did not take basic academic courses in science, English, and mathematics, they scored poorly. Annegret Harnischfeger and David E. Wiley (1975) prepared one of the more objective studies about the decline in test scores and concluded that *no single variable* could be identified to account for these declines.

By the late 1970s, several researchers began to identify public high schools whose graduates had test scores higher than the national average or which were showing growth rather than decline. The totality of this trend became labeled as the "effective schools movement."

Roots of the Movement

One of the leading proponents of the "effective schools movement" was the late Ronald Edmonds—a prominent and well-respected educator and researcher. Edmonds died in 1983, before he could successfully challenge the predominant social science theory that familial effects outweigh any school effects on learning. In short, Edmonds began to collect evidence to repudiate the work of James Coleman and his associates (1966) and of Christopher Jencks and others (1972). The Coleman and Jencks studies tended to establish correlational data that the higher the family's socioeconomic status, the better the school achievement of its children. Coleman and Jencks did provide an easy alibi for teachers and administrators, especially those in urban or predominantly minority schools: we cannot expect much from minority or poor students since social background and luck are far more important than the influence of the school. Thus the untested hypothesis of a sociologist and economist was used in an active, rigorous manner by public educators as an excuse for not improving the schools.

Thomas L. Good's research summary (1982) pointed out that what teachers expect of their students is usually what they get from them. His statement was nothing new, for Robert Rosenthal and Lenore Jacobson (1968) initially had reported this finding as the "Pygmalion effect." However, Good's summary did report that (1) teachers tend to treat low-achieving students with less favorable responses than high-achieving students; (2) teachers demand less from low achievers; (3) teachers interact in a less friendly manner with low achievers; (4) low achievers seldom get the benefit of the doubt in tests, whereas high achievers do; and (5) when expectations are forced on the school through community pressure, the performance of all students is increased. In one early study (Rist 1970), it was found that the teachers of inner-city children tended to expect their students to do poorly. It seems to have been amply demonstrated that if you expect children to perform poorly in school, they will perform poorly (Rosenthal and Jacobson 1968). On the other hand, if you expect them to do well, they will.

You may well ask yourself why teachers and administrators do not rectify such poor instructional expectations. Again, many public school educators have uncritically and unintentionally accepted the familial-effects theory: teachers cannot be held accountable for students' failure to learn when they know that the students come from poor home environments. Just as Ron Edmonds has cautioned all educators, a theory that is not applicable and is not verified may be used as an alibi because it is convenient.

In 1979, Ron Edmonds defined an effective school as one in which the basic skills of the poor or minority children are at least equal to the skills of middle-class children, and that by examining test scores alone, the socioeconomic group could not be identified. Edmonds described four general traits of effective schools: (1) strong instructional leadership that sets the climate for learning, for using a wide array of instructional strategies, and for using school resources that focus on student learning; (2) high expectations for all students; (3) orderly climate and a quiet and pleasant atmosphere conducive to learning; and (4) emphasis on the acquisition of basic skills.

Describing Effective Schools

The most important question for staff developers to address is how to provide the quality training that will produce effective schools. In the previous sentence, the emphasis was deliberately on the institutions—the schools—and not on individuals—the teachers or principals. It is apparent that it takes all the resources of an institution to make learning efficient, excellent, and effective. There are several so-called school effectiveness projects in the United States and Canada, but here we select one project that synthesizes the entire movement: the Alaska Effective Schooling Program.

In the 1980s, the State Board of Education for the state of Alaska inaugurated a school-improvement plan that was subcontracted to the Northwest Regional Educational Laboratory (NWREL). After a review of school effectiveness studies, the NWREL staff identified five major elements that lead to effective school practices:

- Leadership
- School environment
- Curriculum
- Classroom instruction and management
- Assessment and evaluation

If classroom instruction and management is examined in greater detail (selected because the focus of much staff development is on classroom improvements), then there are subsumed at least eleven major elements:

1. Expectations for behavior
2. Student behaviors
3. Class routines and procedures
4. Standards
5. Small and large groups
6. Stage setting
7. Instruction and direction
8. Learning time
9. Reteaching
10. Teacher-student interaction
11. Student rewards and incentives

All of these have implications for staff development. But, what have some researchers reported about effective schools? A selected set follows.

Reports from Effective Schools

Prior to establishing any agenda by which a staff developer can improve a school or make it more effective, much *profiling* must be done. Robert E. Blum and Jocelyn A. Butler (1985) reported a ten-step plan that requires data collection and interpretation from several sources. These data are from reported research, current practices, school-climate surveys, evaluations, student achievements, school attitudes, and social behaviors. Prior to preparing any plan for school improvement, you must first know what really needs improving before acting and then finding out that the wrong action was taken.

Stewart C. Purkey and Marshall S. Smith (1982) cautioned that achievement tests may be overused as an indicator of effective schools. They observed that schools are social systems where change occurs in small increments, not from orders—top down.

Emphasizing the research findings from instructionally related studies, Jere Brophy (1982) reported that there tended to be eight teacher characteristics associated with effective schools: (1) establishing teacher expectations, (2) providing opportunities for children to learn, (3) using coherent classroom management and organization, (4) pacing the curriculum, (5) teaching actively rather than

TABLE 9-1.

EFFECT OF SELECTED ALTERABLE VARIABLES ON STUDENT ACHIEVEMENT

VARIABLE[a]	EFFECT SIZE[b]	PERCENTILE EQUIVALENT
D Tutorial Instruction	2.00	98
D Reinforcement	1.20	
A Feedback-corrective (Mastery Learning)	1.00	84
D Cues and explanations	1.00	
D Student classroom participation	1.00	
A Student time on task	1.00[b]	
A Improved reading/study skills	1.00	
C Cooperative learning	0.80	79
D Homework (graded)	0.80	
D Classroom morale	0.60	73
A Initial cognitive prerequisites	0.60	
C Home environment intervention	0.50[b]	69
D Peer and cross-age remedial tutoring	0.40	66
D Homework (assigned)	0.30	62
D Higher order questions	0.30	
B New science and math curriculum	0.30[b]	
D Teacher expectancy	0.30	
C Peer-group influence	0.20	58
B Advance organizers	0.20	
C Socioeconomic status (for contrast)	0.25	60

Note: [a]Object of change process—A-Learner, B-Instructional material, C-Home environment or peer group, D-Teacher. [b]Averaged or estimated from correlational data or from several effect sizes.
Source: Benjamin S. Bloom (1984). "The 2 Sigma Problem: The Search for Methods of Group Instruction as Effective as One-to-One Tutoring," *Educational Researcher, 13* (6), 4–16. Used with permission of the American Educational Research Association and Benjamin S. Bloom.

passively, (6) teaching to mastery, (7) identifying grade-level differences, and (8) providing a supportive learning environment.

Anthony V. Codianni and Gretchen Wilbur (1983) compared the findings of seventeen major studies on effective schools. They identified six aspects that recurred:

- Strong leadership
- Positive school climate
- Emphasis on basic skills
- High student expectations
- Continuous assessment of learning
- Systematic staff development

Synthesizing the common components of school effectiveness studies from thirty-five states, Beverly A. Bancroft and Laurence W. Lezotte (1985) found that focusing on a single school as the strategic unit for improvement was critical. Further, using a building-based improvement team consisting of teachers and administrators aided in school-improvement efforts. Bancroft and Lezotte also observed that a three- to five-year implementation period was important. Short-term plans simply are not successful.

The implications for staff development are most obvious in all these studies, and are explicitly stated by Codianni and Wilbur and Bancroft and Lezotte.

While not addressing the issue of effective schools, Benjamin S. Bloom (1984) certainly identified instructional practices that have a highly positive impact on student achievement. Bloom illustrated the magnitude of an instructional treatment with two measurement terms: standard deviations and percentile equivalents. His comparisons of treatments are against a conventional subject-matter class. Table 9-1 illustrates the powerful effects of selected instructional strategies on student achievement.

For example, using tutorial instruction with children moves them two standard deviations to the right of what they would predictably do in a conventional classroom. This means that children who would be classified as "average" are now classified as academically gifted! Also, slow learners become high-average learners. As you examine Table 9-1, observe how powerful the top seven treatments are in relation to student achievement.

Obviously, massive and intensive staff-development efforts have to be made to implement these powerful strategies. (None of these was tested, even though several were proposed to do so in the infamous Experimental Schools Program.)

LESSONS FOR REFORMERS

Reformers of any ilk typically race into the "flames of adversity to do good." Educational reformers usually disregard tradition and the complexity of this nation's educational systems. Note the use of the plural—systems! In a previous paper (Orlich 1985), I suggested that two major facets mitigate against educational changes or reforms. The first is a strong tradition of professional or intuitive wisdom coupled with political interferences with the professional aspects of teaching. The second is a rather weak empirical knowledge base in the schools.

The basis for many educational practices is a long, rich, and intuitive oral tradition. The oral tradition is an extremely strong influence on every beginning teacher. Practitioners continually warn new teachers against using "all that theory that you learned at the university."

That bias is supported by continued political interference in educational affairs. State legislatures or state boards of education often make specific laws controlling class size; textbooks to be used; time spent teaching reading, language arts, mathematics, and physical education; who, when, and what to test; and how much money can be spent to provide all the educational services.

If the above conditions were controlling education completely, the schools would truly be in a political mess. But there are emerging some theoretical or research-based perspectives that impact on the oral tradition and politics. These perspectives have a time lag associated with them, as we shall see, so it takes a few years to assess their practical and educational value.

Theoretical Perspectives

An example of an emerging theoretical perspective is inclusion of Mastery Learning in the teacher education and staff-development programs. When John Carroll (1963) and Benjamin S. Bloom (1968) published their initial statements about the mastery concept, there were no methods textbooks discussing the idea. As of 1987, of nine major methods textbooks examined, three carried some treatment of Mastery Learning.

Other examples of emerging theories are observational techniques such as Flanders's Interaction Analysis system; Robert Gagne's hierarchical sequencing; and the taxonomies of the cognitive, affective, and psychomotor domains. Each of these techniques is time dated, and a longitudinal analysis could easily be initiated to determine the time lag from generation of concept to professional acceptance to publication in textbooks. Obviously, such an analysis does not account for actual implementation. For Mastery Learning, the time lag is about twenty years; even now, a large number of in-service projects do not treat the topic, in spite of Mastery Learning being one of the suggested tools for "effective schools."

In May 1985, an ERIC computer search was conducted on entries and documents relating to Mastery Learning. As could be predicted, very few entries—five, to be exact—appeared between 1963 and 1969. Three hundred and fifty-two entries are listed for 1970–79, and 458 for 1980–85. While the number of entries in the journals has increased dramatically, the concept is yet to be widely disseminated in school-reform initiatives. This suggests that a similar analysis should be instituted to determine how long it takes for validated contemporary ideas, theories, and developments to enter the many thousands of school systems in the country.

Research-Based Perspectives

The line that distinguishes research-based perspectives from theoretical ones may be rather arbitrary. Research-based models tend to have stronger empirical and experimental verifications than do theoretical ones. Sources of information for research-based perspectives again emanate from journals and national conventions. Concepts such as "time on task," "wait-time," or "tutorial instruction" can easily be researched experimentally, with valid replications reported on the topics.

To illustrate the point, a May 1985 ERIC computer search was conducted on the concept of "wait-time," popularized by Mary Budd Rowe's (1974) studies. The concept was first entered into the ERIC system and reported in 1971. Between that time and 1985, there have been fifty-four entries listed in ERIC. Here, the lag time spans a period of ten to twelve years. It appears that "wait-time" is being more quickly incorporated into the teaching field than Mastery Learning.

The sequence of (1) asking a question, (2) pausing, and (3) selecting a student was, of course, described by Walter R. Borg and his associates (1970). But the term "wait-time" was not coined by them. Thus the concept of pausing, or "wait-time," might be pegged to the year 1970 (see Tobin 1987).

These two examples support the review of currently published papers as part of any in-service education program to keep all professionals informed of current educational developments.

The research perspective is most important for staff developers, but it is time consuming. It is difficult to remain current with in-service topics ranging from performance objectives to critical thinking. Staff developers must read a wide range of journals and be true cosmopolites.

Thus any reform movement must have a research or theoretical basis and be empirically testable. The initiatives of the Holmes Group and the Carnegie Forum are doomed to failure, for they ignore most of the above and the generalizations that follow.

THE CHANGE PROCESS

Reforms are simply attempts to change the status quo. The reforms of the Ford Foundation, Experimental Schools Project, and *A Nation at Risk* all attempted massive or comprehensive educational changes. While some may argue that changes just happen, there is a higher probability that lasting reforms follow a process of accumulation.

Homer Garner Barnett (1953, 40) summarized the basic tenet for reform or innovation anthropologically, when he wrote that in society "accumulation results from building upon the past, not a discarding of it; and the amount of past development conditions the amount and variety of what can be done at present." Revolution is not a common event when viewed from Barnett's thesis. Thus reforms that attempt massive change efforts (revolutions) may be doomed from the start—including the Carnegie Forum and the Holmes Group. Yet we know that educational innovations and reforms do take hold.

Some Tested Processes of Innovation

One question to be addressed is, "What are some of the processes of successful innovation or reform?" Ivor Morrish (1976) recognized that there are at least six phases in the process of innovation: (1) invention, (2) dissemination, (3) demonstration, (4) implementation, (5) abandonment, and (6) rebirth.

This leads, then, to a set of fourteen generalizations, or conditions, that help explain why successful innovations or reforms take hold. This set is supported by empirical findings or extensive evaluation studies.

1. *The size of a project is unrelated to its success.* Both the Ford Foundation (1972, 38) and Rand studies (Berman and McLaughlin, 1978a) reported that small grants had as much impact as larger ones. Thus the quality of the reform is the critical element. Most innovation and educational reforms simply are fads or simplistic solutions with very short half-lives.

2. *Innovations that rely heavily on technology tend to be short-lived.* Peter W. Greenwood et al. (1975) and Anthony G. Oettinger's (1969) analyses support this second generalization. Sophisticated technology has not yet been designed to take the abuse given it by young adolescents. When any technological component breaks down, the teacher is quick to give up on the innovation. Education is one of our nation's most labor-intensive industries. While the nation's business sector seeks to eliminate the need for humans as workers, greater numbers of teachers are needed. There is no real savings in replacing teachers with machines; you need both to do an effective job.

One caution. By 1958, the basic research had been completed. By 1972, the product was developed (the hand-held calculator). And by 1978, the slide rule—an innovation stemming from 1622, invented eight years after the invention of logarithms—was obsolete. However, such a fate will not occur often. Microcomputers will not replace teachers this century, perhaps not in the next, either.

3. *The implementation of an innovation is directly related to immediate administrator support.* Richard O. Carlson (1965a, 4), Ronald G. Havelock (1968, 77), and Orlich et al. (1972 and 1973) have all substantiated that administrative support is imperative for the implementation of any educational innovation or reform. Teachers cannot implement innovations alone, nor can administrators be reformers alone. This, of course, has implications for the training and preparation of administrators—not just for public schools, but for universities as well!

4. *Curriculum and instructional innovations are easier to implement than changes in the organization or administration.* The review of research conducted by Michael Fullan and Alan Pomfret (1977) tended to support this hypothesis, as does the work by W. W. Charters, Jr. et al. (1973). "Wait-time" is easier to install than Mastery Learning.

5. *There is need for a critical mass of advocates before an innovation can be implemented.* Peter W. Greenwood et al. (1975, 65) supported this hypothesis, as did Orlich et al. (1972 and 1973). Geraldine R. Koller (1977) and Evelyn M. Craven (1978), in two separate studies, tended to verify this conclusion.

6. *Directives alone are seldom effective in stimulating the adoption or implementation of innovations or reforms.* The studies of Harry F. Wolcott (1977, 34–110) and W. W. Charters, Jr. et al. (1973, 62–65) lent support to this generalization.

Evidence for rule six was also reported by Ruth Anne Hansen and I (1980), in examining state mandated innovative projects in higher education. Fifty-eight of the sixty projects studied were abandoned in less than six years, with the bulk dropped in less than four years.

A. Michael Huberman and Matthew B. Miles (1986) reported that administrative support and "strong-arming," plus the provision of timely and sustained assistance, were important attributes for the successful implementation of innovations. They concluded that the failure to maintain innovations is usually accompanied by opportunistic motives, poor planning, lack of commitment, and nonsupportive building administrators. The latter findings tend to appear on virtually every such list. However, Huberman and Miles did caution that users (teachers) can easily subvert rational plans simply by nonuse or by modifying the innovation to look like an already existing practice.

Linda M. McNeil (1988) presented a somewhat dismal report of selected magnet schools, indicating that some administrators are gaining a bureaucratic control of schooling. Orgnaizational dynamics place high school principals in a power position that forces teachers to reflect the values held important by these administrators: for example, control and routine processing of students toward the diploma. McNeil observed that administrative directives were implemented by highly routinized classroom procedures, depersonalized teaching, and simplified student work—all signs of "flatness."

7. *Organizations that build an adaptive capacity to innovate tend to accelerate future adaptions.* The works of J. Victor Baldridge (1974) and Richard A. Schmuck and Matthew B. Miles (1971) provided some evidence supporting this hypothesis. This adaptive capacity is first and foremost contingent on resource availability (Corbett, Dawson, and Firestone 1984).

"Teacher empowerment" is one trait of an adaptive organization. Joan L. Sickler (1988) provided a case study and some convincing test data illustrating how three major steps changed the adaptive capacity of the ABC Unified School District in Cerritos, California. Superintendent Eugene Tucker initiated three major reforms to build a more adaptive organization.

First came a new management structure that reduced to one the organizational levels between principals and superintendent. Then teachers were given complete control over the curriculum. Lastly, teachers were encouraged to become school leaders. Staff development was a critical factor in creating the new vision for this district.

By empowering a critical mass of teachers to make decisions, the superintendent got teachers to spend more time and energy on curriculum design, team work as a way to solve problems, and implementation of needed changes.

8. *Cosmopolites tend to increase the probability of diffusion and adoption of innovations.* Everett M. Rogers (1962, 5), Donald Orlosky and B. O. Smith (1972, 413), and Peter W. Greenwood et al. (1975, 67) all verify this hypothesis. This means that if a person desires to learn about reforms, he or she must travel to various professional meetings where studies about innovations and reforms are being reported.

Susan F. Loucks (1983) and she and David A. Zacchei (1983) indicated that of 146 schools studied, 75 percent continued implementation of National Diffusion Network (NDN) materials. In some cases, ten years had passed since initial adoption. They concluded that if the materials are user friendly and well defined, their probability of being maintained was improved. All NDN projects must pass a rigorous test before being placed in the network, thus fads are eliminated immediately.

9. *It costs additional funds to innovate.* The combined studies of Richard O. Carlson (1965a, 63), Ford Foundation (1972), John Pincus (1974), Stanley P. Heath and I (1977), and Peter W. Greenwood et al. (1975, vi and vii) all substantiate the classic finding that Paul Mort (Ross 1951) originally suggested in the late 1930s. Mort concluded, as did others, that innovative school districts tended to spend more money per student than did noninnovative school districts.

What is novel for the period between 1965 (passage of ESEA) and 1981 is that the federal government, in the form of categorical aid, was the chief financial contributor to local innovations and, in 1984, to national reform initiatives by bankrolling *A Nation at Risk.*

10. *The production of educational innovations and their concomitant acceptance is a political process.* The book, *The Politics of Educational Innovations,* by Ernest R. House (1974), showed the intricate political correlations between federal fiscal efforts and stimulation of innovations. An analysis of the Rand report prepared by Paul Berman et al. (1975; V, 13) and practical experience shows that many federal educational programs are continued for political and social reasons despite the fact they are not achieving their intended educational objectives.

In "Legislated Learning Revisited," Arthur E. Wise (1988) was alarmed by the centralization associated with the current reform movement. Decisions, he noted, are being made by state legislatures and state agencies, in part because local school boards are no longer key political players. Wise asserted that centralized political forces are transforming schools into bureaucratic instruments. Teachers force children to learn a standardized curriculum that reflects the state's standardized testing program. Curriculum is aligned to tests rather than to the needs of the children. Professional leadership and decision making are reduced to implementing procedures prescribed by the state. While several initiatives are attempting to reduce the trend toward centralization, Wise tended to be somewhat pessimistic that the trend can be reversed. An alarming condition indeed, when you consider the cherished belief that decision making be made by those closest to being served.

11. *New curricula do what they intend.* This conclusion may come as a surprise to many. The current feeling that we have a nation of "dummies" because of new curricula is totally unfounded. Decker F. Walker and Jon Schaffarzick (1974) conducted an intensive review of the new curricula. They concluded that the new programs are superior on their own terms. They cautioned that tests developed for "old programs" cannot be used to show favorable results on new curricula. So in this sense, Flip Wilson's comment of "What you see is what you get" is apropos of educational reform efforts.

12. *The project leader is critical.* The Rand Corporation studies collectively interpreted the role of the project leader as not critical to a project's success. The Ford Foundation study contradicted the Rand findings by stating that when the original leader left a project, the project tended to be aborted. At the elementary school level, it appears that the principal plays the critical role in diffusion, implementation, and maintenance of an innovation (Charters et al. 1973; Broughton, Crouch, and Floyd 1978; and Orlich, Ruff, and Hansen 1976). In most institutions, the project leader may be the most critical variable for long-range success (Baldridge 1974).

John I. Goodlad (1955 and 1984) suggested that the basis for any change should be the single school building. Goodlad's proposal tends to run counter to other change advocates, who hold that an entire system must change. However, Goodlad's change concept is most appropriate to innovations in higher education. Seldom can an entire institution make a dramatic break with tradition, but individuals and subgroups within departments can.

13. *Panaceas do not work.* Just as Ponce de Leon was misled about a fountain of youth, educational reformers continue to plan and fund projects that are panaceas. The classic Coleman report (Coleman et al. 1966), which led to busing as *the* integration mechanism, simply led to a white flight from the inner cities. James S. Coleman (1975) reported that the implications of his original analysis had not been adequately analyzed. Of course not; no one was asked to predict the extreme reaction by white residents to rapid desegregation, especially in northern urban areas. Coleman also wrote that when "individuals retain control of some actions that can in the end defeat the policy, the courts are probably the worst instrument of social policy" (1975, 12). It does precious little good to know that many years later. The Coleman report illustrated again the absolute danger of one centralized study leading to the formulation of public policy aimed at school reform. Any wonder that the U.S. Government Accounting Office (1977) published a report entitled, "Social Research and Development of Limited Use to National Policymakers."

Lorraine M. McDonnell and Anthony Pascal (1988) analyzed negotiated contracts of selected teacher organizations and concluded that tradeoffs are made by teacher groups when a major reform is adopted. Institutional reforms are essentially compromises between the players, that is, the many publics. Reforms will modify past practices, not simply discard them. (And anthropologists will know the reason why.)

14. *As loosely coupled organizations, schools can make only moderate change.* Karl E. Weick (1982) described the schools as "loosely coupled." This means that it is meaningless to apply assembly-line metaphors to educational services. Nationally, the schools are organized as state systems. Only occasionally will a federal law have any impact on the states; Public Law 94-142 might be the most recent. The fifty states in turn consist of thousands of school districts. Each district has its own local school board. No reform movement has ever been able to move even a moderate number of school boards to change basic educational policies. (And that includes the very popular Conant Report of 1959.) School systems in turn are loose confederations: elementary, middle, and senior high schools. No one reform or even a series of reforms can have much more than a ripple effect on all these organizations. The loose-coupling principle implies that reforms simply cannot sustain their influence for a long time. The energy is absorbed "in the spaces."

IMPLICATIONS FOR STAFF DEVELOPERS

The current set of educational reforms is politically oriented; that is, its drive and energy comes from noneducational sources. The bulk of contemporary reforms are of poor substance, and the reformers present cliché-ridden, overgeneralized shibboliths for true reform. But what happens when a reform, no matter how poor, becomes a state's operating policy? I may laugh at those responsible for the nonsense, but school boards and superintendents must implement or support the policies. Obviously, the bulk of changes aimed at comprehensive school reform will fail. None has succeeded in the past. Further, Americans have a short attention span when it comes to the schools. *A Nation at Risk* was hardly published when the popular press ran glowing stories that reforms were in place and improvements could be seen! Quick fixes are the hallmark of alledged reform movements, and the track record is very poor for comprehensive or quick-fix reforms.

The "effective schools" thrust offers hope in the reform movement. It is a change that requires a well-documented plan for action. These school-improvement plans resemble needs assessments. With an operationally defined needs assessment, a collaborative staff-development committee can analyze in-service projects aimed at either specific schools or groups of teachers and administrators in the school district.

The "effective schools movement" also focuses much attention on needed organizational and instructional concerns. The literature shows that organizational changes are very complex, time consuming, and difficult to sustain. Instructional changes that affect a classroom or a small group tend to be relatively easy to implement. The critical question for all staff developers is one of payoff. Which needs or, if you wish, reforms have the greatest payoff for the students? That question must be asked of every in-service initiative that boasts of being a reform. The response will probably be subjective. Yet if data are collected and analyzed, the decisions made will have some empirical basis and not be totally subjective.

The now famous Rand studies and some others emerging from the "effective schools movement" show that it takes from three to five years for any meaningful implementation of a major educational change. We cannot assume that adoption is equivalent to implementation. With a three- to five-year time span, a reform requires a great commitment in order to be sustained, supported, and implemented. Huberman and Miles (1986) observed that resources must be committed and that the reform effort must be the *top* administrative priority. Of course, I am assuming that there will be several specific in-service projects under any reform umbrella.

Finally, any reform agenda must have the support of the many publics that constitute a school district. Monolithic movements are for the most part fads; brief enthusiasm exists initially, but in a year or two the fads are replaced by newer and hotter fads. School board members are very susceptible to fads because they lack a historical perspective on education. Administrators, especially superintendents, must please their school boards. So fads often enter the schools because the top level of administrating and policymaking has a weak knowledge base. No amount of staff development will ever implement the latest educational fad.

Finally, if you are to implement a rather complex reform agenda, then the prerequisite skills for all staff must be established before the main thrust is initiated. Mastery Learning requires in-service programs related to small groups, curriculum alignment, materials preparation, and criterion-referenced evaluation. When these four technical prerequisite skills are mastered by teachers and principal, the concept of Mastery Learning can be initiated. But several attendant organizational and support-service elements must be modified if you want success in the implementation. These elements include the staff's perception of learning and their commitment to a philosophy of education consistent with Mastery Learning. The same elements apply to direct instruction, thinking-skills training, cooperative learning, tutorial instruction, learning styles strategies, and manipulative math or science.

The effective implementation of any quality educational reform directly relates to the commitment provided by local staff-development programs. And the enhancement of human resources is the paramount criterion by which to judge any alleged reform.

CHECKLIST FOR SCHOOL REFORMS

_____ 1. The reform movement makes its assumptions and hidden agenda known.

_____ 2. The reform is operationally defined.

_____ 3. The reform has a substantial research base to support it.

_____ 4. The reform is implementable in the schools.

_____ 5. The reform focuses on a subsystem of organizational, curriculum, or instructional practice.

_____ 6. The reform does not require massive outlays of resources.

_____ 7. The reform is student oriented.

_____ 8. The reform shows sensitivity to the best instructional practices or empirically verified treatments.

_____ 9. The school is the unit of reform.

_____ 10. An operational staff-development plan is provided by the reformers.

_____ 11. The period for implementation is adequate—that is, three to five years.

_____ 12. The reform can be evaluated initially.

_____ 13. The reform adds to what already exists, rather than discards the old.

_____ 14. Collegial support is present to endorse the reform.

_____ 15. The reform can exist in a loosely coupled organization.

_____ 16. The staff-development plan addresses real needs.

_____ 17. The reform is truly worth the effort.

_____ 18. Administrative support sustains the adoption and implementation efforts.

CHAPTER 10

IMPLEMENTING A STAFF-DEVELOPMENT VISION

A journey of 1,000 miles begins with a single step.

Chinese Proverb

Planning, organizing, and implementing a staff-development program is an incremental process. No school district suddenly installs a comprehensive model, since these programs must grow and mature. It is important to recognize that many elements of a supportive program may be in place and scattered about the organization. Donald R. Moore and Arthur A. Hyde (1978) made that observation when they calculated budgetary allocations to in-service projects. In nearly all major school districts, staff development, curriculum improvement, curriculum development, instructional improvement, and school improvement are administered through separate departments. Each has a leader who jealously guards the unit from interlopers. (That problem is addressed later in this chapter.)

Nurturing a vision for staff development requires supportive administrative personnel and programs based on client or user needs. Successful projects are important in the vision-making process, since there is nothing better than having the participants enrolled in the staff-development programs make complimentary remarks about them. When teachers leave a workshop highly motivated and then find that what they have learned actually does make a difference in their classrooms, the vision gains momentum and staff development grows in credibility. The bottom line reflects teacher and learner efficiency and efficacy. Recall that teachers are primarily motivated by student success. They achieve pride in their work and gain incentives by a reflective process. That is, their success is a reflection of how well their students succeed in and out of the classroom. Coaches—a critical power group in any school—bask in the success of their teams, especially championship ones. Teachers continually boast about their best students who gain scholarships, recognitions, or appropriate stature. Teachers even enjoy speaking about "characters" with whom they have interacted.

Thus when an in-service project is evaluated, participants rank it as effective if it meets their professional needs. But follow-ups with these individuals and their principals are essential to determine if teaching behaviors change or if students do improve.

IMPLEMENTING AN ORGANIZATIONAL STRUCTURE

To achieve maximum benefits from a staff-development program, you need to develop a flexible structure within the central office. The director of staff development, regardless of the organizational chart, needs organizational access to the superintendent and assistant superintendents charged with instruction and finance. Such access is critical if staff development efforts are to be coordinated, funded at an appropriate level, and recognized as an important part of the school district's mission.

Orlich's Law of In-Service Education

Over the years, I have observed some very effective staff-development programs and made a few conclusions about why they are successful. This book reflects those observations. *Successful* in-service projects are oriented directly to a specified group: janitors, food preparers, fourth-grade teachers, middle-school science teachers, high school English teachers, principals, and so on. *Unsuccessful* in-service programs are those in which every member of the school district is required to attend. The latter is a serious indictment against administrators who believe that something is so important that all staff must attend. Command performances are useless in changing the organization or in bringing about success in teaching.

Successful projects relate to specific persons, thus Orlich's Law: *the relevance of an in-service project is inversely proportional to the number who attend.* I am not being sarcastic or flippant. If three science teachers in the high school need an in-service project that helps them teach earth science better and ultimately improves how science is delivered to the students, then that project should be supported. Conversely, to require all science teachers to sit through an in-service project not related to their specific needs is a waste of taxpayers' money and teachers' time.

In-service education is not cherished by teachers because they have been virtually forced to hear meaningless speeches, participate in inane projects, or attend totally irrelevant workshops. A basic assumption of human development is that individuals have needs to be met. Meeting individual needs is quickly translated into successful projects. More important, teachers who have positive experiences become advocates for the staff-development program. The literature on staff development is replete with case studies and evaluations to support that assertion.

To address the needs of small groups, or even individuals, requires coordination among various school district offices. The staff-development council needs representatives who are committed to keeping communications channels open and to interacting with their colleagues. The sum of these interactions is the process called *collaboration*.

Collaborative Model

The most successful staff-development programs involve the people who are affected by the decision-making processes. Administrators, teachers, staff members, and classified staff personnel must help plan and design activities intended for their own job-related growth. The recent phenomenon of negotiated professional agreements on staff development comes as no surprise. Teacher associations and unions understand the impact that staff development has on their professional well-being, and these groups want to share in that power and decision making.

Smaller school districts tend not to use a legal document to guide staff development. But district officials contemplating such agreements would be wise to examine agreements currently in force, seeking those elements that provide a vision of collaboration rather than a situation that leads ultimately to administrator-teacher confrontation. By having all parties subscribe to the goal of enhancing human potential, those associated with the program will exhibit behaviors that evolve subtly from collective bargaining to thoughtful problem solving.

What does a district gain from collaboration? Perhaps the biggest gain comes from the commitment by all constituencies in a school district. David D. Marsh and Maryalice Jordan-Marsh (1986) discussed the readiness of individuals to serve on collaborative committees that plan for building-based in-service projects. Further, from the ranks of the collaborative group or committee emerge the future leaders of and advocates for quality programs.

Collaboration requires commitment. As Bob Pickles (1988) wrote, collaboration takes time, involvement, trust, and a sense of mission to work effectively. A school district staff-development council or task force is an absolute necessity. Once this group is established and operational, then school-based councils might be set up. Any school that has a school-improvement or "effective school" project needs a school council to support those efforts and ensure commitment by all teachers.

Concomitantly, the concept of "teacher empowerment" (Sickler 1988) is gaining awareness and acceptance. The old, adversarial relationship between administrators and teachers has been unproductive in improving services to children. The emerging concept of empowerment is truly a collaborative one. Teachers are given full responsibility and authority for instructional and curriculum development—two areas that reflect their professional domain. Teachers collaboratively plan the learning experiences and develop honest standards of academic excellence, rather than adhere to political slogans. Empowerment implies efficacy.

Teachers develop into school instructional leaders when the concept is implemented at the school district level.

A school board policy relating to staff development and in support of collaborative planning is the first step toward success. The other elements tend to fall into place after a forward-looking board describes a vision.

Staff Training

After the school board adopts a policy endorsing a comprehensive district program, the policy needs to be implemented through administrative regulations. At this juncture, it is professionally appropriate to involve representatives of the staff-development council or task force. For districts with on-going programs, the above is probably already in force. Districts just approaching a comprehensive program (as compared to a series of disconnected in-service education projects) need to plan for internal staff training.

Just what does such staff training entail? Refer to Table 1-1 and examine the six functions of a complete program: (1) in-service education, (2) organization development, (3) consultation, (4) communication and coordination, (5) leadership, and (6) evaluation. These six functions provide the basis for entry training for staff-development program leaders. In some cases, it is possible to contract with a local university to provide a full course on staff development. Another option is to bring in knowledgeable consultants to help organize a series of readings and other interactive experiences for the initial group of staff developers. A third option is to visit selected school districts with a reputation for quality staff-development programs and work out a training model with them.

The essential point is to bring the initiating group "up to strength," so that the council or task force develops a rationale and philosophy for the training. Of course, the growth approach should be adopted as the philosophical driving force.

Classified staff need an organizational plan so that they can benefit from the overall program. Selected classified personnel should be identified to receive entry-level training (as discussed) in order that they know (1) the rationale for the programs, (2) how to conduct the training projects, and (3) how to gain advancement opportunities through the district's program. Establishing a classified training program brings unanticipated rewards to the schools. The more the nonteaching staff know about their jobs and the jobs of those closely related to their own, the stronger the team. For example, child-abuse identification programs have become an essential area for in-service education. All district employees should receive relevant short-term in-service education concerning this dreadful phenomenon. In numerous cases, classified staff—that is, bus drivers, secretaries, food service personnel, or custodians—are the first in the school setting to observe or be in contact with an abused child.

Again, the training projects and overall program for all employees must be based on needs. Relevance is the key concept for staff development; that point cannot be reiterated too often. As staff training continues, a talent bank should be instituted to identify, on a continuous basis, local human resources who can contribute to the staff-development program.

THE SCHOOL CULTURE

An emerging concept applicable to any school district instituting a comprehensive staff-development program is that referred to as the *school culture*, or the *ecology of school renewal*. Seymour B. Sarason (1982), Ann Lieberman and Lynne Miller (1984), and John I. Goodlad (1987) have written extensively about the impact school culture has on the implementation of innovations, school-improvement projects, and in-service education.

Concepts for Consideration

The primary concept associated with the school culture movement is that of the system. A *system* is an entity comprising many elements or components that interact in a positive manner, so that the system functions effectively. A school district is an example of a system. It is a human creation comprising people, buildings, machinery, materials, rules, conventions, and a host of parts and players. The system has subsystems. A school district has attendance areas, different types of schools, bus routes, and the like. A subsystem such as a high school has even smaller subsystems: athletic teams, specific academic programs, vocational units, service groups, union and nonunion employees, student groups, faculty groups, clubs, and the like.

Systems are important because they function as a whole. Of importance, components of systems interact in a manner that stimulates or retards more interaction. The "effective schools movement" and school-based in-service education advocates understand that the system or subsystem must function at a very high rate of efficiency or the elements will begin to deteriorate.

Lieberman and Miller (1984) summarized several points about the school culture. First, the school culture is characterized by great ambiguity. The goals and values of the schools are not easily identified or agreed upon. The work in a school is not a product, but the schools are continually compared to the industrial, product-oriented model.

Second, the ethos of schools differs greatly among districts. There is no simple prescription that will improve all the schools. As Wise (1988) noted, the more prescriptive a state legislature becomes in making laws to fix possible ills, the more problems arise as a direct effect of those laws, which are rarely well thought out. Local conditions have more to do with school-improvement efforts than changes imposed from the outside. Yes, the local folks are in a position to know more about their schools than political reformers from the state or national capitals.

Third, norms and values are different school by school. Teachers learn their roles through experience, regardless of the amount of formal education. The norms and values differ significantly for elementary and secondary teachers. For the most part, teaching is an isolated activity. Teachers interact with children or adolescents all day, with little professional contact with colleagues.

Fourth, instructional methods and practices are complex acts, having weak research bases. Teachers continuously show "the research" to be wrong by achieving good results and by never using *the* researched method. Perhaps that is what makes teaching so susceptible to charlatans and quick-buck hacks: the knowledge base related to student learning is weak, while teaching artistry is not exactly quantifiable. The Holmes Group is deluding its members and the teaching profession by implying that effective instruction will be defined after the next definitive research study.

The interaction of components within a system is critical for its health. If the business office ignores teacher or principal requests for selected quality instructional materials, then that office can have a negative impact on student learning. If the principal is a weak instructional leader, then that school may show poor morale and poor student achievements. If the central office forces teachers to teach to some "company line," then the teachers will do so half-heartedly and will subvert the policy, no matter how good its intent.

School cultures do not just happen; they develop over periods of time. To determine some of the elements of any school culture, you can complete the profiling processes suggested by Robert Blum and his associates (1985). John I. Goodlad's processes used in *A Place Called School* (1984) would also produce data to identify the critical elements.

Another major problem that faces a school culture is a predominance of educational psychology in teaching training, to the neglect of a study of culture, norms, and interactions. The latter are found in the domains of sociology and anthropology, which are notoriously missing in virtually all teacher preparation programs or even graduate programs.

Implications for Staff Developers

The vision espoused in this book is not novel, but it is threatening to school district personnel who have "called the shots" on in-service education programs. The vision of collaboration is a threat to personal power and organizational prestige. Most school districts do not systematically conduct needs assessments nor do they subscribe to the profiling processes. These two techniques help produce data that indicate the elements constituting a school district or school culture. Whom do faculty members seek when faced with instructional problems? Which cliques attend meetings of professional associations? These are subtle questions illustrating social patterns that help shape a school culture.

Power is knowledge, and those who have knowledge about how schools or districts really operate are not quick to part with it. The vision described in this book demands that power be shared to better all human resources in the school district. Implied in the vision is the need to involve as many constituencies as possible in every major project. The sharing activity (empowerment) is one means to this end—shared decision making. If every project had collaboration for one year, a new norm of collegiality would emerge. The major studies about innovations in our schools have shown that "buying in" is a critical part of implementation.

If school-based staff development is to be one component of the district's operational plan, then it is essential to provide at least a basic organization-development training component to those involved. While this book has just touched the topic of adult learning, it behooves staff developers to examine the highlights of the topic so that staff-development plans recognize the unique needs of adults.

The vision also implies that individuals be provided with some responsibility to shape their own in-service agendas. The key word here is *responsibility*. Teachers and administrators need time to reflect on their specific and unique training needs. Allowing individuals some choice in their professional development quickly establishes the notion that "people are trusted around here."

To encourage personal interaction, the staff-development council could call for RFPs (requests for proposals) that meet the in-service needs of selected groups. Collaboration of efforts to meet a specific training need would be the criterion for eligibility. The usual components of a proposal would also be required: (1) objectives, (2) plan of operation, (3) evaluation model, (4) budget, and (5) personnel. This simple mechanism encourages job-alike individuals to collaborate in achieving a group-determined goal. All these facets help make for meaningful and efficacious staff-development programs and shape a healthy school culture.

LINKING SUPPORTIVE ELEMENTS

Staff development is usually isolated from the total-curriculum or instructional-improvement efforts of a school district. Collaborating and sharing power and responsibility are apparent in smoothly operating bureaucracies. An allowance is made to share overlapping areas of responsibility, and it is strongly recommended that all the school-improvement and curriculum-development programs be organized in the same division as is staff development. This is not to imply that staff development is the driving force of the schools. But it recognizes that school-improvement efforts are attained through staff-development programs. The vision recognizes also that all curriculum-development projects are implemented after in-service education activities have trained staff members for new roles, methods, programs, or strategies.

The total process of school improvement is cyclical. Figure 10-1 illustrates the dynamics of the cycle. It begins with a need or a rationale for change. The needs and rationale are converted into specific program elements, curriculum materials, organizational components, instructional strategies, evaluation models, and

FIGURE 10-1.

CYCLE OF STAFF, SCHOOL, OR PROGRAM IMPROVEMENT

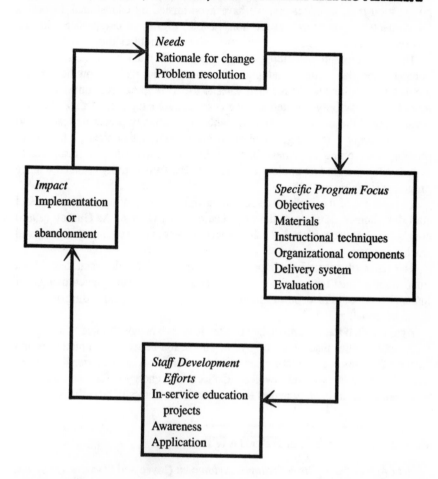

delivery systems. Next come the staff-development activities to develop staff competencies. The impact of the process is implementation if the program is successful or abandonment if unsuccessful. The cycle continues for other programs. Actually, several such cycles operate at any one time.

Recognize that Figure 10-1 is much abbreviated. There are dozens of specific tasks and initiatives that take place simultaneously, and only the general ones are identified in the figure. Let us assume that the figure is a valid representation of reality. As such, key district administrators can better appreciate the plea for consolidation of curriculum, instruction, and school improvement in the same organizational unit as staff development. You can conclude from examining the literature cited in Chapter 9 that major educational innovations fail because of two primary reasons. The first is that the innovation is not worthwhile. A poorly conceived innovation with little intrinsic value, no matter how much staff-development effort is used to support it, is doomed from the start. There is no question that, as educators, we have been misled by educational advocates for products or programs that are not feasible, useful, or compatible with the schools. The so-called modern math curriculum exemplifies this.

The second reason for failure of major programs is that inadequate staff development takes place with the adoption. Teachers do not really know how to use the materials or how to change their roles to use a complex program to its maximum benefit. Activity-oriented science curricula are examples of this. Districts often adopted these science programs without adequately preparing teachers to cope with inquiry teaching, materials management, open-ended problems, or multiple-questioning strategies. Districts that did devote adequate resources to staff development in fact implemented very successfully activity-oriented science programs (see Orlich 1987).

The success of the "effective schools movement" is contingent on successful staff development. People in the organization must change. As Guskey (1986) concluded, educators must first achieve success before they change their personal teaching behaviors.

The vision of instructional improvement, curriculum development, and school improvement must include the concept of staff development. The cultivation of human resources to meet new challenges is a positive part of expanding organizational potential.

Again, collaboration among the program leaders who are charged with making the school a better place leads to greater interaction between administrators and teachers. Groups begin to take pride in accomplishments, and the transition from a reactive to proactive stance evolves. Collectively, energy is focused on a common vision that ultimately makes the students benefactors of the efforts.

A VISION OF THE STUDENT

Student Achievement Through Staff Development (Joyce and Showers 1988) was a novel attempt to emphasize in-service education and learner achievement. While it is interesting to assert such a close link, in practice it is very difficult to observe a direct correlation between a teacher in-service project and greater outcomes on student achievement tests, products, or performances. Coaches attend numerous clinics, worskhops, and the like to sharpen their coaching skills. Yet in every case some team must lose in a competitive situation. Teachers attend workshops, clinics, projects, and classes—and students may or may not show immediate improvement because of organizational structures or competitive grading. Somewhere along the chain of events in staff development we must be concerned about the impact on the student.

The cumulative research is not yet adequate to identify exactly what interventions cause students to behave (that is, to achieve) in a precise, exact, and desired manner. B. F. Skinner (1984) bemoaned this fact and suggested that his theory of behavior modification was the answer to the problem. Unfortunately, research is not completely supportive of Skinner's theory, either. Current in-service education efforts obviously make claims for student efficacy or improvement. You would hardly advertise that "Our project will cause student failures." You only find out how well the program does after longitudinal evaluations.

For example, Ted Bredderman (1983) provided evidence that students who were the beneficiaries of activity-oriented science programs in the elementary schools did as well as or better on science achievement tests than students in science reading-only classes. The children in activity classes did better on process tests than children exposed to textbooks alone. However, Bredderman did not correlate in-service education programs with student test scores.

You could argue or speculate about this matter, but each school with an improvement project must examine student achievements and records to determine program success. If a school makes a massive effort to enhance student achievements through a staff-develement program, then the evidence for success comes through the interpretations of many different evaluative instruments or direct observations of specific behaviors. Evaluation must be planned for very early in the establishment of major or minor programs. Refer to Figure 10-1 to observe that evaluation is addressed in the improvement cycle. While there is a tendency to evaluate some in-service projects for participant reactions, we need to expand the concept of evaluation to measure the impact of in-service education on the students. Thus the vision of effective staff-development efforts must ultimately focus on the predicted impact on students.

ATTENDANT ISSUES

Comprehensive staff-development programs are affected by many issues and questions that may not be directly related to the topic. Let us identify some emerging questions.

1. How can we reconcile the reality and expectation differences in the school cultures of elementary, middle, and high school staff members?
2. In what ways can the stature of in-service education be raised?
3. What fiscal aid can be made available on a continued basis to support longitudinal staff-development efforts?
4. In what ways can incentives play a more significant role in supporting efforts for individual improvement?
5. How can administrators be encouraged to collaborate in staff-development efforts?
6. How can high technology be integrated effectively into the delivery system for staff development?

7. What roles will bargaining associations continue to play in stressing professional development?
8. How can staff development be institutionalized as a proactive organizational element?
9. What political restraints work against implementing a comprehensive staff-development program?
10. What impact will endless legislation have on school-improvement and staff-development efforts?
11. What lessons are truly transferable from the mounting literature about implementation of innovations?
12. How can staff development become a means to solve new social agendas that have a subtle but direct impact on the schools?
13. What coalitions will emerge to help educators respect continued learning in an era of unprecedented social change?
14. Assuming a stable or declining teacher corps, how will school districts cope with severe competition for talent on a national or local basis?

There are many more issues that could be listed. (See "Current Issues in Staff Development" in the *Journal of Staff Development*, Volume 7, Number 1, Spring 1986; and Gene E. Hall's *Beyond the Looking Glass*, 1986, for extended lists.) But issues are identified to be resolved. The faster the issues are recognized and addressed, the less negative influence they have on the schools.

CONCLUSION

Based on a growth perspective, staff development is a long-term, complex process, not a series of singular events. Staff development will gain in importance as a necessary and integral part of all school districts. Further, district administrators will need to analyze the preservice education of their new people so that in-service education programs can augment the induction experience. You can argue that there must be closer links between preservice and in-service education. However, that argument may not be supportable. There are about 15,000 school districts and over 1,200 teacher-training institutions. To suggest a tight linkage implies a centralization of power. Centralization of American education has had very few supporters over the past 200 years. Some collaboration is possible, but I see no realistic initiative that can create closer coordination between pre- and in-service teacher or administrator preparation programs. The critical element for staff-development planners is knowing what special competencies are needed to function in a specific instructional environment. Having those competencies is a powerful motivator for new professionals or classified staff.

State legislatures will undoubtedly be involved in staff-development issues, as more on-the-job training is required. Legislators will carefully evaluate the trend among school districts to use in-service education as a mechanism for augmenting teacher salaries. With anticipated legislative involvement, there will be the usual flurry of crisis-oriented laws to "fix" perceived problems.

Accomplishing the agenda for staff development as outlined in this book requires greater intra- and inter-district cooperation to plan and deliver high-quality in-service projects. Institutions whose resources must be shared in these efforts are community colleges, vocational-technical institutes, and universities. When the public schools are linked with the very excellent training opportunities of the business sector and the postsecondary educational facilities, the schools have a boundless resource base. Indeed, networks and networking must be established to exploit all these resources. Staff developers must be integrated into the many networks that now exist, especially among administrators. Through networking, mutually cooperative agreements can be worked out (Ward and Pascarelli 1987).

Professional associations must provide more intensive experiences at their conventions. Listening to a smorgasbord of speakers is not effective in-service education for attendees. Conventions must evolve into major training experiences that reflect the best in adult learning techniques.

The major responsibility for staff development resides with the local school districts. It is here that staff development makes a genuine contribution toward improving educational services to youth. It is at the local level that staff development gains employee endorsement. Effective staff development is the culmination of efforts by individuals who truly believe in the enhancement of human potential. Staff development is the very least that can be done to improve professional practices. Perhaps it is the very most.

CHECKLIST FOR IMPLEMENTATION

_____ **1.** A vision for staff development is promulgated for the entire school organization.

_____ **2.** The organizational structure reflects the importance of staff development.

_____ **3.** The size of an in-service project is not a criterion for support.

_____ **4.** A collaborative model for staff development is institutionalized.

_____ **5.** Training for staff developers is incorporated into the district's overall plans.

_____ **6.** The school district culture is analyzed so that staff-development activities can have a positive impact.

_____ **7.** School-improvement projects use the school culture to maximize all resources.

_____ **8.** Student achievements are correlated to in-service projects.

_____ **9.** Issues that affect staff development are examined on a systematic basis so that needs are addressed.

_____ **10.** Networks are constructed to expand the school's human resources base.

_____ **11.** Staff development is viewed as a renewal process.

"Continuous learning is not an option for educators; it is a mandatory and professional responsibility."

Adam Urbanski
Vice President
American Federation of Teachers
July 28, 1988

APPENDIXES

APPENDIX A

THE DELPHI TECHNIQUE

The Delphi Technique requires *at least* a month or more to accomplish, depending on the size of the group and the complexity of the questionnaire. Its value is that the selected sample has an opportunity to identify those issues it perceives as important. Further, this method allows administrators to add their opinions, since they too are concerned with the problems that occur as changes take place. Administrators may desire to send out their own Delphi questionnaires to identify administrative priorities.

The following set of materials illustrates a case study in which the Delphi technique was institutionalized in the planning process of a regional administrators' group. This study reviews all the details of the Delphi Technique. As a needs-assessment method, the Delphi technique has proved to be a valuable asset in decision making.

DELPHI CASE STUDY: INITIAL SURVEY BY COUNTY ADMINISTRATORS, DELPHI INSTRUMENTATION

OCTOBER

TO: Area Administrators
FROM: Planning Committee
SUBJ: Administrators' Retreat

The Planning Committee is using the Delphi Technique to determine a consensus for selecting the keynote topic for next year's Administrators' Retreat in Sandpoint. This technique is being administered to ensure maximum participation for principals and superintendents in our group.

Listed below are 5 possible keynote topics. Please add 1 or 2 topics of your own to the list. Later, you will receive an entire list of possible topics, and you will have an opportunity to rank them. As part of this technique, on the next form we also ask for your assistance in selecting the mini-sessions for the retreat.

POSSIBLE KEYNOTE TOPICS

1. Learning Styles
2. Computers in the Classroom
3. Staff Development/In-Service Planning
4. Gifted Education
5. Collective Bargaining
6. _____
7. _____

Please return this form to the contact person for your group as soon as possible. Your contact person is: Audrian Fowler

---

DELPHI CASE STUDY: ROUND 1

NOVEMBER
TO: Area Administrators
FROM: Planning Committee
SUBJ: Administrators' Retreat

As you are aware, the Planning Committee is using the Delphi Technique to determine a consensus for selection of the keynote topic for the Administrators' Retreat in Sandpoint. Keep in mind that the keynote topic involves an all-day presentation (6 to 7 hours). This technique is being utilized to ensure maximum participation from principals and superintendents in our group.

Listed below are 36 suggested keynote topics. Please select your top 5 choices and rank them from 1 to 5, with 1 being high and 5 being low. On your second round we will present only the top 8 topics. Further, you have 2 copies of this form. Keep one completed form for your own files and return the other completed form to your contact person. You will shortly receive a copy of how the entire group reacted. Two additional rounds will be completed following this same procedure. By always keeping a copy of how you ranked the items, you can then compare your rankings with the entire group. Any topics suggested for the keynote topic may also be included as a topic for mini-sessions.

SUGGESTED KEYNOTE TOPICS

_____   1. Learning Styles
_____   2. Computers in the Classrooms
_____   3. Staff Development/In-Service Planning
_____   4. Teaching the Gifted Child in the Regular Classroom
_____   5. Collective Bargaining
_____   6. Compliance (Salary Procedure, M-808)
_____   7. Project Leadership
_____   8. Effective School Research
_____   9. Positive School Climate
_____   10. Beyond Stress to Effective Management
_____   11. Stress Reduction
_____   12. Time Management
_____   13. Drug and Alcohol Education

—— **14.** Effective Schooling (Models) Evaluation Included
—— **15.** Teacher Evaluation as Instructional Improvement
—— **16.** Administrator Evaluation
—— **17.** Working with the Underachiever/Mainstreaming
—— **18.** Staff Motivation—Theory—Morale
—— **19.** Leadership Styles
—— **20.** Legislation—Legislative Priorities
—— **21.** Deskbook in Writing
—— **22.** Declining Enrollment—RIF
—— **23.** Developing Educational Coalitions
—— **24.** School Management Team
—— **25.** Instructional Theory Into Practice (ITIP)
—— **26.** Budgeting Problems in Buildings
—— **27.** Curricular Trends
—— **28.** Discipline
—— **29.** Personnel Management
—— **30.** Follow-Up on Brain Research—Curriculum
—— **31.** Censorship
—— **32.** Futures Planning
—— **33.** Communications
—— **34.** Multidisciplinary Team, Programming, and Meetings
—— **35.** In-Service Delivery Models
—— **36.** Legal Issues in Education

Please return one copy of the completed form to the contact person for your group by November 22. Your contact person is: Audrian Fowler.

DELPHI TECHNIQUE: RESULTS OF ROUND 1

DECEMBER

TO: Area Administrators
FROM: Planning Committee
SUBJ: Delphi Technique, Results of Round 1

Below are the results of the Delphi questionnaire rankings of the suggested keynote topics for the Administrators' Retreat. Sixty responses were returned to the committee. Those topics with the highest rank order, having 10 or more responses, and the lowest mean were considered for the final 8 topics. Compare your copy of Round 1 with the entire group.

Rank Order	Number of Responses	Mean	Topic
1	24	2.375	Computers in the Classroom
2	24	2.75	Positive School Climate
3	22	2.77	Staff Motivation—Theory—Morale
4	17	2.41	Learning Styles
5	18	3.00	Teacher Evaluation as Instructional Improvement
6	15	2.40	Leadership Styles
7	14	2.86	Legal Issues in Education

Rank Order	Number of Responses	Mean	Topic
8	14	3.14	Follow-Up on Brain Research—Curriculum
9	11	3.45	Beyond Stress to Effective Management
10	9	3.00	Compliance (Salary Procedure)
11	9	3.22	Collective Bargaining
11	9	3.22	Time Management
11	12	3.92	Curricular Trends
14	7	2.57	Effective Schooling (Models)
15	8	3.50	Communications
15	7	3.14	Project Leadership
17	7	3.29	School Management Team
18	7	3.43	Personnel Management
19	7	3.57	Staff Development/In-Service Planning
20	5	3.00	Legislation—Legislative Priorities
20	5	3.00	Futures Planning
22	4	2.50	Drug and Alcohol Education
22	5	3.20	Teaching the Gifted Child in the Regular Classroom
24	4	2.75	ITIP
25	6	4.00	Discipline
25	4	3.00	Multidisciplinary Team
25	3	2.00	In-Service Delivery Models
28	4	3.25	Developing Educational Coalitions
29	4	3.50	Budgeting Problems in Buildings
30	2	2.50	Deskbook in Writing
30	2	2.50	Declining Enrollment—RIF
32	3	2.00	Stress Reduction
33	2	3.50	Effective School Research
34	2	4.00	Censorship
35	2	4.50	Administrator Evaluation
36	0	0.00	Working with the Underachiever/Mainstreaming

DELPHI TECHNIQUE: RESULTS OF ROUND 3

JANUARY
TO: Area Administrators
FROM: Planning Committee
SUBJ: Delphi Technique, Results of Round 3

The results of Round 3 of the Delphi Technique are listed below. Sixty-six responses were returned to the committee.

Rank Order	Weighted Mean	Topic
1	2.697	Staff Motivation—Theory—Morale
2	3.136	Positive School Climate
3	3.758	Computers in the Classrooms
4	4.393	Learning Styles

Rank Order	Weighted Mean	Topic
5	4.758	Teacher Evaluation as Instructional Improvement
6	4.970	Leadership Styles
7	5.939	Legal Issues in Education
8	6.409	Follow-Up on Brain Research—Curriculum

Three members of the committee have met with Dr. Walt Gmelch, education professor at Washington State University, and discussed the keynote topic. Walt has agreed to be the keynote speaker. Many of you are acquainted with Walt already, and if you have not met him, you are in for a treat. He is an exceptional teacher who involves members of the group throughout his presentation.

The committee will now deal with topics for the mini-sessions, so the agenda can be completed.

Thank-you for participating in this Delphi Technique. This method has made the committee's task much easier and helped to identify your greatest interests.

BRIEF ANALYSIS

The Delphi case study illustrates how priorities of the respondents slowly evolved. Originally, the topic of staff motivation was not an example. However, that topic slowly climbed to number-one priority during the three rounds of questionnaires. Positive school climate tended to stabilize its position at number two, while the remaining top eight items gradually shifted. The planning group for this particular administrators' conference has commented that each subsequent conference is better than the last. They should be; after all, the conference topics are very relevant to the intended audience. And that is what staff development is all about.

Advantages of the Delphi Technique

Through the use of repeated questionnaires, needs tend to become clarified; thus an investigator can distinguish critical, short- or long-range concerns from more ephemeral ones. Group consensus is gained through each subsequent issuance of the instrument, allowing each individual to reexamine his or her original position and reconsider whether there is need for change in position based on information about the group response. Supportive and opposition elements within the organization are made known. Such data aid in implementing or postponing the programs, and in determining if internal support is needed or lacking. Priorities are clearly identified. In short, the Delphi Technique is a powerful tool by which information is gathered for planning and decision making.

Disadvantages of the Delphi Technique

You might assume that the Delphi Technique readily identifies problem areas or conflicting opinions and attitudes. However, when there is a lack of clear consensus, the method for ranking might, in fact, shift the priorities. Several techniques can be used to determine arithmetical scales, such as a total weighted average, a median ranking, frequency rankings, an unweighted frequency, or rank orders. In determining the weights of a Delphi survey, Dr. Toshio Akamine, a colleague of mine, noted that items shift upward or downward in priority because each treatment meets specific statistical assumptions that affect a

TABLE A-1.

GENERAL TASKS FOR DELPHI TECHNIQUE

1. Decision is made to collect the data.
2. The concept, policy, or statement being evaluated is stated.
3. The initial list is prepared *or* a call for items is circulated.
4. The initial sets of statements are prepared.
5. The first questionnaire, with directions, is distributed (Round 1).
6. The results are collected and tabulated.
7. The minority items are added and the revised questionnaire is edited.
8. Each participant receives the results of Round 1 plus group consensus.
9. New rankings are requested (Round 2).
10. Round 2 rankings are tabulated and edited.
11. New minority items are added.
12. Each participant receives the results of Round 2, plus group consensus.
13. New rankings are requested (Round 3).
14. Final rankings are tabulated *or* Round 4 proceeds, if needed.
15. Results are disseminated.

numerical listing. In our particular use, the top and bottom items remained in those positions, respectively, regardless of method. But the other six items—especially the second, third, and fourth—shifted about. Akamine's observation illustrates a subjective characteristic of the Delphi Technique when an attempt is made to quantify the responses. Although the Delphi Technique is a powerful tool, our experience points out that there is a slight problem in ranking items when they are quantified to reduce bias.

A second major factor is how the statements are written. Value-laden terms cause a shifting in rank upward or downward. It becomes extremely crucial that statements either be value free or reflect operationally defined terms. If included, value-laden items can cause a biased set of responses.

Stating or developing an initial set of items can be a problem. All selected respondents have some "intuitive" or "felt" needs or concerns, and it may be well to begin with these concerns. Or it may be even better to begin with an open-ended needs survey in which all respondents list what they consider the two or three major needs associated with the topic (as was done in Washington). These lists are then sent to a task force for editing and compilation. However, if the lists are very lengthy, additional editing, classifying, and grouping must take place so that a meaningful response pattern can be generated. Subjectivity may enter into the editing to select the second-round statements.

One last caution. Lists generated by a group can be biased from their inception, and valid needs or positions may therefore not even be listed by the respondents. If planners are to accomplish a major policy determination by the Delphi Technique, it may be prudent to retain an outside consultant to analyze each round of statements for its implied meanings and to synthesize statements or priorities that were not explicitly identified.

Since minority opinions are appended to the basic questionnaire, the chances of their moving up to top priorities are highly improbable if only three distributions of the questionnaire are used. However, if you desire to give respondents an opportunity to prioritize the appended minority opinions, then at least *four* questionnaires must be distributed. The second questionnaire contains the minority items for the first time. The third questionnaire shows how respondents ranked the minority items. And the fourth questionnaire requires further ranking and evaluating by the respondents. In my experience, *no* minority item has ever moved into the top-priority areas.

Table A-1 is a general summary of the Delphi Technique.

A Conference Planning Checklist*

Here are some tasks that may apply to the conference (or staff-development activity) that you have in mind.

Who does it?	When?	
		A. Arrange for Resource Persons
_____	_____	Contact prospective speakers
		Request speakers to
_____	_____	identify needed audiovisual equipment
_____	_____	prepare manuscript and photos for proceedings
_____	_____	supply photo for publicity
		Arrange for speakers'
_____	_____	transportation
_____	_____	lodging
_____	_____	meals
		Inform speakers about
_____	_____	total program and audience
_____	_____	meeting facilities
_____	_____	interviews with news staff
_____	_____	personal arrangements
		B. Arrange Meeting Facilities
_____	_____	Confirm availability of meeting rooms
_____	_____	Arrange podium and head table
		Arrange for the control of
_____	_____	lights
_____	_____	temperature
_____	_____	ventilation
_____	_____	P.A. system
_____	_____	recording equipment
_____	_____	Arrange props: ashtrays, signs, banners, water
		C. Arrange Teaching Materials for Registrants
_____	_____	Identification badges

*Adapted from "Conference Planning," prepared by James S. Long, Washington State University, Cooperative Extension Service, Pullman. Reprinted with permission.

Who does it?   **When?**

_____   _____   Requisition to reproduce
_____   _____   Distribute materials

D. Provide Audiovisual Support

_____   _____   Request projection equipment
_____   _____   Request operators
_____   _____   Design, prepare charts, slides
_____   _____   Supply easel, chalkboard

E. Publicize

Brochure

_____   _____   develop mailing list
_____   _____   draft copy
_____   _____   have duplicated
_____   _____   distribute brochures

Media

_____   _____   select appropriate media
_____   _____   determine dates of releases
_____   _____   prepare releases, ads; get photos
_____   _____   arrange for reporter at conference

F. Arrange Refreshments, Meals, Social Hour

_____   _____   Request written quotation
_____   _____   Select menu, price
_____   _____   Prepare tickets, distribute
_____   _____   Arrange seating, head table
_____   _____   Arrange program entertainment, MC

G. Conduct Preregistration and Final Registration

_____   _____   Plan clerical help and arrangement

Supply materials

_____   _____   receipts
_____   _____   parking permits
_____   _____   maps
_____   _____   facilities directory
_____   _____   conference readings
_____   _____   final schedule
_____   _____   Report tally

H. Determine Budget and Financial Terms

_____   _____   Estimate expenses and income (budget form attached)
_____   _____   Complimentary registrations, student registrations
_____   _____   Registration deadline, limit, refunds
_____   _____   Fees (registration, materials, meals proceedings, transportation)
_____   _____   Disposition of surpluses, deficits
                                   Pay speakers

Who does it?	When?	
_____	_____	per diem
_____	_____	honorarium
_____	_____	travel
_____	_____	Pay time-slip help
		I. Make Final Program Arrangements
_____	_____	Prepare and post directional signs
_____	_____	Plan for ushers
_____	_____	Orient speakers
_____	_____	Introduce speakers and other guests
_____	_____	Handle questions from the floor
_____	_____	Select someone to operate the house
		lights, project equipment, PA
		system, record talk
_____	_____	Introduce the method of evaluation
		Announce
_____	_____	late registration procedures
_____	_____	meal schedule
_____	_____	phone, info desk, postal service,
		paging system
_____	_____	list of participants
_____	_____	transportation, parking
		J. Evaluate
_____	_____	Establish criteria
_____	_____	Design
_____	_____	Conduct
_____	_____	Tally and summarize
_____	_____	Report
		K. Prepare Auxiliary Program for
		Spouses, Children
_____	_____	**L. Prepare Exhibits**
		M. Submit Forms
_____	_____	Request for conference facilities, lease
		agreement
_____	_____	Visiting Professor Form
_____	_____	Travel Authorization
_____	_____	Requisitions
_____	_____	Memoradum of Agreement
_____	_____	Vouchers
		N. Paper Sessions (Optional)
_____	_____	Criteria prepared
_____	_____	Call for papers
_____	_____	Panel reviews proposals
_____	_____	Sessions schedules
_____	_____	Participants informed
_____	_____	Program prepared

APPENDIX C

In-Service Activity Organizer*

School _____

Contact Person at School _____

Address _____

Telephone Area Code _____ Number _____ Extension _____

Conductor of Proposed Activity _____

Purpose of activity:

Objectives of activity:

Type of in-service activity:

_____ Awareness   _____ Application

_____ Implementation   _____ Maintenance (Follow-up for new
                                            personnel)
Participants:

_____ Teachers   _____ Administrators from central office

_____ School building administrators _____ Classified staff

Level of participants:

_____ Districtwide   _____ Secondary school   _____ Junior high school

_____ Elementary   _____ Other: specify

Expected number of participants _____

Length of activity: _____ Hours _____ Days _____ Weeks

Place _____

*Prepared by Donald C. Orlich, but adapted from Phillip T. Larson, "Conducted Metric Education Workshops—A Model" in *Successful Experiences in Teaching Metric*, Jeffrey V. Odom, ed., U.S. Department of Commerce, National Bureau of Standards (Washington, D.C.: USGPO, 1976) 58–59.

Address _____ Room number _____
Contact person at the site _____

Time of activity:
  Day of week _____ Date _____
  Beginning time _____ Ending time _____

Requested activity was initiated by:
  _____ Administrators _____ Teachers _____ Educational association representatives
  _____ Others: specify

Incentives:
  _____ In-service day contributed by district
  _____ College credit from (specify) _____
  _____ Participants paid to attend
  _____ Local education association sponsored
  _____ Credit granted for salary scale advancement
  _____ Released time for participants
  _____ Continuing Education Units (CEU)
  _____ Other: specify

Desired structure for conduct of activity:
  _____ Lecture   _____ Hands-on experiences
  _____ Discussions   _____ Laboratory
  _____ Films   _____ Demonstrations
  _____ Small groups   _____ Demonstration with school students

Media needed for activity:
  _____ Overhead projector   _____ Audiocassette recorder
  _____ 16 mm projector   _____ Playback unit
  _____ 35 mm slide projector   _____ Screen
  _____ 35 mm carousel projector   _____ Extension cords
  _____ VTR setup (specify type)   _____ 3-prong plug adaptor
  _____ Other: specify

Desired facilities:
  _____ Flat-top tables   _____ Electrical outlets   _____ Sinks
  _____ Desks   _____ Movable chairs   _____ Chalkboard
  _____ Water taps   _____ Tablet arm chairs   _____ Gas supply
                                                       _____ Other: specify

NOTE: If the furniture is to be arranged in some specific manner, sketch out here.

Needed print materials:

Other needed materials:

Backgrounds (i.e., to what extent are participants familiar with the topic to be presented):

What curriculum, textbook, or program will this in-service activity address? (Provide grade levels, series, or general description):

Under what educational organization pattern will the topic be used?
_____ Traditional classrooms   _____ Team-taught classes
_____ Open classrooms   _____ Other: specify

Status of those attending activity:
_____ Learners—Participants will learn from activity.
_____ Trainers—Participants will train others in the districts.
_____ Change-Agents—Participants will be initiators of change.
_____ Demonstration Personnel—Participants will demonstrate activities on call within district.

Long-range plans for this in-service activity:

Follow-up activities:

Other:

Microcomputers:
Specify exact brand, model and type of microcomputer to be used:
Brand:
Model:
Type:

Software Requirements:

APPENDIX D

MICROTEACHING

Experience is a great teacher. Those who administer or teach in the school know the value of preservice or university classes at the beginning of their educational careers. But the real payoff comes from the experience obtained through working with children, adolescents, young adults, or adults. The vast majority of educators learn from both positive and aversive school experiences. Of course, there are many who have had "one year of experience simply repeated twenty times." There is even a truism among faculty members who have taught for twenty or twenty-five years: if you watch the educational scene, you'll see the same techniques recycled about every ten years. But there have been several instances in which some new educational technique or method was implemented in the system, and teachers and administrators were forced to change some previously cherished behavior.

How do you practice new behaviors in an in-service setting? First, in-service environments must be safe. A "safe" environment means that, as teachers try out new techniques, they are not ridiculed for early failures. It means they can take some extra time to practice new techniques, and receive positive feedback and constructive criticism. This safe environment is not in the classroom, in front of twenty-eight or thirty-eight students.

Microteaching has long been used in preservice education as a means of providing practice in skill or behavior development. This technique also affords both beginning and advanced teachers excellent opportunities to plan and practice a wide array of new instructional strategies. My goal is not only to extend the use of microteaching but also to provide instructions to educators in applying this very effective method as an in-service technique.

What Is Microteaching?

Microteaching is a scaled-down teaching experience. Essentially, it is an opportunity for experienced professionals to develop or improve specific teaching skills with a small group of students (four to six) by means of brief (ten to fifteen minutes) single-concept lessons. These lessons are recorded on videotape for reviewing, refining, and analyzing of very specific teaching processes. Microteaching is a technique that allows the teacher to place small aspects of teaching "under the microscope."

Specifically, microteaching is an empirically tested procedure that allows an experienced teacher to:

_____ 1. Practice a new technique, strategy, or procedure in a supportive environment.
_____ 2. Prepare and deliver a lesson with a reduced amount of anxiety.
_____ 3. Test new ways of approaching a topic or lesson.
_____ 4. Develop very specific delivery techniques, such as introducing a topic, giving an assignment, or explaining an evaluation procedure.
_____ 5. Be evaluated both by others and by him or herself.
_____ 6. Gain immediate feedback of his or her performance by viewing the video playback.
_____ 7. Risk little but gain much in valuable experience.
_____ 8. Subdivide complex teaching interactions into related components.
_____ 9. Manage his or her own behavior in a systematic manner.

The microteaching approach to developing competencies is not without its drawbacks, and two questions have been raised about its effectiveness. How do you apply the effects of microteaching to real classes? Does it matter significantly that peers are not authentic students?

Answering these questions is easy. First, a teacher masters a teaching strategy through microteaching, and slowly and systematically uses the strategy in the classroom. Second, experiences with microteaching have shown that it is the practice that counts, not the composition of the "student" group.

But microteaching has considerable merit in its own right because, outside of the actual classroom setting, it provides the closest simulation of teaching yet devised. Staff-development directors strive for excellent, not merely satisfactory, performance, so educators need to practice skills with the constant goal of self-improvement. The Far West Educational Laboratory report shows that microteaching is a powerful way to change teaching behaviors (Borg and associates 1970).

As its basic objective, microteaching subdivides multifaceted teaching acts into simpler components so that the teacher learning new instructional skills can break the skills into manageable components. When in-service teachers engage in a microteaching lesson, they focus on a specific aspect of teaching until they develop a satisfactory minimum competency in that skill. If the skill is not mastered, then a "reteach" session is scheduled to perfect it. The teacher proceeds to a new skill only after achieving success with the preceding one. In some cases, it can take from ten to twenty trials.

Before developing microteaching lesson plans, however, there are several considerations to be discussed. First, not every topic, concept, or process automatically lends itself to every teaching method. Each concept needs to be analyzed to determine whether it is appropriate for a particular teaching method or for the time allotted to conduct the microclass.

Second, in situations where it is not possible to obtain school-age students for the teaching sessions, a modified form of microteaching can be used. For example, colleagues can be recruited to act as students. Because of limited time, the reteach sessions may need to be kept to a minimum.

Both cognitive skills (in the form of single-concept lessons) and processes can be perfected through microteaching. Single-concept lessons are described later in this section, but what are the processes of instruction?

The term *instructional process* refers to how a teacher performs a specific teaching act. Processes that can be learned through microteaching include:

____ **1.** Introducing a new topic or concept
____ **2.** Giving an assignment to a class
____ **3.** Specifying how students will be evaluated in the course
____ **4.** Asking questions
____ **5.** Handling complex explanations
____ **6.** Tutoring an individual or small group
____ **7.** Leading a discussion
____ **8.** Practicing inquiry and problem-solving skills
____ **9.** Providing summaries of student statements
____ **10.** Closing a discussion or a class period

This list is far from complete; you may think of many other processes. What is comforting to the in-service teacher is that microteaching allows him or her to practice a skill in safety. The reality is there, but not the harsh realism of a classroom. With microteaching, a teacher can isolate one tiny segment of the totality of teaching and practice it until he or she masters the process. In the past, few teachers had the opportunity to practice a skill before using it in a classroom.

Preparing for Microteaching

Microteaching is not just "getting up front and teaching." The technique requires that the behaviors to be practiced are prescribed carefully. As in "regular" daily lessons, the objective(s) must be specified. Furthermore, a set of criteria must be established by which to judge how effective the teacher is in accomplishing the desired skills, processes, or behaviors. The whole idea of microteaching is to help improve teaching techniques through practice, feedback, and evaluation.

Usually, microteaching sessions are only ten minutes long. To conduct a lesson, the instructor needs a portable videotape recorder, a TV camera, and a microphone for a videotape recorder (VTR) setup. Plan for at least one or two technicians (perhaps students or your peers in class) to help operate the equipment. If a VTR setup is not available, use a cassette audiotape recorder, which will be nearly as effective.

In preparing a microteaching lesson plan, the teacher should now be able to combine all the competencies he or she has learned. Here is an instructional objective to use in designing and demonstrating the lesson:

Within the prescribed time limit and focusing on a specific teaching process or technique, teach a preselected concept to either a peer group of approximately five students or five "real" students. The members of your mini-class must achieve the performance objective as stated in the lesson plan, or you must accomplish the teaching process that you have specified in the plan.

To accomplish this objective, perform the following tasks for each microteaching session:

____ **1.** Prepare a lesson plan, using an appropriate format.
____ **2.** Make two copies of your lesson plan: one for your group leader and one for your own use while microteaching.

____ 3. Teach the lesson to the student or peer group within the time limit stipulated for the particular microteaching session.

____ 4. Evaluate student achievement or your teaching performance by using a stated performance objective and a specific evaluation device.

____ 5. Play the role of student when not teaching: operate the recording equipment or evaluate other microteaching performances.

____ 6. Critique in writing, by using an evaluation instrument, the teaching of the other students in the group. Each group should also provide immediate oral feedback to the microteacher following each microlesson.

____ 7. Critique your own lesson after viewing and listening to the recording of the teaching. You may want to use a critique checklist or other evaluation criteria to aid in your self-evaluation.

____ 8. Reteach the lesson, time permitting, to master the new technique.

Deciding on Content and Lesson-Plan Format

One of the teacher's most critical decisions in preparing for a microteaching lesson is how to narrow the topic. The purpose of microteaching is to focus directly on one aspect of the teaching process at a time. To accomplish this, the teacher should select a single subconcept from the material to be learned and develop a lesson aimed at helping the microsession students learn this concept in the short span of time.

Initially, making a decision about the content is often difficult. It requires isolating those concepts, principles, rules, and facts that are most significant.

Once the concept has been selected for the microlesson, the next step is to develop a limited number (perhaps only one) of performance objectives. That is, the teacher needs to determine what behavior the microstudent is to manifest in relation to the concept and to what extent he or she is expected to recall, recognize, or apply the concept. The ulti-

MODEL D-1.
MICROTEACHING PLANNING CHECKLIST

CHECK WHEN COMPLETED	ACTIVITIES
_____	1. Entry level known.
_____	2. Instructional objective for unit properly written.
_____	3. Focus of single-concept lesson identified.
_____	4. Rationale clearly stated.
_____	5. Content determined.
_____	6. Instructional processes specified.
_____	7. Microsession evaluation or critique developed.
_____	8. Audiovisual materials and special instructional items prepared.
_____	9. Two copies of lesson plan completed (original for instructor; copy for self).
_____	10. Lesson delivered.
_____	11. Peer evaluations given.
_____	12. Tape replayed.
_____	13. Self-critique conducted.
_____	14. Decisions made on whether to reteach.

mate criterion of a plan's effectiveness is this, *Does it work during the actual implementation in the classroom?*

Microteaching Feedback

Once the teacher completes the lesson and receives immediate verbal and written feedback, he or she is ready for what may be the most significant aspect of the technique: self-evaluation. Replaying the microteaching sessions can be invaluable in helping to identify strengths and weaknesses in the particular teaching approach and strategy. The playback (learner feedback) of microteaching gives a teacher an approximation of how he or she appears, sounds, and interacts with students. In the interest of effectiveness and efficiency, the teacher should view the video recording as soon as possible after the session, preferably immediately.

Keep in mind that "feedback" implies constructive criticism. If an error is made, provide a positive suggestion, not merely "you missed. . . ." Microteaching is only as effective as the quality of the feedback given.

While observing the replay of a microsession, it is helpful to use an evaluation form that reflects appropriate criteria by which to judge the effectiveness of the teaching skills. Microteaching evaluation forms should address the specific techniques that are being practiced. Thus individual forms may have to be created. Model D-1 is a planning checklist to aid in conducting microsessions systematically.

REFERENCES

Alaska Effective Schooling Program (1981). Portland, Oreg.: Northwest Regional Educational Laboratory.

Aldridge, Bill G. (May 1988). "Federal Program Alert," *NSTA Report.* Washington, D.C.: National Science Teachers Association, 3 and 8.

Alkin, Marvin C. (1970). "Products for Improving Educational Evaluation." *Evaluation Comment, 3*(1), 1–4.

Ames, Carole and Russel Ames, eds. (1985). *Research on Motivation in Education, Volume 2: The Classroom Milieu.* Orlando: Academic Press.

Andrews, Richard (1987). "On Leadership and Student Achievement." *Educational Leadership, 45*(1), 9–16.

Andrews, Theodore E. (1981). "Improving Adult Learning Programs." In *Adult Learners: A Research Study,* Theodore E. Andrews, W. Robert Houston, and Branda L. Bryant. Washington, D.C.: Association of Teacher Educators.

Andrews, Theodore E., W. Robert Houston, and Branda L. Bryant (1981). *Adult Learners: A Research Study.* Washington, D.C.: Association of Teacher Educators.

Ashton, Patricia (1985). "Motivation and Teacher's Sense of Efficacy." In *Research on Motivation in Education, Volume 2: The Classroom Milieu,* Carole Ames and Russell Ames, eds. Orlando: Academic Press.

Aslin, Neil C. and John W. DeArman (1976). "Adoption and Abandonment of Innovative Practices in High Schools." *Educational Leadership, 33*(8), 601–606.

Baca, Robert B. (1979). *A Study of In-Service Effectiveness on Activity-Oriented Science Teaching.* Unpublished doctoral dissertation. Pullman: Washington State University.

Bacharach, Samuel B. and Sharon C. Conley (1986). "Education Reform: A Managerial Agenda." *Phi Delta Kappan, 67*(9), 641–645.

Bacharach, Samuel B., Scott C. Bauer, and Joseph B. Shedd (1986). *The Learning Workplace: The Conditions and Resources of Teaching.* Ithaca, N.Y.: Organizational Analysis and Practice.

Bacharach, Samuel B., Sharon Conley, and Joseph Shedd (1986). "Beyond Career Ladders: Structuring Teacher Career Development Systems." *Teachers College Record, 87*(4), 563–574.

Baldridge, J. Victor (1974). "Political and Structural Protection of Educational Innovations." In *What Do Research Findings Say About Getting Innovations into Schools: A Symposium*, Sanford Temkin and Mary V. Brown, eds. Philadelphia: Research for Better Schools, Inc., Publication No. OP-305, 12–15.

Bandura, Albert (1982). "Self-Efficacy Mechanism in Human Agency." *American Psychologist, 3*(2), 122–147.

Bancroft, Beverly A. and Laurence W. Lezotte (1985). "Growing Use of Effective Schools Model for School Improvement." *Educational Leadership, 42*(6), 23–27.

Banner, James M., Jr. (1985). *The Anatomy of Teacher Institutes: A Design For Professional Development*. Washington, D.C.: Council for Basic Education.

Barnett, Homer Garner (1953). *Innovation: The Basis of Cultural Change*. New York: McGraw-Hill.

Barth, Roland S. (1987). "The Principals' Center at Harvard University." *NASSP Bulletin, 71*(495), 23–29.

Barth, Roland S. (1986). "Principal Centered Professional Development." *Theory Into Practice, 25*(3), 156–160.

Bass, Gail V. (1978). *A Study of Alternatives in American Education, Vol. I: District Policies and the Implementation of Change*. Santa Monica, Calif.: Rand Corporation, R-2170/1-NIE.

Beck, William (1978). "Testing a Noncompetency In-Service Education Model Based on Humanistic or Third Force Psychology." *Education, 98*, 337–340.

Beiber, Roger L. (1979). *A Study of Decision-Making for In-Service Teacher Education*. Unpublished doctoral dissertation. Pullman: Washington State University.

Bell, Harry H., Jr., and John W. Peightel (1976). *Teacher Centers and In-Service Education*. (Fastback No. 71). Bloomington: Phi Delta Kappa Educational Foundation.

Bell, Terrel H. (1984). "American Education at a Crossroads." *Phi Delta Kappan, 65*(8), 531–534.

Berlin, Barney M., John G. Conyers, Walter Fricker, Kathleen B. Jensen, and Joanne Rooney (1987). "Teacher-2-Teacher: The Palatine Peer Coaching Program." *Journal of Staff Development, 8*(1), 21–24.

Berman, Barbara and Fredda J. Friederwitzer (1985). "The Turnkey Strategy: Multiplying the Benefits of Staff Development." *Journal of Staff Development, 6*(2), 33–40.

Berman, Paul, Perter W. Greenwood, Milbrey Wallin McLaughlin, and John Pincus (1975). *Federal Programs Supporting Educational Change, Vol. V: A Summary of the Findings in Review*. Santa Monica, Calif.: Rand Corporation, R-1589/4-HEW (ABR.)

Berman, Paul and Milbrey W. McLaughlin (1978). *Federal Programs Supporting Educational Change, Vol. VIII: Implementing and Sustaining Innovations*. Santa Monica, Calif.: Rand Corporation. (a)

Berman, Paul and Milbrey W. McLaughlin (1978). *Rethinking the Federal Role in Education*. Santa Monica, Calif.: Rand Corporation, Rand Paper Series, P-6114. (b)

Bethel, Lowell J. and Shirley M. Hord (1981). "A Case Study of Change: In-Service Teachers in a National Science Foundation Environment Science Education Program." Paper presented at the annual meeting of the American Educational Research Association, Los Angeles, Calif.

Betz, Loren, Darrell Jensen, and Patricia Zigarmi (1978). "South Dakota Teachers View In-Service Education." *Phi Delta Kappan* (Research notes), *59*(7), 491–493.

Bickel, William E., Stanley E. Denton, Judy A. Johnston, Paul G. LeMahieu, Deborah

Saltrick, and John R. Young (1987). "Clinical Teachers at the Schenley Teacher Center: Teacher Professionalism and Educational Reform." *Journal of Staff Development,* 8(2), 9–15.

Bickman, Leonard (1987). "The Functions of Program Theory." In *Using Program Theory in Evaluation,* Leonard Bickman, ed. San Francisco: Jossey-Bass, New Directions for Program Evaluation, No. 33.

Bierly, Margaret M. and David C. Berliner (1982). "The Elementary School Teacher as a Learner." *Journal of Teacher Education, 33*(6), 37–40.

Black, Max (1973). "Models and Archetypes." In *Philosophy of Educational Research,* Harry S. Broudy, Robert H. Ennis, and Leonard I. Krimerman, eds. New York: John Wiley and Sons, 483–501.

Blackwell, Ben (1987). Interview regarding Public School Employee Association's role in staff development, September 14, 1987.

Blase, Joseph J., Marlene I. Strahe, and Edward J. Pajak (1986). "A Theory of Teacher Performance: Preservice and Inservice Implications." *Contemporary Education, 57*(3), 138–143.

Blewett, Evelyn J., ed. (1969). *Elementary Teacher Training Models.* Washington, D.C.: U.S. Department of Health, Education, and Welfare, Office of Education, Bureau of Research, OE-58033.

Bloom, Benjamin S. (1968). "Learning for Mastery." *Evaluation Comment, 1*(1), 1–2.

Bloom, Benjamin S. (1982). "The Master Teachers." *Phi Delta Kappan, 63*(10), 664–668, 715.

Bloom, Benjamin S. (1984). "The 2 Sigma Problem: The Search for Methods of Group Interaction as Effective as One-to-One Tutoring." *Educational Researcher, 13*(6), 4–16.

Bloom, Benjamin S. et al. (1956). *Taxonomy of Educational Objectives: The Classification of Education Goals. Handbook I. Cognitive Domain.* New York: David McKay.

Blum, Robert E. and Jocelyn A. Butler (1985). "Managing by Improvement by Profiling." *Educational Leadership, 42*(6), 54–58.

✓ Blum, Robert E., Jocelyn A. Butler, and Nancey L. Olson (1987). "Leadership for Excellence: Research-Based Training for Principals." *Educational Leadership, 45*(1), 25–29.

Bolan, R., ed. (1982). *School-Focused In-Service Training.* London: Heinemann Education Books.

Boone, Edgar J. (1985). *Developing Programs in Adult Education.* Englewood Cliffs, N.J.: Prentice-Hall.

Borg, Walter R., Marjorie L. Kelley, Phillip Langer, and Meredith Gall (1970). *The Mini-Course: A Microteaching Approach to Teacher Education.* Beverly Hills, Calif.: Macmillan Educational Services, Inc.

Boschee, Floyd and Dennis D. Hein (1980). "How Effective is In-Service Education?" *Phi Delta Kappan* (Research notes), 61(6), 427.

Bredderman, Ted (1983). "The Effects of Activity-based Elementary Science on Student Outcome: A Quantitative Synthesis." *Review of Educational Research, 53,* 499–518.

Brickell, Henry M. (1964). "State Organization for Education Change: A Case Study and a Proposal." In *Innovation in Education,* Mathew B. Miles, ed. New York: Teachers College Press, Columbia University, 503.

Brimm, J. L. and D. J. Tollet (1974). "How do Teachers Feel About In-Service Education?" *Educational Leadership, 31,* 521–524.

204

Brodbeck, Mary (1973). "Models." In *Philosophy of Educational Research*, Harry S. Broudy, Robert H. Ennis, and Leonard I. Krimerman, eds. New York: John Wiley and Sons, 475–482.

Brookfield, Stephen D. (1986). *Understanding and Facilitating Adult Learning*. San Francisco: Jossey-Bass.

Brophy, Jere (1982). "Successful Teaching Strategies for the Inner City Child." *Phi Delta Kappan, 63*(8), 527 and 529.

Brophy, Jere and Thomas L. Good (1986). "Teacher Behaviorism and Student Achievement." In *Handbook of Research on Teaching*, Myron C. Wittrock, ed. (3rd ed.). New York: Macmillan.

Broughton, Diane K., Mark E. Crouch, and Gary W. Floyd (1978). *A Successful Implementation of an Innovation*. Unpublished field study. Pullman: Washington State University.

Cady, Lillian V. and Mark Johnson (1981). *The Joint Study of In-Service in Washington State*. Olympia: Washington State Board of Education and Council for Postsecondary Education.

Caldwell, Sarah DeJarnette (1986). "Effective Practices for Principals' Inservice." *Theory Into Practice, 25*(3), 174–178.

Carlson, Laurence B. and Robert E. Potter (1972). "Training Classroom Teachers to Provide In-Class Educational Services for Exceptional Children in Rural Areas." *Journal of School Psychology, 10*(2), 147–151.

Carlson, Richard O. (1965). *Adoption of Educational Innovations*. Eugene, Oreg.: University of Oregon, Center for the Advanced Study of Educational Administration. (a)

Carlson, Richard O. (1965). "Barriers to Change." In R. O. Carlson et al., *Change Processes in the Public Schools*. Eugene, Oreg.: University of Oregon, Center for the Advanced Study of Educational Administration, 4–7. (b)

Carmichael, Oliver C. (1962). "A Hundred Years of the Land-Grant Movement." *Saturday Review, 45*(April 21), 58–59, 71–72.

Carney, Maureen, Evelyn M. Davila, Morile Graubard, Meg Gwaltney, Marvinia Hunter, and Nicki King (1979). *In-Service Training in Desegregated School Districts: Eastern Region Case Studies*. Santa Monica, Calif.: Rand Corporation, a Rand Note prepared for the National Institute of Education, Rand-N-1251-NIE. (a)

Carney, Maureen (ed.), Evelyn M. Davila, Rita Mahard, and Beth Osthimer (1979). *In-Service Training in Desegregated Districts: Midwest Region Case Studies*. Santa Monica, Calif.: Rand Corporation, a Rand Note prepared for the National Institute of Education, Rand-N-1252-NIE. (b)

Carroll, John (1963). "A Model of School Learning." *Teachers College Record, 64*(1), 723–733.

Caruso, Joseph J. (1985). "The Role of Teacher Advisors in Improving Writing Instruction." *Journal of Staff Development, 6*(2), 67–73.

Charters, W. W., Jr., et al. (1973). *The Process of Planned Change in the School's Instructional Organization*. Eugene, Oreg.: University of Oregon, Center for the Advanced Study of Educational Administration.

Clinton, Bill (1986). "Who Will Manage the Schools?" *Phi Delta Kappan, 68*(4), 208–210.

Codianni, Anthony V. and Gretchen Wilbur (1983). *More Effective Schooling from Research to Practice*. ERIC Clearinghouse on Urban Education, New York: Teachers College, Columbia University. ERIC/CUE Urban Diversity Series No. 83. ERIC/EDRS 236 299.

Cogan, Morris L. (1975). "Current Issues in the Education of Teachers." In *Teacher Education*, Kevin Ryan, ed. National Society for the Study of Education Yearbook, Part II. Chicago: University of Chicago Press, 5.

Cohen, Elizabeth G. and Theresa R. L. Perez (1980). *Organizational Model for School Change Memorandum*. Final Report (Grant No. OB-NIE-78-0212), (P-4). Palo Alto, Calif.: Stanford University, National Institute of Education.

Cole, Richard D. (1987). *A Model to Determine the Fiscal Impact of the Legislative Evaluation and Accountability Program (LEAP) on Staff Development in Selected Washington School Districts*. Unpublished doctoral dissertation. Pullman: Washington State University.

Coleman, James S., Ernest Q. Campbell, Carol J. Hobson, James McPartland, Alexander M. Mead, Frederick D. Weinfeld, and Robert L. York (1966). *Equality of Educational Opportunity*. Washington, D.C.: U.S. Government Printing Office.

Coleman, James S. (1975). "Recent Trends in School Integration." *Educational Researcher, 4*(7), 12.

Coleman, James S. (1977). "Population Stability and Equal Rights." *Society, 14*(4), 34–36.

Combs, Arthur W., ed. (1962). *Perceiving, Behaving, Becoming*. Washington, D.C.: National Education Association, Yearbook for Association for Supervision and Curriculum Development.

Commission of the Reorganization of Secondary Education, National Education Association (1918). *Cardinal Principles of Secondary Education*. Washington, D.C.: U.S. Government Printing Office.

Comptroller General of the United States (1977). *Social Research and Development of Limited Use to National Policymakers*. Washington, D.C.: U.S. Government Printing Office, HRD-77-34, Report to the Congress.

Conant, James B. (1959). *The American High School Today: A First Report to Interested Citizens*. New York: McGraw-Hill.

Conran, Patricia C. and Aurora Chase (1982). "The Extended Year Program in Suburban Chicago: A Different Approach to In-Service Training. *Phi Delta Kappan, 63*(6), 398–399.

Corbett, H. Dickson, Judith A. Dawson, and William A. Firstone (1984). *School Context and School Change: Implications for Effective Planning*. New York: Teachers College Press, Columbia University.

Costello, John (1986). Interview, Ellensburg, Washington, State Staff Development Conference, April 30.

Coward, Raymond T., ed. (1977). *Planned Educational Change: The Experimental Schools Experience*. Washington, D.C.: U.S. Department of Health, Education and Welfare, National Institute of Education.

Craven, Evelyn M. (1978). *An Evaluation of an Implementation Model for Elementary Schools Science*. Unpublished doctoral dissertation. Pullman: Washington State University.

Criteria of Excellence: District In-Service (1979). Juneau: Alaska Department of Education.

"Critical Issues in Staff Development" (Spring, 1986). *Journal of Staff Development, 7*(1), 80–98.

Cross, Ray (1981). "Teachers Know Their Own In-Service Needs." *Phi Delta Kappan*, *62*(7), 94–98.

Cruickshank, Donald R., Christopher Lorish, and Linda Thompson (1979). "What We Think We Know About In-Service Education." *Journal of Teacher Education*, *30*(1), 27–32.

Cuban, Larry (1982). "Persistent Instruction: The High School Classroom, 1900–1980." *Phi Delta Kappan*, *64*(2), 113–118.

Cuban, Larry (1986). "Persistent Instruction: Another Look at the Constancy in the Classroom." *Phi Delta Kappan*, *68*(1), 7–11.

Culberston, Jack A. and Luvern L. Cunningham, eds. (1986). *Microcomputers and Education*, Eighty-fifth Yearbook of the National Society for the Study of Education, Part 1. Chicago: University of Chicago Press, ix–x.

Dale, E. Lawrence (1985). "Proposed Staff Development Model." Unpublished paper. Pullman: Washington State University.

Daresh, John C. and James C. LaPlant (1985). "Developing a Research Agenda for Administrator Inservice." *Journal of Research and Development in Education*, *18*(2), 39–43.

Daresh, John C. (1986). "Support for Beginning Principals: First Hurdles are Highest." *Theory Into Practice*, *25*(3), 168–173.

Davis, Edward and Tom Morgan (1986). *Wellness—A Staff Development Program for Any District*. Paper presented at the National Staff Development Council Annual Conference, Atlanta, December 16, 1986.

Deal, Terrance E. and Lynn D. Celotti (1980). "How Much Influence Do (and Can) Educational Administrators Have on Classrooms? *Phi Delta Kappan*, *61*(7), 471–473.

Digest of Education Statistics 1983–84. (1983). U.S. Department of Education, National Center for Education Statistics, Washington, D.C.: U.S. Government Printing Office, table 65, 80.

Dillman, Don A. (1978). *Mail and Telephone Surveys: The Total Design Method*. New York: John Wiley & Sons.

Dillon-Peterson, Betty, ed. (1981). *Staff Development/Organization Development*. Alexandria, Va.: Association for Supervision and Curriculum Development.

Dimperio, Joseph C. (1987). "The Teaching Clinic." *Journal of Staff Development*, *8*(2), 16–17.

Directory of Inservice Training Programs for Principals (1982). Washington, D.C.: National Institute of Education, Program on Educational Policy and Management.

Donaldson, Gordon A., Jr. (1987). "The Maine Approach to Improving Principal Leadership." *Educational Leadership*, *45*(1), 43–46.

Duke, Daniel L. (1987). *School Leadership and Instructional Improvement*. New York: Random House.

Edelfelt, Roy A., ed. (1977). *In-Service Education: Criteria for and Examples of Local Programs*. Bellingham, Wash.: Western Washington State College.

Edelfelt, Roy A. and Margo Johnson, eds. (1975). *Rethinking In-Service Education*. Washington, D.C.: National Education Association.

Edmonds, Ronald (1979). "Effective Schools for the Urban Poor." *Educational Leadership*, *37*(1), 15–27.

Edmonds, Ronald (1979). "Some Schools Work and More Can." *Social Policy*, *9*(5), 28–32.

Edson, C. H. (1983). "Risking the Nation." *Issues in Education*, *1*(2 & 3), 171–184.

Eisner, Elliot W. (1984). "Can Educational Research Inform Educational Practice?" *Phi Delta Kappan*, 65(7), 447–452.

Eisner, Elliot W. (1985). *The Art of Educational Evaluation: A Personal View.* Philadelphia: Falmer Press.

Ellis, Susan (1982). "Matching Evaluation to the Type of Staff Development Activity at the Building Level." *Journal of Staff Development*, 3(1), 48–55.

"Employers Lead in Job Training, Study Suggests." *Education Week* (July 27, 1983), 3.

Engelking, Jeri L. (1986). "Teacher Job Satisfaction and Dissatisfaction." *ERS Spectrum*, 4(1), 33–38.

Fayol, Henri (1949). *General and Industrial Management*, translated by C. Stores. London: Sir Isaac Pitman and Sons.

Feiman, Sharon, ed. (1978). *Teacher Centers: What Place in Education?* Chicago: University of Chicago Press, Center for Policy Study.

Feiman, Sharon (1981). "Exploring Connections Between Different Kinds of Educational Research and Different Conceptions of In-Service Education." *Journal of Research and Development in Education*, 14(2), 11–21.

Feistritzer, C. Emily and Rhonda J. McMillion (1979). *The 1980 Report on Educational Personnel Development.* Washington, D.C.: Feistritzer Publications.

Fennell, B. H., W. L. Hill, and S. J. Thiessen (1980). *Teacher In-Service Training Costs: A Staff Study.* Edmonton, Alberta: Alberta Department of Education. ERIC/EDRS No. ED 198 072.

Fenstermacher, Gary D. and David C. Berliner (1983). *A Conceptual Framework for the Analysis of Staff Development.* Santa Monica, Calif.: Rand Corporation, N-2046-NIE.

Ferver, Jack C. (1980). *University Collaboration in School In-Service.* Unpublished report. Madison: University of Wisconsin Extension.

A Five-Year Plan for Professional Development (1985). Madison, Connecticut: Madison Public Schools, 57 pp.

Flakus-Mosqueda, Patricia (1983). *Survey of States' Teacher Policies.* Denver: Education Commission of the States, Working Paper No. 2.

Fontana, Jean (1986). "Teacher Centers: A Costly Innovation." *Delta Kappa Gamma Bulletin*, 53(1), 27–30.

A Foundation Goes to School (1972). New York: Ford Foundation.

Franco, James and Donald Zundel (1986). "Project Impact: A Comprehensive Approach to Staff Development." *Journal of Staff Development*, 7(1), 67–79.

Fullan, Michael (1982). *The Meaning of Educational Change.* New York: Teachers College Press, Columbia University.

Fullan, Michael and Alan Pomfret (1977). "Research in Curriculum and Instruction Implementation." *Review of Educational Research*, 47(2), 335–397.

Fullan, Michael, Matthew B. Miles, and Gib Taylor (1980). "Organization Development in Schools: The State of the Art." *Review of Educational Research*, 50(2), 121–183.

Gage, N. L. (1963). "Paradigms for Research on Teaching." In *Handbook of Research on Teaching*, N. L. Gage, ed. Chicago: Rand McNally and Company, 94–141.

Gall, Meredith D. and Ronald S. Renchler (1985). *Effective Staff Development for Teachers: A Research-Based Model.* Eugene, Oreg.: ERIC Clearinghouse on Education Management, University of Oregon.

Gardner, John W. (1961). *Excellence: Can We Be Equal and Excellent Too?* New York: Harper & Row.

Garman, Noreen B. and Helen M. Hazi (1988). "Teachers Ask: Is There Life After Madeline Hunter?" *Phi Delta Kappan, 69*(9), 669–672.

Gerla, Samuel E. (1987). "Inservice Needs of Superintendents in Small Sized School Districts." Paper/panel presented at the National Staff Development Council, Annual Conference, Seattle, December 2, 1987.

Getzels, Jacob W. (1959). "Administration as a Social Process." In *Administrative Theory*, D. E. Griffiths, ed. New York: Appleton-Century-Crofts, 150–165.

Glassberg, Sally and Sharon N. Oja (1981). "A Developmental Model for Enhancing Teachers' Personal and Professional Growth." *Journal of Research and Development in Education, 14*(2), 58–70.

Glickman, Carl D. (1986). "Developing Teacher Thought." *Journal of Staff Development, 7*(1), 6–21.

Goldberg, Herman R. (1986). "In the Works: AASA Assessment Center." *School Administrator, 43*(3), 16–17.

Gomery, Jill and Rex Crouse, (1987). "The Oregon Consortium for Instructional Coaching." *Journal of Staff Development, 8*(2), 18–20.

Good, Carter V., ed. (1973). *Dictionary of Education* (3rd ed.). New York: McGraw-Hill.

Good, Thomas L. (1982). "How Teachers' Expectations Affect Results." *American Education, 18*(10), 25–32.

Good, Thomas and Douglas A. Grouws (1987). "Increasing Teachers' Understanding of Mathematical Ideas Through In-Service Training." *Phi Delta Kappan, 68*(10), 778–783.

Goodlad, John I. (1955). "The Individual School and its Principal: Key Setting and Key Positions in Educational Leadership." *Educational Leadership, 13*(1), 2–6.

Goodlad, John I. (1975). *The Dynamics of Educational Change: Toward Responsive Schools*. New York: McGraw-Hill.

Goodlad, John I. (1978). "A Preview of Schooling in America." *Phi Delta Kappan, 60*(1), 47–50.

Goodlad, John I. (1984). *A Place Called School*. New York: McGraw-Hill.

Goodlad, John I., ed. (1987). *The Ecology of School Renewal*. Eighty-sixth Yearbook of the National Society for the Study of Education, Part I. Chicago: University of Chicago Press.

Goodlad, John I. and M. Frances Klein (1970). *Behind the Classroom Door*. Worthington, Ohio: Charles A. Jones Publishing Co.

Gordon, Jack (1986). "Where the Training Goes." *Training, 23*(10), 49–63.

Gray, James and Miles Myers (1978). "The Bay Area Writing Project." *Phi Delta Kappan, 59*(6), 410–413.

Greenwood, Peter W., Dale Mann, and Milbrey Wallin McLaughlin (1975). *Federal Programs Supporting Educational Change Vol. III: The Process of Change*. Santa Monica, Calif.: Rand Corporation, R-1589/1-HEW.

Greer, C. (1970). *The Principal as Educator*. New York: Center for Urban Education. ERIC/EDRS No. ED 054 537.

Griffin, Gary A., ed. (1983). *Staff Development*. Part II, Eighty-second Yearbook of the National Society for the Study of Education. Chicago: University of Chicago Press.

Gross, Albert C. (1978). *Human Factors in Productivity Improvement Project. Volume I: Case Study*. San Diego, Calif.: General Services Department. ERIC/EDRC No. ED 736, 269, PB-300 232/6.

Gudridge, Beatrice M. (1980). *Teacher Competency: Problems and Solutions*. (AASA

Critical Issues Report). Sacramento, Calif.: American Association of School Administrators.

Guide for In-Service Instruction: Science—A Process Approach (1967). (AASA Misc. Publication 67-9). Washington, D.C.: Commission on Science Education.

Gulick, Luther (1937). "Notes on the Theory of Organization." In *Papers on the Science of Administration*, Luther Gulick and L. Urwick, eds. New York: Institute of Public Administration.

Guskey, Thomas R. (1984). "The Influence of Change in Instructional Effectiveness Upon the Affective Characteristics of Teachers." *American Educational Research Journal, 21*(2), 245–259.

Guskey, Thomas R. (1986). "Staff Development and the Process of Teacher Change." *Educational Researcher, 15*(5), 5–12.

—Hackman, Elaine (1982). "Staff Development Data Banks: Taking Evaluation Beyond 'Happiness Quotients.'" *Journal of Staff Development, 3*(1), 71–83.

Hagstron, David (1987). "The Alaska Principals' Center." *NASSP Bulletin, 71*(495), 30–34.

Hall, Burnis, Jr. (1985). "A Building Level Staff Development Model That Works." *Catalyst for Change, 14*(3), 8–11.

Hall, Gene E. (1986). *Beyond the Looking Glass: Recommendations & Critical Warnings for Teacher Educational Practitioners, Policymakers & Researchers.* Austin, Tex.: Research and Development Center for Teacher Education. ERIC/EDRS No. ED 270 451.

Hall, Gene E. and Shirley M. Hord (1987). *Change in Schools: Facilitating the Process.* Albany: State University of New York Press.

Hall, Gene E. and Susan F. Loucks (1978). "Teacher Concerns as a Basis for Facilitating and Personalizing Staff Development." *Teacher College Record, 80*(1), 36–53.

Hall, Gene E. and Susan F. Loucks (1981). "Program Definition and Adoption: Implications for Inservice." *Journal of Research and Development in Education, 14*(2), 46–58.

✓ Hall, Gene E., Susan F. Loucks, William L. Rutherford, and Beulah N. Newlove (1975). "Levels of Use of the Innovation: A Framework for Analyzing Innovation Adoption." *Journal of Teacher Education, 26*(1), 52–56.

✓ Hannaford, Marion E. and Donald C. Orlich (1987). *Applying Evaluation Theory to Assess an Inservice Program.* Unpublished paper. Pullman: Washington State University.

Hansen, Ruth Anne and Donald C. Orlich (1980). "A Preliminary Study of Legislated Innovations For Higher Education (or) Do Shotgun Weddings Really Endure?" *Phi Delta Kappan, 61*(6), 426–427.

Hardie, C. D. (1973). "Research and Progress in Education." In *Philosophy of Educational Research*, Harry S. Broudy, Robert H. Ennis, and Leonard I. Krimerman, eds. New York: John Wiley & Sons, 90–91.

Harnischfeger, Annegret and David E. Wiley (1975). *Achievement Test Score Decline: Do We Need To Worry.* Chicago: ML-Group for Policy Studies in Education, Central Mid-Western Regional Educational Laboratory.

Harris, Ben M. (1980). *Improving Staff Performance Through In-Service Education.* Boston: Allyn and Bacon.

Harris, Ben M. (1986). *Developmental Teacher Evaluation.* Boston: Allyn and Bacon.

Harris, Elayne M. (1984). "Planning and Managing Workshops for Results." In *Designing and Implementing Effective Workshops.* Thomas J. Sork, ed. San Francisco: Jossey-Bass, New Directions for Continuing Education, No. 22, 39–53.

Havelock, Ronald G. (1968). "Dissemination and Translation Roles." In *Knowledge Production and Utilization in Educational Administration*, Terry L. Eidell and Joanne M. Kitchel, eds. Eugene, Oreg.: Center for the Advanced Study of Educational Administration, University of Oregon, 74–119.

Hearn, Norman E. (1969). *Innovative Educational Programs: A Study of Their Influence of Selected Variables Upon Their Continuation Following the Termination of Three-Year ESEA Title III Grants.* Unpublished doctoral dissertation. Washington, D.C.: George Washington University. ERIC/EDRS No. ED 032 448.

Hearn, Norman E. (1970). "A Study of the Adoption Rate of ESEA Title III Innovations When Federal Funds Were Terminated." *Phi Delta Kappan, 52*(1), 59–61.

Heath, Rachael, Marilyn Miller, Wanda McDaniel, and Fern Mann (1987). "The Teacher Renewal Institute." *Journal of Staff Development, 8*(2), 30–33.

Heath, Stanley P. and Donald C. Orlich (1977). "Determining Costs of Educational Technology: An Exploratory Review and Analysis." *Educational Technology, 17*(2), 26–33.

Helmer, Olaf (1967). *Analysis of the Future: The Delphi Method.* Santa Monica, Calif.: Rand Corporation.

Henderson, Euan S. (1979). "The Concept of School-Focused In-Service Education and Training." *British Journal of Teacher Education, 5*, 17–25.

Hersey, Paul W. (1986). "Selecting and Developing Educational Leaders." *School Administrator, 43*(3), 16–17.

Hersey, Paul and Kenneth H. Blanchard (1982). *Management of Organizational Behavior: Utilizing Human Resources* (4th ed.). Englewood Cliffs, N.J.: Prentice-Hall.

Herzberg, Frederick (1976). *The Managerial Choice to be Human.* Homewood, Ill.: Dow Jones-Irwin.

Hill, Glenys (1987). *A Study of Teacher Compensation Plans.* Unpublished paper. Pullman: Washington State University.

Hofstadter, Richard (1963). *Anti-Intellectualism in American Life.* New York: Alfred Knopf.

Hord, Shirley M., William L. Rutherford, Leslie Huling-Austin, and Gene E. Hall (1987). *Taking Charge of Change.* Alexandria, Va.: Association for Supervision and Curriculum Development.

Houle, Cyril O. (1980). *Continuing Learning in Professions.* San Francisco: Jossey-Bass.

House, Ernest R. (1978). "Assumptions Underlying Evaluation Models." *Educational Researcher, 7*(3), 4–12.

House, Ernest R. (1983). "How We Think About Evaluation." In *Philosophy of Evaluation*, Ernest R. House, ed. San Francisco: Jossey-Bass, New Directions for Program Evaluation, No. 19.

House, Ernest R. (1974). *The Politics of Educational Innovation.* Berkeley: McCutchan Publishing Corporation.

Houston, W. Robert, ed. (1986). *Mirrors of Excellence.* Reston, Va.: Association of Teacher Educators.

Houston, W. Robert and H. Jerome Frieberg (1979). "Perpetual Motion, Blindman's Bluff and In-Service Education." *Journal of Teacher Education, 30*(1), 7–9.

Howey, Kenneth R. (1977). "A Framework for Planning Alternative Approaches to In-service Education." In *Planning In-service Teacher Education: Promising Alternatives.* Washington, D.C.: American Association of Colleges for Teacher Education and the ERIC Clearinghouse on Teacher Education.

Howey, Kenneth R., R. Bents, and Dean Corrigan, eds. (1981). *School-Focused In-Service: Descriptions and Discussions*. Reston, Va.: Association of Teacher Educators.

Howsam, Robert B. (1967). "Effecting Needed Changes in Education." In *Planning and Effecting Needed Changes in Education*, Edgar L. Morphet and Charles O. Ryan, eds. Denver: Publishers Press, Designing Education for the Future: An Eight State Project, 65–81.

Howsam, Robert B. (1974). "Governance of Teacher Education by Consortium." In *Governance by Consortium*, J. H. Hansen, ed. Syracuse: Multi-State Consortium on Performance-Based Teachers Education, 18.

Huberman, A. Michael and Matthew B. Miles (1986). "Rethinking the Quest for School Improvement: Some Findings from the DESSI Study." In *Rethinking School Improvement: Research, Craft, and Concept*, Ann Lieberman, ed. New York: Teachers College Press, Columbia University.

Huddle, Eugene W. and Jane Hammond. (1987). "The Maryland Professional Development Academy." *NASSP Bulletin, 71*(495), 14–16.

Huefner, Robert P. (1967). "Strategies and Procedures in State and Local Planning." In *Planning and Effecting Needed Changes in Education*, E. L. Morphet and C. O. Ryan, eds. Denver: Publishers Press.

Hughes, Larry W. (1986). "Applying Assessment Center Technology: A Modest Proposal to School Study Councils." *Catalyst for Change, 15*(3), 17–20.

Huling-Austin, Leslie (1986). "What Can and Cannot Reasonably Be Expected From Teacher Induction Programs." *Journal of Teacher Education, 37*(1), 2–5.

Hunter, Madeline (1985). "What's Wrong with Madeline Hunter?" *Educational Leadership, 42*(6), 59–60.

In-Service Education of Teachers; Research Summary 1966-SI (1966). Research Division, National Education Association. Washington, D.C.: National Educational Association, 3. ERIC/EDRS No. ED 002 728.

Interim Progress Report: In-Service Training for School District Personnel (1974). Unpublished document. Tallahassee: Florida Department of Education.

Jackson, Philip W. (1971). "Old Dogs and New Tricks: Observations on the Continuing Education of Teachers." In *Improving In-Service Education: Proposals and Procedures for Change*, Louis J. Rubin, ed. Boston: Allyn and Bacon, 19–36.

Jackson, Philip W. (1986). *The Practice of Teaching*. New York: Teachers College Press, Columbia University.

Jencks, Christopher et al. (1972). *Inequality: A Reassessment of the Effect of Family and Schooling in America*. New York: Basic Books.

Johnson, Margo (1980). *In-Service Education: Priority for the '80s*. Syracuse: National Council of States on In-Service Education.

Johnson, Susan Moore (1986). "Incentives for Teachers: What Motivates, What Matters." *Educational Administration Quarterly, 22*(3), 54–79.

Jordan, William (1987). *Thirteen Evaluation Methods for In-Service Education Projects*. Unpublished paper. Pullman: Washington State University.

Joyce, Bruce R. and Beverly Showers (1982). "The Coaching of Teaching." *Educational Leadership, 40*(1), 4–8, 10.

Joyce, Bruce and Beverly Showers (1987). "Low Cost Arrangement for Peer Coaching." *Journal of Staff Development, 8*(1), 22–24.

Joyce, Bruce and Beverly Showers (1988). *Student Achievement Through Staff Development*. New York: Longman.

Joyce, Bruce R., K. M. McNair, R. Diaz, F. McKibbin, Floyd T. Waterman, and Michael G. Baker (1976). *Interviews: Perceptions, Purposes, and Practices.* In-Service Teacher Education Report II. Palo Alto, Calif.: Stanford Center for Research and Development in Teaching.

Joyce, Bruce R., Kenneth R. Howey, Sam J. Yarger, William C. Hill, Floyd T. Waterman, Barbara A. Vance, Donald W. Parker, and Michael G. Baker (1976). *Issues to Face.* In-Service Teacher Education Report I. Palo Alto, Calif.: Stanford Center for Research and Development in Teaching.

Kalbacken, Joan (1986). "Employee Assistance Programs: Costly Innovations?" *Delta Kappa Gamma Bulletin, 53*(1), 53–57.

Kane, Michael and Cheryl Chase (1983). *Staff Development.* Denver: Education Commission of the States, Working paper No. TF-83-4.

Kaplan, Philip (1980). *The Cost and Efficient Utilization of Resources. Synthesis Report. In-Service Education and Training of Teachers: Towards New Policies.* Paris, France: Organization for Economic Cooperation and Development, Centre for Educational Research and Innovation. ERIC/EDRS No. ED 198 097.

King, Nicki (1980). *The Role of School Administrators in Staff Development.* Santa Monica, Calif.: Rand Corporation, the Rand Paper Series, P-6536.

Kingrey, Joan (1987). "Instructional Equity." *School Directors Signal, 34*(6), 5–6.

Kipp, William, Arthur N. Thayer, and James L. Olivero (1981). *Project Leadership—Introductory Component* (Fifth printing and revised edition). Newport Beach, Calif.: Association of California School Administrators.

Knowles, Malcolm S. (1984). *Andragogy in Action.* San Francisco: Jossey-Bass.

Knowles, Malcolm S. (1986). *Using Learning Contracts: Practical Approaches to Individualizing and Structuring Learning.* San Francisco: Jossey-Bass.

Knox, Alan B. (1986). *Helping Adults Learn.* San Francisco: Jossey-Bass.

Kohlberg, Lawrence (1971). "From Is to Ought." In *Cognitive Development and Epistemology,* T. Mischel, ed. New York: Academic Press.

Koller, Geraldine R. (1977). *The Effectiveness of an Implementation of an Elementary School Science Program with a Science Resource Supply Center.* Unpublished doctoral dissertation. Pullman: Washington State University.

Korinek, Lori, Rex Schmid, and Martha McAdams. (1985). "Inservice Types and Best Practice," *Journal of Research and Development in Education, 18*(2), 33–38.

Kottkamp, Robert B., Eugene F. Provenzo, Jr., and Marilyn M. Cohen (1986). "Stability and Change In a Profession: Two Decades of Teacher Attitudes, 1964–1984." *Phi Delta Kappan, 67*(8), 559–567.

Krathwohl, David R., Benjamin S. Bloom, and Bertram B. Masia (1964). *Taxonomy of Educational Objectives: The Classification of Educational Goals. Handbook 2. Affective Domain.* New York: David McKay.

Kuhn, Thomas S. (1962). *The Structure of Scientific Revolutions.* Chicago: University of Chicago Press.

LaBolle, Larry D. (1983). *A Model to Determine the Fiscal Impact of Staff Development in Selected Alaskan School Districts.* Unpublished doctoral dissertation. Pullman: Washington State University.

LaPlant, James C. (1986). "Collegial Support for Professional Development and School Improvement." *Theory Into Practice, 25*(3), 185–190.

Lawrence, Gordon (1982). "A Synthesis of Research on the Effectiveness of Staff Development Programs." *In-Service*. Syracuse: National Council of States on In-Service Education, 10.

Lee, Chris (1986). "Training Profiles: The View from Ground Level." *Training, 23*(10), 76–83.

Lemke, Cheryl (1985). "Report on Computer/Technology Education Programs." Olympia, Wash.: State Superintendent of Public Instruction.

Levine, Sarah L. (1986). "The Principals' Center Movement: When School Leaders Become Learners." *The Journal of Staff Development, 7*(2), 28–41.

Lieberman, Ann, ed. (1986). *Rethinking School Improvement: Research, Craft, and Concept*. New York: Teachers College Press, Columbia University.

Lieberman, Ann and Lynne Miller, eds. (1979). *Staff Development: New Demands, New Realities, New Perspectives*. New York: Teachers College Press, Columbia University.

Lieberman, Ann and Lynne Miller (1984). *Teachers, Their World and Their Work*. Alexandria, Va.: Association for Supervision and Curriculum Development.

Lipham, James M. (1981). *Effective Principal: Effective School*. Reston, Va.: National Association of Secondary School Principals.

Little, Judith Warren (1982). "Norms of Collegiality and Experimentation: Workplace Conditions of School Success." *American Educational Research Journal, 19*(3), 325–340.

Litzenberger, Jerry P. (1979). "Behavioral In-Service." *In-Service*. Syracuse: National Council of States on In-Service Education, 4, 5, 7–10.

Loacker, Georgine (1986). "The Springfield Link: What Research Says About Learning." *NASSP Bulletin, 70*(486), 38–40.

Lortie, Dan C. (1975). *School Teacher: A Sociological Study*. Chicago: University of Chicago Press.

Lortie, Dan C. (1986). "Teacher Status in Dade County: A Case of Structural Strain?" *Phi Delta Kappan, 67*(8), 568–575.

Lottich, Kenneth V. (1974). *New England Transplanted*. Dallas: Royal Publishing Company.

Loucks, Susan F. (1983). "At Last: Some Good News From a Study of School Improvement." *Educational Leadership, 41*(3), 4–5.

Loucks, Susan F. and Gene E. Hall (1977). "Assessing and Facilitating the Implementation of Innovation: A New Approach." *Educational Technology, 17*(2), 18–21.

Loucks, Susan F. and Marge Melle (1982). "Evaluation of Staff Development: How Do You Know It Works?" *Journal of Staff Development, 3*(1), 102–117.

Loucks, Susan F. and David A. Zacchei (1983). "Applying Our Findings to Today's Innovations." *Educational Leadership, 41*(3), 28–33.

Loucks-Horsley, Susan, Catherine K. Harding, Margaret A. Arbuckle, Lynn B. Murray, Cynthia Dubea, and Martha I. Williams (1987). *Continuing to Learn: A Guidebook for Teacher Development*. Andover, Mass. and Oxford, Ohio: Regional Laboratory for Educational Improvement of the Northeast and Islands and National Staff Development Council.

Loucks-Horsley, Susan and Patricia L. Cox (1985). "What the National Commissions and Studies of Education Overlooked: The 'How' of School Change." *Journal of Staff Development, 4*(1), 21–28.

Lowney, Roger G. (1986). *Mentor Teachers: The California Model*. Bloomington, Ind.: Phi Delta Kappa Educational Foundation, Fastback Series, No. 247.

Lutz, J. P. (1976). "Statewide Survey with Implications for In-Service Education." *In-Service*. Syracuse: National Council of States on In-Service Education, 1–2.

Marsh, David D. and Maryalice Jordon-Marsh (1986). "Addressing Teachers' Personal Concerns about Innovations Through Staff Development." *Spectrum*, 4(2), 41–47.

Marshall, Jon C. and Sarah D. Caldwell (1984). "How Valid Are Formal, Informal Needs Assessment Methods for Planning Staff Development Programs?" *NASSP Bulletin*, 68(475), 24–30.

Maryland Department of Education (1978). *Process Evaluation: A Comprehensive Study of Outliers*. Baltimore, Md.: Maryland State Department of Education, Center for Education Research and Development, University of Maryland. ERIC/EDRS No. ED 160 644.

McCormack-Larkin, Maureen (1985). "Ingredients of a Successful School Effectiveness Project." *Educational Leadership*, 42(6), 31–37.

McDonald, F. (1980). "The Problem of Beginning Teachers: A Crisis in Training." (Vol. 1) *Study of Instruction Programs for Beginning Teachers*. Princeton: ETS. As cited in James V. Hoffman, Sara A. Edwards, Sharon O'Neal, Susan Barnes, and Margaret Paulissen (1986), "A Study of State-Mandated Beginning Teacher Programs," *Journal of Teacher Education*, 37(1), 16–21.

McDonnell, Lorraine M. and Anthony Pascal (1988). *Teacher Unions and Educational Reform*. Santa Monica, Calif.: Rand Corporation, Center for the Study of the Teaching Profession, JRE-02.

McGregor, Douglas (1960). *Human Side of Enterprise*. New York: McGraw-Hill.

McIntyre, Patrick (1976). *Cost, Benefit and/or Liabilities Model for the Western Washington State College Teacher Corps Teacher Designed In-Service Project*. Washington, D.C.: U.S. Office of Education, Teacher Corps.

McLaughlin, Milbrey W. and Paul Berman (1977). "The Art of Retooling Educational Staff Development in a Period of Retrenchment." Santa Monica, Calif.: Rand Corporation, Rand Paper Series, P-5985.

McLaughlin, Milbrey W. and David D. Marsh (1978). "Staff Development and School Change." *Teachers College Record*, 80(1), 69–94.

McNeil, Linda M. (1988). "Contradictions of Control, Part 1: Administrators and Teachers." *Phi Delta Kappan*, 69(5), 333–339.

McQuigg, Beverly (1980). "The Role of Education in Industry." *Phi Delta Kappan*, 61(5), 324–325.

Miles, Matthew B., ed. (1964). *Innovation in Education*. New York: Teachers College Press, Columbia University.

Miller, Lynne (1980). "The High School and its Teachers. Implications for Staff Development." *Journal of Staff Development*, 1(1), 1–11.

Miller, Stephen K., Shelley R. Cohen, and Kathleen A. Sayre (1985). "Significant Achievement Gains Using the Effective Schools Model." *Educational Leadership*, 42(6), 38–43.

Moore, Donald R. and Arthur A. Hyde (1978). *Rethinking Staff Development: A Handbook for Analyzing Your Program and Its Costs*. New York: Ford Foundation.

Moore, Donald R. and Arthur A. Hyde (1980). *An Analysis of Staff Development Programs and Their Costs in Three Urban School Districts*. Chicago: Design for Change.

Moore, Donald R. and Arthur A. Hyde (1981). *Making Sense of Staff Development Programs: An Analysis of Staff Development Programs and Their Costs in Three Urban School Districts*. Chicago: Design for Change.

Morelli, Louis (1987). Telephone interview on January 23, 1987 with administrator of In-Service/Staff Development, State Department of Education, Tallahassee, Florida.

Morrish, Ivor (1976). *Aspects of Educational Change.* New York: John Wiley & Sons.

Mortimore, Peter and Pam Sammons (1987). "New Evidence on Effective Elementary Schools." *Educational Leadership, 45*(1), 4–8.

Moye, M. Jack and Katherine M. Rodgers (1987). "Teachers as Staff Developers: A Success Story." *Journal of Staff Development, 8*(1), 42–45.

Murphy, Joseph and Philip Hallinger (1986). "Some Encouraging Signs in Staff Development for School Administrators." *Journal of Staff Development, 7*(2), 13–27.

Murphy, Peter J. (1985). "A New Professional Education Experience." *Education Canada, 25*(1), 35–39.

A Nation at Risk: The Imperative for Educational Reform (1983). Washington, D.C.: National Commission on Excellence in Education, U.S. Department of Education.

A Nation Prepared: Teachers for the 21st Century (1986). New York: Carnegie Forum on Education and the Economy, Task Force on Teaching as a Profession.

National Association of Secondary School Principals (1975). *Secondary Schools in a Changing Society: This We Believe.* Reston, Va.: National Association of Secondary School Principals.

National Education Association (1971). *Project on Utilization of In-Service Education R & D Outcomes.* Washington, D.C.: National Education Association. ERIC/EDRS No. ED 167 558.

National Education Association (1973). "In-Service Education & Teacher Centers." *Briefing Memo on Instruction and Professional Development.* Washington, D.C.: National Education Association, 1–2.

National Education Association, Research Division (1963). *Personnel Administration in Urban School Districts, 1961–62.* Research Report 1963-R13. Washington, D.C.: National Education Association.

National Education Association, Research Division (1956). *Teacher Personnel Practices, Urban School Districts, 1955–56.* Special memo. Washington, D.C.: National Education Association.

NEA Reporter (1974). "Teachers Rap Administrator-Run In-Service Days," *13*, April.

Neil, Roger (1985). "Inservice Teacher Education: Five Common Causes of Failure." *Action in Teacher Education, 7*(3), 49–55.

Neill, Shirley Boes (1981). "The National Diffusion Network." *Phi Delta Kappan, 62*(10), 726–728.

Nickolai-Mays, Susanne and Jerry L. Davis (1986). "Inservice Training of Teachers in Multicultural Urban Schools: A Systematic Model." *Urban Education, 21*(2), 169–179.

Nicholson, Alexander M., Bruce R. Joyce, Donald W. Parker and Floyd T. Waterman (1976). *The Literature on In-Service Teacher Education: An Analytic Review.* ISTE Report III. Washington, D.C.: Office of Education, Teacher Corps. ERIC/EDRS No. ED 129 734.

Oettinger, Anthony G. (1969). *Run, Computer, Run: The Mythology of Educational Innovation.* Cambridge, Mass.: Harvard University Press.

Oja, Sharon N. (1980). "Adult Development is Implicit in Staff Development." *Journal of Staff Development, 1*(2), 7–56.

Olivero, James L. (1982). "Principals and Their Inservice Needs." *Educational Leadership, 39*(6), 340–344.

Olson, Lynn (1987). "An Overview of the Holmes Group." *Phi Delta Kappan, 68*(8), 619–621.

Orlich, Donald C., F. B. May, Robert J. Harder, Thomas P. Ruff and Jacqueline Ormsby (1972). "A Change Agent Strategy: Preliminary Report." *Elementary School Journal, 72*(6), 281–293.

Orlich, Donald C., F. B. May, and Robert J. Harder (1973). "Change Agents and Instructional Innovations: Report 2." *Elementary School Journal, 73*(7), 390–398.

Orlich, Donald C. (1978). *Designing Sensible Surveys.* Pleasantville, N.Y.: Redgrave Publishing Co.

Orlich, Donald C. (1979). "Establishing Effective In-Service Programs by Taking . . . AAIM." *The ClearingHouse, 53*(1), 53–55. (a)

Orlich, Donald C. (1979). "Federal Educational Policy: The Paradox of Innovation and Centralization." *Educational Researcher, 8*(7), 4–9. (b)

Orlich, Donald C. (1979). "Planning as an Evaluation Model." *Educational Technology, 19*(6), 22–27. (c)

Orlich, Donald C. (1982). "In-Service Education: Fiscal Implications for Policy-Makers." *Planning & Changing, 13,* 214–222.

Orlich, Donald C. and James R. Ezell (1975). "Evaluating the Efficacy of an Elementary Science In-Service Education Program." *Science Education, 50*(1), 59–71.

Orlich, Donald C., Thomas P. Ruff, and Henry R. Hansen (1976). "Stalking the Curriculum: Or Where do Elementary Principals Learn About New Programs." *Educational Leadership, 33*(8), 614–621.

Orlich, Donald C., Robert J. Harder, Richard C. Callahan, Constance H. Kravas, Donald P. Kauchak, R. A. Pendergrass, and Andrew J. Keogh (1985). *Teaching Strategies: A Guide to Better Instruction,* (2nd. ed.). Lexington, Mass.: D.C. Heath and Company.

Orlich, Donald C. (1985). "The Dilemma of Strong Traditions and Weak Empiricism." *Teacher Education Quarterly, 12*(3), 23–32.

Orlich, Donald C. (1986). *A Longitudinal Evaluation Strategy for Staff Development Programs.* Paper presented at the National Staff Development Council Annual Conference, Atlanta, Georgia, December 15.

Orlich, Donald C. (1987). *Findings From In-Service Education Research for Elementary Science Teaching.* Washington, D.C.: National Science Teachers Association, Council for Elementary Science International, Monograph and Occasional Paper Series #2.

Orlosky, Donald and B. O. Smith (1972). "Educational Change: Its Origin and Characteristics." *Phi Delta Kappan, 53*(7), 412–414.

O'Sullivan, P. S., M. K. Piper, and J. P. Carbonari (1981). "A Model for the Effect of an In-Service Program on Junior High School Student Science Achievement." *Journal of Research in Science Teaching, 18,* 199–207.

Otto, Henry John and D. C. Sanders (1964). *Elementary School Organization and Administration.* New York: Meredith Publishing Co.

Parkay, Forrest W. (1986). "A School/University Partnership That Fosters Inquiry-Oriented Staff Development." *Phi Delta Kappan, 67*(5), 386–389.

Patton, Michael (1982). "Reflections on Evaluating Staff Development: The View From an Iron Cow." *Journal of Staff Development, 3*(1), 6–24.

Piaget, Jean. *Science of Education and the Psychology of the Child.* New York: Viking Press, 1970.

Pickles, Bob (1988). "Decision-Making for Staff Development." In *A Handbook for Staff*

Development, Donald C. Orlich, ed. Dubuque, Iowa: Kendall/Hunt, Washington State Staff Development Council, 11–16.

Pincus, John (1974). "Incentive for Innovation in the Public Schools." *Review of Educational Research, 44*(4), 113–144.

Peper, John B. (1986). "Implementing Computer-Based Education in Jefferson County, Colorado." In *Microcomputers and Education,* Jack A. Culbertson and Luvern L. Cunningham, eds. Eighty-fifth Yearbook of the National Society for the Study of Education, Part 1. Chicago: University of Chicago Press, 132–155.

Polemeni, Anthony J. (1969). "A Study of the Status of Title III Projects." *Phi Delta Kappan, 55*(1), 41–43.

Postlethwait, Samuel N., Joseph Novak, and H. T. Murray, Jr. (1972). *The Audio-Tutorial Approach to Learning Through Independent Study and Integrated Experiences.* Minneapolis, Minn.: Burgess Publishing Co.

Pruzek, Robert M. (1987). *A Statewide Evaluation Report on Teacher Resource and Computer Training Centers.* Unpublished paper. Albany, N.Y.: State University of New York.

Purkey, Stewart C. and Marshall S. Smith (1982). "Too Soon To Cheer? Synthesis of Research on Effective Schools." *Educational Leadership, 40*(3), 64–68.

Pundiak, Jean, Betsy Barnard, and Marine Brizius (1974). *Needs Assessment in Education: A Planning Handbook for Districts.* Trenton, N.J.: State Department of Education.

Puuri, Carl R. and Raymond G. Weinmann (1981). "Continuing Education and Certification of Silviculturists on the USDA Forest Service." *Journal of Forestry, 79,* 204–206.

Rasp, Alfred F. (1974). "Delphi: A Strategy for Decision Implementation." *Educational Planning, 1*(2), 42–47.

Ravitch, Diane (1983). *The Troubled Crusade: American Education, 1945–1980.* New York: Basic Books.

Reigal, Marc S. (1987). "Motivation and Commitment Through Teacher-Initiated Staff Development." *Journal of Staff Development, 8*(2), 50–53.

A Report by the Commissioner on Education to the Governor and Legislature on the New York State Teacher Resource and Computer Training Center Program (1987). Albany, N.Y.: University of the State of New York, State Education Department, No. 87-6590, March.

Revised Codes of Washington (1977). 28.A.71.200.

Rist, Ray C. (1970). "Student Social Class and Teachers Expectations: The Self-Fulfilling Prophecy in Ghetto Education." *Harvard Educational Review, 40,* 411–451.

Rogers, Carl (1969). *Freedom to Learn.* Columbus, Ohio: Charles E. Merrill.

Rogers, Everett M. (1962). *Diffusion of Innovations.* New York: Free Press.

Rosenholtz, Susan J. (1984). *Political Myths About Reforming Teaching.* Denver: Education Commission of the States. No. TQ 84-4.

Rosenthal, Robert, and Lenore Jacobson (1968). *Pygmalion in the Classroom.* New York: Holt, Rinehart & Winston.

Ross, Donald H., ed. (1951). *Administration for Adaptability, Vol. III.* New York: Metropolitan School Study Council, 23.

Rowe, Mary Budd (1974). "Wait-time and Rewards as Instructional Variables: Their Influence on Language, Logic and Fate Control: Part 2. Rewards." *Journal of Research In Science Teaching, 11*(4), 291–308.

Rubin, Louis J., ed. (1971). *Improving In-Service Education Proposals and Procedures for Change.* Boston: Allyn and Bacon.

Rubin, Louis J. (1984). *Artistry in Teaching*. New York: Random House.

Runkel, Phillip J., Spencer H. Wyant, Warren E. Bell, and Margaret Runkel (1980). *Organizational Renewal in a School District: Self-Help Through a Cadre of Organizational Specialists*. Eugene, Oreg.: University of Oregon, Center for Educational Policy and Management.

Rutherford, William L. (1978). "The Madness of Educational Change." *Educational Technology, 18*(6), 19–21.

Samuelson, Everett V. and Donald C. Orlich (1985). *Enhancing the Quality of a Professional Workplace In Public Education Through a Comprehensive Teacher Education Incentive Plan*. Moscow, Idaho: University of Idaho, U.S. Department of Education, No. G 00 8400 203.

Sarason, Seymour B. (1982). *The Culture of the School and the Problem of Change* (2nd ed.). Boston: Allyn and Bacon.

Saxl, Ellen R., Ann Lieberman, and Matthew B. Miles (1987). "Help is at Hand: New Knowledge for Teachers as Staff Developers." *Journal of Staff Development, 8*(1), 7–11.

Schiff, Susan J., Carol Irwin, and Chrysann McBride (1987). "Everyone's a Winner! Alternatives for Beginning and Exemplary Teachers." *The Journal of Staff Development, 8*(2), 34–37.

Schild, Robert J. (1964). "A Survey of Certain Practices and Some Proposed Directions for In-Service Education Programs in Selected Schools." Doctoral dissertation, Columbia University. *Dissertation Abstracts, 25*(1), 315.

Schmuck, Richard A. (1987). *Organizational Development in Schools: Contemporary Conceptual Practices*. Eugene, Oreg.: Center on Organizational Development in Schools, University of Oregon.

Schmuck, Richard A. and Matthew B. Miles, eds. (1971). *Organization and Development in Schools*. Palo Alto, Calif.: National Press Books.

Scholl, Shirley S. and Phyllis McQueen (1985). "The Basic Skills Articulation Plan: Curriculum Development Through Staff Development." *Journal of Staff Development, 6*(2), 138–142.

Schultz, Theodore W. (1960). "Capital Formation by Education." *Journal of Political Economy, 68*, 571–583.

Schultz, Theodore W. (1963). *The Economic Value of Education*. New York: Columbia University Press.

Schwaller, Anthony E. (1980). "The Need For Education/Training Programs in Industry." *Phi Delta Kappan, 61*(5), 322–323.

Science Education Databook (1980). Washington, D.C.: Directorate for Science Education, National Science Foundation, SE 80-3, 19.

Scriven, Michael (1967). *The Methodology of Evaluation*. AERA Monograph Series on Curriculum Evaluation, No. 1, 39–83.

Scriven, Michael (1972). "Prose and Cons About Goal Free Evaluation." *Evaluation Comment, 3* (4).

Sewell, Paul J. (1978). *Identification of Future Educational Administrators Through Inservice Leadership*. Unpublished master's paper. Pullman: Washington State University.

Showers, Beverly (1983). "Transfer of Training: The Contribution of Coaching." Eugene, Oreg.: University of Oregon, Center for Educational Policy and Management.

Showers, Beverly (1985). "Teachers Coaching Teachers." *Educational Leadership, 43*(8), 43–48.

Shulman, Lee S. (1986). "Paradigms and Research Programs in the Study of Teaching: A Contemporary Perspective." In *Handbook of Research on Teaching* (third ed.), Merlin C. Wittrock, ed. New York: Macmillan.

Sickler, Joan L. (1988). "Teachers in Charge: Empowering the Professionals." *Phi Delta Kappan, 69*(5), 354–356, 375–376.

Sieber, Sam D., Daren S. Louis, and Loya Metzger (1972). *Evaluation of Pilot State Dissemination Programs.* New York: Columbia University, Bureau of Applied Social Research.

Silberman, Charles E. (1970). *Crisis in the Classroom: The Remaking of American Education.* New York: Random House.

Simpson, Elizabeth J. (1966). "The Classification of Educational Objectives, Psychomotor Domain." *Illinois Teacher of Home Economics, 10,* 110–114.

Sirotnik, Kenneth A. and Richard W. Clark (1988). "School-Centered Decision Making and Renewal." *Phi Delta Kappan, 69*(9), 660–664.

Sizer, Theodore R. (1983). *A Celebration of Teaching: High Schools in the 1980's.* Reston, Va.: National Association of Secondary School Principals and Commission on the Educational Issues of the National Association of Independent Schools.

Skinner, B. F. (1969). *Contingencies of Reinforcement: A Theoretical Analysis.* Englewood Cliffs, N.J.: Prentice-Hall.

Skinner, B. F. (1984). "The Shame of American Education." *American Psychologist, 39,* 947–954.

Smith, Eugene R. and Ralph W. Tyler (1942). *Appraising and Recording Student Progress.* New York: Harper and Row.

Sparks, Georgea, Marsha Nowakowski, Burnis Hall, Rudi Alec, and Joseph Imrick (1985). "School Improvement Through Staff Development." *Educational Leadership, 42*(6), 59–62.

Staff Recognition . . . Unlocking the Potential for Success (1985). Arlington, Va.: National School Public Relations Association, Staff Recognition Packet.

Stahlecker, Jim (1979). *Bay Area Writing Project Cost Report. Evaluation of the Bay Area Writing Project.* Technical Report. Berkeley: University of California, Berkeley. ERIC/EDRS No. ED 191 064.

Stallings, Jane A. (1976). "How Instructional Processes Relate to Child Outcomes in a National Study of Follow Through." *Journal of Teacher Education, 27*(1), 43–47.

Stallings, Jane A. (1982). "Effective Strategies for Teaching Basic Skills." In *Developing Basic Skills Programs in Secondary Schools,* Daisy G. Wallace, ed. Reston, Va.: Association for Supervision and Curriculum Development, 1–19.

Stanley, Julian C. (1954). *Measurements in Today's Schools.* New York: Prentice-Hall.

Stoller, Jane E. (1975). *Cost Analysis of NSF Sponsored Programs: An Exploratory Study.* (Research Paper No. 18). Minneapolis, Minn.: University of Minnesota. ERIC/EDRS No. ED 148 636.

Stufflebeam, Daniel L. (1970). "Programmatic Change." Paper presented to Annual Convention of the American Vocational Association, New Orleans, December 5.

Stufflebeam, Daniel L. (1971). "The Relevance of the CIPP Evaluation Model for Educational Accountability." *Journal of Research and Development in Education, 5*(1), 19–21.

Sullivan, Maureen A. (1987). "Staff Development Through Professional Reading and Discussion." *Journal of Staff Development, 8*(1), 39–41.

Swanson, Beverly B. and Peggy M. Koonce (1986). "Teacher Incentives: Is Merit Pay Enough?" *Action In Teacher Education, 8*(3), 87–90.

Tallerico, Kathryn M. (1987). "Building Level Staff Development: A Personal Account of a Peer Helping Peers." *Journal of Staff Development, 8*(1), 32–35.

Thomas, Margaret A. (1978). *A Study of Alternatives in American Education, Vol. II: The Role of the Principal.* Santa Monica, Calif.: Rand Corporation, R-2170/2-NIE.

Thompson, Jay C., Jr. and Van E. Cooley. (1986). "A National Study of Outstanding Staff Development Programs." *Educational Horizons, 64*(2), 94–98.

Tillman, Murray (1985). "Relationships of Inservice Training Components and Changes in Teacher Concerns Regarding Innovations." *Journal of Educational Research, 78*(6), 364–371.

Tobin, Kenneth (1987). "The Role of Wait-Time in Higher Cognitive Level Learning." *Review of Educational Research, 57*(1), 69–96.

Tomorrow's Teachers: A Report of the Holmes Group (1986). East Lansing, Mich.: Holmes Group, Inc.

Tomsich, Bob and Barbara Pond (1986). *Maximizing Your Effectiveness: Staff Development Programming That Works.* Paper presented at the National Staff Development Council Annual Conference, Atlanta, December 16.

Tuckman, Bruce W. (1985). *Evaluating Instructional Programs,* 2nd ed. Boston: Allyn and Bacon.

Tyler, Ralph W. (1951). "The Functions of Measurement in Improving Instruction." In *Educational Measurement,* W. F. Linquist, ed. Washington, D.C.: American Council on Education.

Tyler, Ralph W. (1971). "In-Service Education of Teacher: A Look at the Past and Future." In *In-Service Education: Proposals and Procedures for Change,* Louis J. Rubin, ed. Boston: Allyn and Bacon.

U.S. Congress (1967). House of Representatives, Committee on Education and Labor. *Study of the United States Office of Education.* Washington, D.C.: U.S. Government Printing Office, House Document No. 193.

U.S. Department of Education, National Center for Education Statistics (1983). *Digest of Education Statistics 1983–84.* Washington, D.C.: U.S. Government Printing Office, table 65, 80.

U.S. Department of Education, Office of Planning, Budget and Evaluation (1983). *Annual Evaluation Report, Fiscal Year 1983.* Washington, D.C.: U.S. Government Printing Office.

U.S. Department of Education, Office of Planning, Budget and Evaluation (1984). *Annual Evaluation Report, Fiscal Year 1984.* Washington, D.C.: U.S. Government Printing Office.

U.S. Department of Health, Education, and Welfare, Office of Education (1971). *Experimental Schools Program.* "1971 Experimental School Projects: Three Educational Plans." Washington, D.C.: U.S. Government Printing Office. DHEW Publication No. (OE) 72-42.

U.S. Government Accounting Office (1976). *Experimental Schools Program: Opportunities to Improve the Management of an Educational Research Program.* Washington, D.C.: U.S. Government Printing Office, MWD-76-64.

Valiant, Robert J. (1985). *The Fiscal Impact of Staff Development Programs In Selected Washington School Districts.* Unpublished doctoral dissertation. Pullman: Washington State University.

Vaughan, Joseph (1983). "Using Research on Teaching, Schools and Change to Help Staff Development Make a Difference." *Journal of Staff Development*, 4(1), 6–24.

Verduin, John R., Jr., Harry G. Miller, and Charles E. Greer (1986). *The Lifelong Learning Experience*. Springfield, Ill.: Charles E. Thomas Publishing Co.

Wagoner, W. H. (1964). *Staff Development: An Emerging Function for Schools*. Washington, D.C.: Department of Rural Education, National Education Association.

Walker, Decker F. and Jon Schaffarzick (1974). "Comparing Curricula." *Review of Educational Research*, 44(1), 83–112.

Ward, Beatrice A. and Joseph T. Pascarelli (1987). "Networking for Educational Improvement." In *The Ecology of School Renewal*, John I. Goodlad, ed. Eighty-sixth Yearbook of the National Society for the Study of Education, Part I. Chicago: University of Chicago Press.

Warren-Little, Judith (1982). "Making Sure: Contributions and Requirements of Good Evaluation." *Journal of Staff Development*, 3(1), 25–47.

Washington Administrative Code (1977). Chapter 392-195-015. Washington State Board of Education, Chapter 392-195 or WAC (WAC392-195-010).

Watts, Heidi (1985). "When Teachers Are Researchers, Teaching Improves." *Journal of Staff Development*, 6(2), 118–127.

Waxman, Hersholt C. (1985). "Research on School-Based Improvement Programs: Its Implications for Curriculum Implementation." *Education*, 105(3), 318–322.

WEA Action (1975). "WEA Chosen for In-Service Study." Publication of the Washington Education Association, 12(1), 1–2.

Weick, Karl E. (1982). "Administering Education in Loosely Coupled Schools." *Phi Delta Kappan*, 63(10), 673–676.

Wenz, Adele (1987). "Teacher Centers: The New York State Experience." *Journal of Staff Development*, 8(2), 4–8.

Westhoff, Maggie, Yvonne Carter, and Lyn Bailey (1987). "Collaborative Roles to Improve Instructional Skills." *Journal of Staff Development*, 8(2), 25–29.

Widman, Terry M. and Jerry A. Niles (1987). "Essentials of Professional Growth." *Educational Leadership*, 44(5), 4–11.

Williams, Richard L. (1978). *A Comparative Study of Metric Skills of Intermediate Students in Calgary, Alberta, and Spokane, Washington*. Unpublished doctoral dissertation. Pullman: Washington State University.

Wilson, John A. (1973). *Banneker: A Case Study of Educational Change*. Homewood, Ill.: ETC Publications.

Wise, Arthur E. (1988). "Legislated Learning Revisited." *Phi Delta Kappan*, 69(5), 328–333.

Wolcott, Harry F. (1977). *Teachers Versus Technocrats: An Educational Innovation In Anthropological Perspective*. Eugene, Oreg.: University of Oregon, Center for Educational Policy and Management.

Wood, Fred H. (1983). "A National Assessment of Valued and Neglected Staff Development Practices." Paper presented to the AREA, April. ERIC/EDRS No. ED 239 374.

Wood, Fred H., Sarah D. Caldwell, and Steven R. Thompson (1986). "Practical Realities for School-Based Staff Development." *Journal of Staff Development*, 7(1), 52–66.

Wood, Fred H. and Sharon A. Lease (1987). "An Integrated Approach to Staff Development, Supervision, and Teacher Evaluation." *Journal of Staff Development*, 8(1), 52–55.

Woodring, Paul (1975). "The Development of Teacher Education." In *Teacher Educa-*

tion, Kevin Ryan, ed. 74th Yearbook, Part II, National Society for the Study of Education. Chicago: University of Chicago Press.

Woodring, Paul (1987). "Too Bright to Be a Teacher?" *Phi Delta Kappan*, 68(8), 617–618.

Wu, P. C. (1987). "Teachers as Staff Developers: Research, Opinion, and Cautions." *Journal of Staff Development*, 8(1), 4–6.

Yager, Robert E., Eddy M. Hidayat, and John E. Penick (1985). "Features Which Separate Least Effective From Most Effective Science Teachers." Iowa City: Science Education Center, University of Iowa.

Yarger, Sam J., Kenneth R. Howey, and Bruce R. Joyce (1979). *In-Service Teacher Education*. Palo Alto, Calif.: Booksend Laboratory.

Youngs, B. Bettie and James L. Hager (1982). "A Cooperative Plan for Personal and Professional Growth in Lake Washington School District." *Phi Delta Kappan*, 63(6), 415–416.

INDEX